Womb

of

Diamonds

Womb

of

Diamonds

**A TRUE ADVENTURE
FROM CHILD BRIDE OF SYRIA
TO CELEBRITY BUSINESSWOMAN
OF JAPAN**

EZRA CHOUEKE

WOMB OF DIAMONDS

Ezra Choueke

Copyright© 2021 by Ezra Choueke

Jacket Illustration by Dany Paragouteva

Book Design by *the*BookDesigners

Hardcover ISBN: 978-0-578-58860-5

Paperback ISBN: 978-0-578-97873-4

For My Family

Acknowledgements

Thank you...

to Tetta for your enthusiasm

to my parents for their support

to Leigh

to Lisa

to Jack, Nicole, Frieda, and Simone

to David, Edith, and Tony Esses

to Lisa Sopher and David Moche

to Laura Haupt, Madeline Hopson, and Peter Park

to Dany Paragouteva, Tomoko Lew, and Clark Miller

Author's Note

These stories are all vivid memories from my grandmother's life. After listening to her stories for years, I wanted to make an effort to preserve them. Some aspects of these accounts were difficult for me to believe at first, although my independent research not only suggested their accuracy, but in many cases confirmed it. An example is when my grandmother insisted that she had witnessed the aftermath of a bombing in 1942. I assumed this could not be the case until I became acquainted with the Doolittle Raid. In situations when I could not support or contradict her memories through research or other interviews, I took her word for an event after I had confirmed the consistent details over months of questioning. While I did my best to re-tell true events, all errors were unintentional and mine alone.

Most names and a few stories have been altered to protect the innocent and the not so innocent... I also made a few changes to aid the flow of the narrative. I added two of Lucie's Japanese neighbors during World War 2 into the Tanaka family, so that their stories could be told together. In a few scenes, I reduced the number of people present in order to tell the stories more quickly and efficiently. I attributed a few backhanded schemes Lucie had to endure over the years to a man named Sigmund. While these schemes are true events, it was not one person who perpetrated them all. So, please don't waste any effort on the search for the real Sigmund.

Lucie had a persistent feud with her mother-in-law. These arguments were real but please keep in mind that I am telling one side of the story. I never had the honor to meet my great-grandmother and would have loved to hear her history as well. I like to judge a person or enterprise by the good they accomplish, and by this barometer I must conclude that she was an amazing person. For this reason, among others, her words were chosen for the title of this book.

Table of Contents

287 BOOK THREE: MY INDEPENDENCE

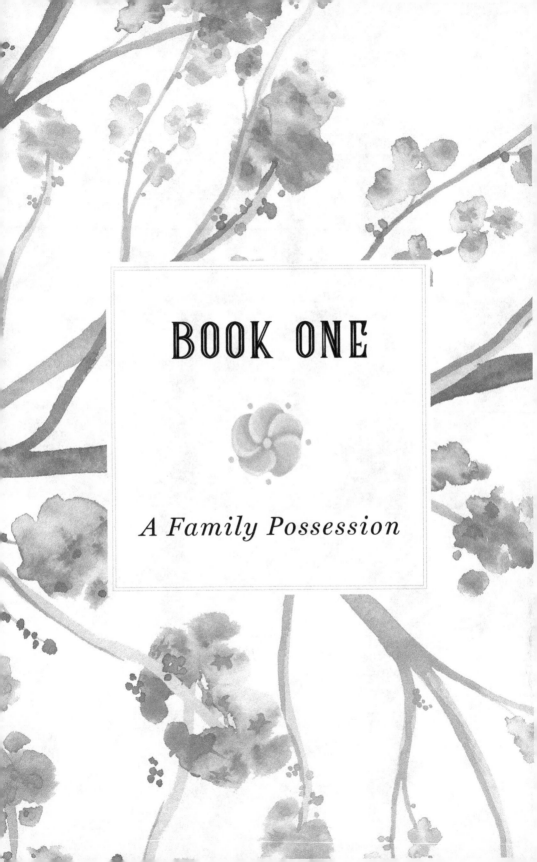

BOOK ONE

A Family Possession

There is No Such Thing
as a Free Lunch...
or a Free Dessert Either

My *mother took me out for ice cream,* and gave me much more than the two scoops I asked for... I got married off instead! Please my friend, sit down, relax, and let me explain.

Everyone calls me Lucie, which is the more glamorous French version of my real name, Polissa. We were poor in 1933 and very seldom spent money on such luxuries but, in my defense, when a 13-year-old girl in French-occupied Aleppo Syria was offered sweets, they seldom asked any questions. I suppose I was so focused on the promised desserts that I ignored the signs that would change my life forever. I didn't know it then, but I would soon be removed by virtual strangers from the country of my youth, taken to far off lands with extremely different languages and cultures, have to fight my way out of poverty, and ultimately battle for my life.

On that hot summer afternoon, Mama carefully applied my makeup and made certain my beige dress fit correctly, then studied her own pretty face and three-quarter-length navy-blue dress in the mirror.

We left around three o'clock and walked down Djemaliyeh, the large main street running by our house. First we saw a street vendor that sold orange ice cream. My mother asked kindly in a soft voice, "Lucie, do you want one?"

I exploded, "Of course!"

This snack was a poor woman's ice candy: a little orange juice mixed together with a lot of water and frozen with a stick in it. We were not rich, so I was very happy to have this frozen orange treat. I took my time savoring each sweet taste, as a girl like me never knew how long she would have to wait for the next one. In the heat of the day, it was heaven...

My mother glanced at her watch and said, "Lucie, let's keep walking." How could I argue when she was in such a generous mood?

After about fifteen minutes, we came to a patisserie. My mother asked again, "Lucie, do you want one?"

"Of course!" I almost shouted.

I chose a *chou a la crème*, as this was my absolute favorite dessert. The cream was cold and refreshing, and the sugar on top was absolutely divine. Again, I took time to enjoy each densely whipped bite.

After I finished, she looked at her watch and asked, "Lucie, do you want another one?"

"YES!" I replied, perhaps too quickly to be polite. I could not believe my good fortune. I chose an éclair very quickly— not allowing my mother any time to change her mind. This one had soft bread, chocolate sauce on top, and a custard center. As soon as it reached the table, I gobbled down the first bite so the owner of the patisserie would not allow her to return it. This dessert was better than the last and it tasted as though I were eating a sweet delicious cloud. I was already disappointed when I finished the last bite because my luck must have run out.

But my mother looked at her watch and said, "Lucie, do you want another one?"

"Are you sure?" I jumped in my seat, holding my breath.

"Yes, I'm sure," she answered with a smile.

"Please!" I fired back, close to ecstasy.

This time I chose more carefully. I figured, she hadn't changed her mind before; there was no reason for her to do it now. Sure enough, the *sahlab*, a sweet, pudding-like Middle Eastern treat, was eaten without any change of heart from the other side of the table. Maybe Mama had finally realized what a good daughter I was?

When I was only halfway done, Mama told me to hurry up and finish. She was apparently running late for an appointment.

No sooner had the last of the *sahlab's* cinnamon and pistachio crumbs disappeared from my plate, than we hurried off down the road at full speed. My mother didn't talk about her appointment, and I didn't ask. I was too busy enjoying the memory of the pastries and orange ice cream to talk about life's trivial little details.

At the end of the street, there was a coffee shop. Mama sat down at a large table facing the road and pulled me down beside her. She looked nervously at her watch and said, "Would you like anything else? I am getting a coffee."

This was like a beautiful dream and I was doing everything in my power not to wake up. It was possibly my life's best memory up to that point, and I wasn't going to let anything like logic get in my way of ordering another dessert. This place had the best ice cream. Not frozen water, but actual frozen cream, and to turn it down was not an option. I ordered two scoops at one time: one scoop chocolate and one scoop vanilla.

I had just started eating when Meyer Shebetai, a religious man, sat down at the table and greeted my mother. I was mildly surprised because I could not imagine why Mama would have an appointment with Meyer. My curiosity was stirred but not enough to pull my concentration away from the amazing bowl of real, smooth ice cream I was devouring.

Mama interrupted me with a sour look. "Why didn't you say hello? Remember, Mr. Shebetai is a friend of your brother's."

"Hello," I said curtly, barely looking at him, and rapidly returned my full attention to the ice cream.

What happened next was a complete blur. Life seemed to go on without me, as the pieces of the day's strange happenings started to fall into place. However, I had sugar rushing through my body and was powerless to act.

A horse-drawn carriage pulled up in front of the coffee shop. Ezra Choueke got out and came straight to the table. He said hello politely to my mother and glanced shyly at me. He announced that he had a customer waiting at his shop, so he had to hurry. Meyer pulled out a prayer book from his jacket and put it on the table. He told me to put my hand on it. Mama grabbed my arm, put it on the book, and then released her grip slowly. Ezra put his hand on top of mine.

Everything happened so fast, my mind drew a complete blank, and I was frozen stiff in surprise. Meyer read a Hebrew prayer very quickly, and Mama instructed me to say, "*Amen*" ("I agree").

I was bewildered by the sudden action. "Why? What am I saying '*Amen*' to?" I asked slowly.

"Just say it!" Mama demanded emphatically.

"*Amen*," I replied cautiously. I rationalized that Meyer was likely just saying a prayer before having a coffee.

Ezra quickly added an *Amen* and before I knew what had happened both of our guests had left in the carriage.

We finished our ice creams and coffees in silence. I knew something big had taken place... I just did not know what.

On the way back home, Mama asked me quietly, "Do you know what you just did?"

"No... What was it?" I replied.

"You and Ezra are engaged now..." she gushed with an enthusiastic smile. "You are to be married!"

I don't know what I had expected her to say, but when I heard those words, I panicked.

"WHAT?????????" I shouted, sugary blood pumping through my heart at thousands of beats per second. "What do you mean??? How can I marry him—he is a big man already!!! How old is he... thirty???"

Mama, matching my energy, looked at me with disgust and impatience, her face immediately taking on a bright crimson color. "What makes you think you are so special??? Who will marry *YOU* without a dowry??? You are lucky to be marrying a man like him!"

"I'm not marrying him, Mama," I said sullenly but adamantly, with my gaze fixed on the street's worn stones. I lowered my voice considerably because my mother was not one to let me yell at her with such disrespect. I did not want to get a spanking.

"You shut up!" she shot back with venom in her voice. "What makes you think you know better than me? You are only thirteen years old. What makes you think you know what is important in life?"

There was a twenty-second silence. The words unspoken created more and more noise between us until the silence was completely deafening. When her next words finally came, it felt as though she had plunged a dagger into my heart, and twisted it 180 degrees.

"Why do you always think of yourself? I am a widow with three girls in the house and no dowry for any of them! You will marry him. If you do not, you will no longer get anything from me!"

Tears started to flood my beet-red face as everything that had happened in the last hour started to really set, like mortar, in my mind. As I rushed from thought to thought about my new fast-approaching life, I realized that I couldn't even form a mental picture of what was to be. It scared me that I would have to live with a man whom I did not know. It scared me that I would no longer be with my family. It scared me that I would no longer be with my friends in school. Everything was so overwhelming that I said the only thing that made sense to me.

"If—you insist that I—marry this man—or you will not support me anymore..." I stammered with the salty taste of tears in my mouth, "I will get a job and move out of the house."

That night, I slept at my Auntie Latife's. My mother and I didn't speak for two weeks.

Aleppo School Days

Let me back up several years to tell this story correctly. I would wake up every ordinary morning to the shouts of Rabbi Azar calling my eldest brother, Abraham, to prayer. If the shouts were not enough to wake him, the Rabbi pulled on a string that hung suspended in the air. The other end was tied around Abraham's wrist and that quickly ended his slumber on the third-floor veranda. This was our version of an alarm clock.

It was the Rabbi's job to wake up every eligible male in our section of Aleppo's Jewish Quarter and make sure they arrived at the morning prayer on time. He would call to Abraham, saying, "We need two more for a *minyan*," the required ten men to begin a Jewish group prayer. Invariably, he would get to the synagogue and greet forty or more men—four times the necessary number. But Abraham was not going to be the one to complain about this misinformation.

Anyway, this was my cue to get out of bed, pull on my Allianz School uniform—a long-sleeved black dress, stopping six centimeters above the knee, with accompanying white blouse and belt—and walk the three and a half blocks of flat, beige stones paving the way to school.

The grayish white limestone brick school building had beautiful arched entrances and tiled floors. Classes started every morning at seven-thirty and were almost exclusively in French, since Syria was a French protectorate at the time. It was at the breakfast recess at half past eight that I learned to take care of myself.

I was a little over average height, with long wavy auburn hair carefully brushed and pinned in place, sapphire blue eyes, a gently sloping nose, a mostly cautious but sometimes enthusiastic smile, and more feminine than imposing. Nonetheless, it was easy for me to "negotiate" my way into a good portion of other girls' breakfasts. My negotiating tactics were not all that complicated. I demanded one fourth of the breakfast of as many classmates as I could find in the schoolyard. If my proposal was ever met with a "No!" the entire meal was promptly hijacked from its owner. While these methods were admittedly heavy-handed, they assured that next time my proposal would be accepted. These robberies were the only way to satiate my perpetual hunger, since there was never enough food in the house.

Some saw me as a bully, but my friends saw me as a Robin Hood type, as everything I procured would be shared with them. You could say that the have-nots of the class went home with fuller bellies because of my efforts. Zatar, bread, cheese, oil, and olives were among the ingredients of my daily fare.

While I did not lack for toughness, I did not rush into a fight either. Some girls, such as Nina Harari, slapped me hard when presented with my proposal. One time was enough for me not to bother her again. It's not that I couldn't have won the fight. It's just that such violent practices are not good business. If she had won, a slew of other challengers would have come out of the stone work.

I also worked hard in the classroom. My poetry, recitations, French, and Arabic were consistently at the top of the class. My geometry and arithmetic were not fantastic but not bad enough to keep me from the honor board.

However, do not confuse being good in school with being a teacher's pet, because even the adults' limits were tested. An excellent example of my troublemaking took place in our sewing class, where not all the sewing done was purely for our educational benefit. The school curtains and other items in need of repair were often the subject of the week's lesson.

Mrs. Nigri, our sewing teacher, was not an adult I felt needed to be obeyed. Even though it was against the rules, I sang loudly while sewing. This resistance to authority was infectious, and after a few weeks, no one in the class would listen to her. One day, I did more than the usual to annoy our teacher, and she discreetly went to La Directrice to complain about me. The Directrice simply said to call her over the next time it happened.

Now Directrice Penso, head of the girls' school, was not one to be trifled with, and everybody knew that! She was strong and fat, and while she was only around one hundred and fifty centimeters tall, her high-heeled shoes made her seem much taller. Her stern, chubby face boasted healthy color in her cheeks, surrounded by a mane of thick, curly black hair with stark white streaks running through it. Whenever she walked down the school's hallways, her shoes made a loud clicking noise as they crashed into the tile on each forceful step. The noise accompanied her wherever she went, giving her an aura of effortless invincibility that thwarted most mischievous girls' plans for the day.

While I did have a profound fear of the Directrice, her aura did not penetrate the door to the sewing class. One week after Mrs. Nigri's complaint, I was belting out a popular Arabic tune when the entire class went silent. I guess the force with which the tune escaped from my mouth masked even the telltale sounds of the *click*, *clack*, *click* as the Directrice stomped down the hallway and into the classroom. I was singing so loudly that even when she stood right behind me, I had no idea that anything was amiss.

Glancing up from mending a gaping hole in a navy-blue sock, I saw the terrified expressions of my classmates come into view. Swiveling my head and shoulders around slowly, I just caught view of the hulking figure behind me as she violently yanked my arm upwards and dragged me to the front of the class.

What came next would linger painfully in my memory many years later. Pulling my hand open in front of her, she brandished a stout ruler—four fingers wide and fifty centimeters long—above her head like a scimitar and brought it down hard with a resounding slap.

She yelled "One!" at the top of her lungs and looked expectantly out at the class as they all answered "One!" in a chorus back to her.

She brought the second stroke down with all her force, and it made a dull thud as it hit my wrist hard. "Two!" she crowed loudly, and the class echoed back, "Two!"

Her third stroke was better placed than the first two and made a huge bang as it collided with my already stinging skin. "Three!" she yelled, and "Three!" the class shouted.

4, 5, 6, 7, 8

After the eighth crushing blow, I looked her in the eyes, bit my lip, and knew I wasn't going to give her the pleasure of seeing me cry.

9, 10, 11, 12

A redness, welts, and blood appeared where my fair skin had been. But I wouldn't cry. I would not give her the satisfaction. I stared stoically into her eyes until it was over and slumped back into my chair at the end of the punishment. Ironically, there was enough time left in the sewing class for me to finish mending her husband's blue socks.

Truthfully, the painful incident neither improved my discipline in Mrs. Nigri's class nor decreased the frequency of my singing. However, it did increase my respect for authority... but, then again, mainly only with people who demanded it.

An exception to this was Mademoiselle Fortune Toledo, my poetry teacher. She pushed us to work hard, but also encouraged us to find happiness in most of the day's activities. She let us sing and talk, as long as we were respectful, and this supported an environment of creative thinking. Her classroom was one of the only places I remember where we could mentally break out of our constricting surroundings. We were told to let our minds approach the limits of the horizon, searching for new places to explore with our imaginations.

Unfortunately for me, Mademoiselle Toledo was a very beautiful woman and people noticed. She was almost one hundred and seventy centimeters tall (about five foot, seven inches), with long blonde hair, a creamy complexion, and her eyes spoke. Since the Syrian-Jewish community of Aleppo was known as an exceptional place to find a serious, pious, young girl, bachelors from overseas often came to the school to find a wife. One morning, a rich man from Argentina met with the Directrice, inquiring as to the availability of any eligible women. He already had children, but his wife had died at a young age. He was looking for a partner in life, and a helper to care for his kids. My suspicion was that the latter need made it more urgent that he find a bride immediately. After he had agreed to the commission proposed by the Directrice, a lunch was set up between Mademoiselle Toledo and the foreign man. Of course, the Directrice was present to preserve the honor of my favorite teacher and, more importantly, her investment.

The next day, I saw Mademoiselle Toledo walking with the Argentinean man. A friend and I approached her and started reciting our lessons for the week. Although we did receive a kind smile, she told us to go home immediately when I asked her to introduce us to her boyfriend. Since I really liked her, I did not protest but left her alone. I did not want to get in the way of her finding a husband, as she was already old by Aleppo standards. She had to be at least eighteen! Two weeks later, my favorite teacher did not show up to class. An announcement confirmed the suspicion that our treasure had been shipped off to Argentina. Everyone in the school was sad—everyone, that is, except for Directrice Penso, who modeled her new mink coat won in the transaction.

My Arabic teacher was also someone I did not test. He was a devout Muslim sheik who wore a long white robe complemented by a large wine-colored tarbush, only partially hiding a generous amount of thick, straight black hair. We did not study Arabic every day, but when we did, we showed nothing but respect. Usually in class, it was acceptable to wear skirts and short sleeves. But with the sheik, every inch of skin, except for our hands and faces, had to be covered. It was even forbidden for us to look in his intelligent eyes as he was a very religious man. I especially loved our teacher's Arabic writing instruction because composing each letter was like drawing a beautiful picture. The sheik and I never had disagreements, as his every command was obeyed to the letter.

Muslim Friends

After school, I hurried home to help prepare the dinner, clean the house, study, and spend time with my family. If it happened to be Friday night, we would enjoy a large meal with lamb or chicken to welcome the Sabbath. In my earliest memories, my father would say the blessings over the wine and bread before all nine of us dined together in the glow of two candles. If it was a weekday, my father and eldest brother would discuss business as the rest of us listened in silence.

My father owned a men's clothing store in the souk, the town market, and did daily business with the Muslim community. In the 1920s and early 1930s, the Aleppo souk had almost magical properties that made it unlike any other place in the world. Jews, Muslims of different traditions, Christians, and members of other religions worked together, side by side, in friendship. The market inhabited a long stone tunnel virtually suffocating with bustling shops. Fierce sunlight often illuminated the tunnel's edges and poured in through the occasional skylight. Beyond the natural light's reach, oil lamps bathed the interior's ancient worn stone arches in a soft golden glow. The customers entered from one side, marveling at fiery persimmons; coal-black figs; deeply tanned pistachios; jumbo Jaffa oranges; vibrant spices of foreign textures and aromas; sumptuous, intricately detailed Persian carpets; large rolls of multicolored fabrics; rich red blankets; elaborate tobacco pipes; hand-stitched clothing; and imported shoes. They inspected a myriad of luxuries and necessities before exiting at the other end of the tunnel. The shopkeepers worked together feverishly to sell the brightly colored items compressed into their small workspaces. If a store did not contain the desired product, the shopkeeper would graciously escort the customer to a friend's.

Merchants visited from Baghdad, Tehran, Beirut, and all over the Middle East. They would load up their camels with fabric, clothing, and dried fruits, among other goods, and caravan back home across the desert. An experienced camel driver could reach Baghdad safely in a mere thirty days. They would travel by day and rest by night, skillfully avoiding bandits and thieves lying in wait, hoping to lighten their loads prematurely.

My father, like many others, imported cotton fabric, Western dress shirts, slacks, and business suits from Manchester, England. After his contacts checked the product quality at the factory, he imported the goods to Aleppo via Beirut. Merchants came to Aleppo from all over the Middle East to buy these foreign goods, creating a thriving marketplace. Jewish merchants were mainly involved in the fabric trade since they could converse in the various languages required to operate an international import/export business. The Arab merchants were fluent in the many dialects required to conduct business with the Middle East and were mainly involved in selling shoes, housewares, gold, food, and other finished products.

Aleppo was such a thriving commercial center that most business owners usually kept an overabundance of merchandise in stock to attract the many daily customers. Especially after a shopkeeper received a new shipment from England or elsewhere, the new products would spill out the doors and clutter the souk's main artery, which led the foreign and domestic buyers from stall to stall.

Once time came to close the market for the day, the merchants, shopkeepers, messengers, and store employees all returned to their families to discuss the day's successes or failures over a warm meal. Those who left a few minutes afterwards, having stayed to attend to their last customer, often heard the front and back gates of the marketplace clang shut behind them. However, all merchandise remained where it was, magically in a state of suspended animation. The store owners simply covered their goods, inside the store and out, with cloth and quickly departed. The Muslims, Jews, Christians, and others respected each other's property as if it were their own, and there was never any theft or vandalism. If a store owner was particularly successful on a given day and left the market with a large bundle of cash, he needn't worry about being robbed. Everyone knew everyone and understood that even a small act of thievery could stain a family's reputation for generations.

In Aleppo, Muslim ideals were woven into the fabric of everyone's existence. The religion and accompanying culture permeated narrow meandering streets, passed through magnificent gates, inhabited quiet courtyards, and baked in the ever-present sun. They flowed from ancient mosques with multicolored stone towers, rough weathered brick walls, smooth domed roofs, and narrow façades adorning arched entranceways—sometimes trimmed, like a king's crown, with diamond-shaped stones. The mosques' interiors boasted numerous high, elegant archways supported on round, decorated columns, while dark basalt and contrasting creamy

marble tiles alternated to cover the floors in decorative geometric designs. Everything in Aleppo was guarded by the cit-
adel, an ancient, gigantic castle watching solemnly over the
city from its sky-piercing observation towers.

Our family had close relationships with Muslims at work,
and I found that many of their customs are not very different from ours. One example concerns Jewish and Muslim
religious dietary laws. Both Kosher and Halal guidelines
forbid eating pork and require the supervised ritual slaughter of cows, goats, and sheep. Personally, I have nothing but
good memories of my everyday experiences with Muslims.
However, we did live in the Jewish quarter, so our neighbors were eighty percent Jewish and twenty percent Arab
Christian, Armenian Christian, and Catholic. For this reason, most of my friends were of these faiths.

Often, Muslims from the souk came to meet my brothers at home, but my brothers quickly left together with them
for a walk. This was mainly because most of the Muslims
we knew were very conservative. The men wore very long,
plain robes with rounded hats, and the women often were
completely covered, except for their eyes. This led to uncomfortable situations when we did not have time to prepare for
a Muslim guest. However, when we had time to dress appropriately, everyone felt comfortable.

One of my brother's best friends was named Salech Sultan.
He was a handsome boy of around fifteen or sixteen, so once
I reached age eleven, my brothers did their best not to have
him stay around the house. They did not want him to fall in
love with the Esses girls or for the Esses girls to fall in love
with him. I was always happy when Ramadan came to an end,
as Salech would bring baskets of sweets left over from their
elaborate feasts. We, in turn, would send him baskets of food
on Purim, a Jewish celebration of survival under Persian rule.
On top of cooperation in business, we would extend each other
additional courtesies. For example, according to both Jewish

and Muslim traditions, Salech would lend our family money with no interest, and we would do the same for him.

Once a member of Salech's family was getting married, and he invited us to the wedding. My brothers were already there, but he met my mother, Auntie Latife, and I halfway to the venue. This was to make sure we didn't run into trouble going through the Muslim area, as it was periodically dangerous for Jewish women to walk through it close to nightfall.

Salech escorted us to the celebration and directed us to the appropriate area. The party was in two different rooms: one for the women and one for the men. The women arrived almost completely covered in long dark robes, scarves, and veils, revealing only luminescent pairs of eyes. However, upon entering the women's room, they uncovered their magnificent embroidered dresses, beautifully made-up faces, and large smiles hiding beneath. The extraordinary celebration included music on the oud (a guitar-like stringed instrument), plenty of Arabic singing, and mountains of fruit and pastries, which was the part I liked best. I danced with most of the women late into the night, while others played *towla* (backgammon) or cards on the fringes of the celebration. Upon departure, each woman once again covered up, hiding her gorgeous gown and the enjoyment we had experienced under large amounts of all-encompassing dark fabric.

While Salech and our friends from the souk made an excellent impression on me, one Muslim boy in particular gave me a most invaluable gift. In another of my earliest memories, Mama often let my sisters and I travel to the countryside with our Auntie Latife on the weekends. One such weekend, at age six, I decided to learn how to swim. Many people of different cultures gathered at a deep circular stone-walled pool fed by a natural spring. On certain days, the men were permitted to swim, and on other days, the women were given a chance. Encircling the ten-meter-wide pool was a heavy curtain so that each sex was given its privacy in the water. Since everyone swam in the nude, this barrier was of profound importance.

My sisters, Auntie, and I arrived early at the pool to avoid the crowds. No one in our family knew how to swim, so at first we only watched a twelve-year-old girl dart back and forth from wall to wall, while we dangled our feet in the water. Watching her for a few minutes, I decided that propelling myself through the water didn't look that difficult. Without warning, I took a running start and jumped as far as I possibly could into the abyss, paddling furiously towards the middle. It was then I realized that swimming was harder than it looked. Even with all my frenetic, furious paddling, I sank slowly into the depths.

Luckily, the girl swam by, taking another lap, and I grabbed onto her back in extreme panic. I wrapped my arms and legs around her, knowing only that I wasn't going to let go for anything. With an additional twenty kilos added to her weight and her legs and arms partially restrained, the girl sank quickly. I held my breath as the water crawled up my nose, and I tightened my grip on the girl's body, my only chance at life. The girl managed to free one leg and kicked frantically until she could steal a breath from the surface. Seeing the sunlight get closer and closer, I craned my neck to inhale a valuable breath as well. Heaving my body upwards to break the surface, I only pushed the girl back down into the icy depths. I heard yelling and screaming from all sides of the stone walls as we descended once again into the blackness.

Auntie Latife immediately realized two things of vital importance: one, she was the only adult present; and two, the only swimmer at the pool was currently being drowned by her niece. She ran outside of the curtain and found three local teenage Muslim boys sitting under a tree. "Come quickly!!! Come quickly!!!" she yelled in abject terror. "There are two girls drowning in the pool!!!"

All three of them jumped up and, right before running over, hesitated and looked quizzically at one another. "Are they dressed?" the youngest one asked.

Auntie Latife screamed: "They are not dressed, but never mind!!! We need your help now!!!"

The boys looked quickly from one to another. Religiously, it was discouraged to see women, other than their wives, with their bodies uncovered. The eldest, a tall boy with bronze skin and dark-brown hair, barked at his two friends to stay where they were. He kicked off his sandals and ran as quickly as a rabbit towards the curtain. In one motion he burst through the barrier, kicked his lead foot onto the stone wall, and using all his momentum, launched himself headfirst into the water.

Spots were swirling in front of my eyes, and an elbow slammed forcefully into my stomach, emptying my entire lung contents into the cold, dark water. Just when I thought death was imminent, two muscular arms enclosed us. I must have slipped into unconsciousness because my next recollection was suddenly waking in agony, like from a terrifying dream, and vomiting up freezing water on a sun-warmed stone floor. It was a few interminable seconds before I could manage a simple painful gasp or cough. Following the ten minutes it took to compose myself and dress painfully, I apologized profusely to the girl and repeatedly thanked the Muslim boy who had saved my life.

Roh Abuki

At around this time, my father passed away. I only have a few memories of him. My favorite happened one day when I was continually pestering my mother for some jewelry. I wanted a ring, a bracelet, and a chain, and I wasn't going to stop asking until I got them. I was a six-year-old with champagne tastes.

That day, as usual, I asked my mother for the jewelry, so she would not forget. Instead of saying no, she told me to go ask my father.

My father was bedridden. He looked very small and tired when I approached his bed. I sat next to him, looked into wise, watery, pale blue eyes, kissed his hand, and said softly, "Papa, Papa."

"Yes, *Roh Abuki?*" he answered, welcoming me in the usual way, meaning "the soul of your father." Smiling weakly at me, he struggled to sit up in bed. He placed his hand on my head and carefully enunciated a Hebrew prayer.

"Papa, I want a gold ring, a bracelet, and a chain," I pleaded hopefully.

"Describe them for me just as you want them," he answered. At this, I got more excited; no one had ever taken my request this seriously before.

I answered carefully. "Well...I want a gold chain-link necklace with a Star of David on it. I also want a matching gold bracelet with a charm, so it makes a jingling noise when my wrist moves. Last, I want a gold ring with a beautiful blue turquoise stone in it. I want the stone to be this big." I measured out around one centimeter with my fingers.

"They sound beautiful," he declared with as much enthusiasm as he could summon. "As soon as I get well, the first thing I will do is go buy them for you."

"Thank you, Papa! Thank you!" I replied. I ran around for the next few days with a body full of enthusiasm and excitement.

A week later, my elder brother, Moise, was instructed to take us to *Tetta's* (Grandmother's) house quite suddenly. My mother gave Moise some of our clothes, money, and bread with cheese for us to eat. We were supposed to take a carriage, but Moise instead decided we should walk, as he had something pressing on his mind. He walked quickly, his attention fixed on the narrow path's irregular beige stones, worn smooth by centuries of pounding with feet and hooves. In the afternoon light, I studied the large monolithic houses rising menacingly to a few stories immediately on each side of our comparatively small bodies. Occasionally, a wooden front door would open, revealing a cool, tranquil courtyard with a gurgling water fountain surrounded by various types of green plants. We walked silently, occupied in our own worlds, when the Muslim call to prayer boomed simultaneously from a few minarets towering proudly in the distance. The rhythmic singing soothed our spirits and steadied our pace.

We stayed at Tetta's for one week, until we got the bad news that would shape our lives from that day forward. When I saw my brother Rafoul crying, I intuitively knew what had happened.

I never saw Papa again...

My Brothers, My Keepers

After the funeral, we immediately needed to change the way we lived in order to make enough money to survive. My mother, Seto, had given birth to nine children, but two had died at early ages. In Aleppo, it was common to lose several children, so everyone had as many children as possible. This was fine as long as there was plenty of money in the house, but when money was short, it was difficult to satisfy so many stomachs. After the death of my father, there were eight stomachs that needed filling two or three times a day: my mother's, Abraham's, David's, Moise's, Rafoul's, Victoria's, Linda's, and mine. My four elder brothers needed to work; my two younger sisters and I needed to take care of the home.

Abraham, the number one son, needed to undertake the enormous responsibility of running an international textile business. The task would have been difficult at any age, but it was thrust upon him when he was only fourteen. Fortunately,

Abraham was powerful, confident, and adapted quickly to his new world. Over time, his position at the head of the business naturally extended his authority to the head of the household. He didn't hesitate to shout at my mother, my sisters, and me, demanding that we keep the home orderly and respectable. He saw the maintenance of the Esses family name as his responsibility since one could not strive to be viewed as honorable in business if there was disorder permeating his household. Abraham quickly developed many good relationships with the Muslims and Jews in Aleppo.

At first, I was very shy around Abraham and almost never spoke to him, as he had a very serious personality. One day, I wanted to go buy some sweets, but didn't have any money. Mother was not in the house, so I convinced Victoria to join me and ask Abraham. He was studying in his room, and, as usual, we brought him his breakfast. When he came to the door and took his food, I looked at Victoria, and Victoria looked at me, but we said nothing. Both of us were too scared to speak! After he had closed the door, we continued to stand in front of it and started arguing loudly.

"What is going on?" Abraham shouted and threw open the door. "Is everyone crazy in this house? Can I not have some peace and quiet?"

My sister and I stood paralyzed in front of him until I found the courage to speak. "Victoria wants enough money to buy two *choux a la crème*, but I told her not to bother you." I said quickly before she could get a word in.

Victoria was about to defend herself when Abraham smiled and said, "Ahhh, is that all?", and gave us enough money to buy ten between us.

Needless to say, Abraham got the best service from that day forward. When he had to go to the train station to sell some goods in Damascus, we were the first to volunteer to help carry his bags. When he returned from the train station, we were there waiting for him. We made sure he always received the best breakfasts and that everything he needed was brought to him without delay.

It was well understood that Abraham could not run the business by himself, so David, my number two brother, joined him immediately. They both worked together developing new customers and expanding the fabrics they could supply by importing additional merchandise from Italy. David had the same dark, wavy hair as Abraham but otherwise was younger by two years, shorter by twelve centimeters, and slimmer. He had inherited the same hypnotic azure blue eyes as the rest of my brothers—although in David's case, they were guarded by a pair of thick glasses.

The glasses were a reflection of David's enthusiasm for learning. He had distinguished himself as the family scholar from a very young age. His photographic memory allowed him to memorize, completely by heart, entire weekly Torah readings, hour-long prayers, and certain lengthy Talmudic arguments—revered teachings covering all aspects of Jewish life, from the legal to the moral, from marriage to business.

Despite my father's zeal for Judaism, his death meant that David had no choice but to join the family business at the age of twelve. My father had been an enthusiastic supporter of the synagogue and had even been protected as a synagogue employee when the government was drafting Jewish men for the army. Even so, it was never an option for my brother to study full time by soliciting the charity of others since he needed to help Abraham support all of us.

Unlike Abraham, David did not fall for our tricks. We tried to ask David for extra pastry money when delivering his breakfast every morning. However, he was usually in the middle of putting on his *tefilin* for the Jewish morning prayer. He shouted at us to keep quiet and leave him in peace, as it was his responsibility to pray for the well-being of the family. We would always close the door in disappointment and wait until he was done, but as soon as he would finish, he would rush out the door on his way to work. This daily ritual made him a master of avoiding the not-so-subtle hints of my sisters and I in our search for extra pocket money. In all fairness to him, though, it was not easy to run the business and support us in those days.

Moise, my next eldest brother, had a difficult time as well. His muscular frame, stylishly cut curly brown hair, easy smile, and dimpled cheeks did not hurt his chances with the females of Aleppo. But the fact that he was the third son ensured he would have to look outside the family for employment. It was well-known in our community that a business could support only so many people. Having too many family members in a business not only required that profits were split more ways but also led to a huge clash of egos that could ultimately throw a family into ruin. A two-headed camel would have a huge problem deciding which path to take in the desert. A three-headed camel would have to spend so much time discussing where to go, it probably wouldn't go anywhere. To avoid arguments, and to preserve the family business, it was understood that Moise would have to look for work elsewhere.

He decided to work with our cousin Albert Esses, who had a contact in the record business. They borrowed some money, imported popular records from France, opened a retail store, and worked for long hours, six days a week. They could not pay an assistant and, therefore, could not leave even to have lunch. There were many poor people in Aleppo and music was a luxury, so it was no small accomplishment that they managed to stay employed.

My sisters and I didn't bother Moise for money. We knew he was starting his business and needed to be careful with what he spent. However, Moise and I did work out our own special relationship. He did not have a lot, but he did have a big shiny chrome bicycle. He would ride it to work and back all week. In Aleppo, it was not a small thing to have a bicycle, so he spent a lot of time taking care of it. Here is where I seized my opportunity. I made a deal with him that, in exchange for the cleaning and maintenance of his bicycle, I would get to ride it around the block on Sunday. I polished the spokes, oiled the chain, removed any rust, and cared for it as if it were my own. It was only a minor detail that when it came time to go on my weekly ride, I was too short to reach the pedals.

With the bike gleaming in the sunlight, Moise would push me around the block. I was not merely riding a bicycle down Djemaliyeh—I was the Queen of England being driven down Oxford Street in the latest model Rolls Royce. The wind in my hair, the ground rushing under my feet, and the majesty of that chrome machine made me feel like the luckiest girl in the world.

As my brother Moise's business improved, he needed to hire someone to help him in the record store. Rafoul, my number four brother, started helping Moise after his eleventh birthday and picked up the business very quickly. His short stature, curly brown hair, crooked teeth, and bad posture were all forgotten after one of his serene, confident, welcoming looks, which could warm even the coldest of hearts. After proving his worth as a salesman, he often traveled to Damascus by train and then to Beirut by car in order to replenish their stock of imported records. While doing so, he cultivated many Arab and Jewish contacts who not only saved his life but also ultimately gave it meaning. However, that is a story I will unravel at the appropriate time.

Since Rafoul was eight years younger than Abraham and the closest in age to my sisters and me, he was the only brother who stayed home and attended school with us for any significant length of time. Yet while he was being groomed to go out into the business world, my sisters and I were being groomed to manage a home.

My Sisters, a Well, and a Veranda

All eight of us lived together in a three-story, white stone house complete with a well in the kitchen and a third-floor veranda. The floors were reddish clay tiles, warmed by bright woven carpets. A Persian carpet with a forest-green background, interrupted by royal-blue flowering vines, was the first sight welcoming guests at the first-floor entrance. They were entertained in a small salon containing an overstuffed blue sofa; an old wooden dresser; an octagonal wooden table, inlaid with geometric floral designs in mother of pearl; and a few handcrafted chairs made from solid walnut. If the guests stayed for a meal, we would make use of the adjacent kitchen and small dining room. On the second story, my sisters and I all slept together on a beige Pakistani carpet with apricot floral accents. Thin mattresses were placed on top for comfort. My mother remained next door in the room she had shared with my father. On the third floor, my four brothers shared two rooms. It was definitely a full house.

Victoria, Linda, and I fought all the time, as normal sisters do. I usually prevailed since I was two years older than Vicky and four years older than Linda. My sisters and I prepared the evening meal every afternoon. Starting the fire in the kitchen charcoal pit, drawing up the well water to cook with, and preparing the ingredients would take hours from start to finish. Most of the food was served to my brothers and mother, as they needed the energy to provide for us. Before we ate our portions, the meat was carefully divided up into even amounts so no one received too much or too little. We would then all slowly eat together out of one big bowl.

We often escaped the hot summer heat by sleeping outdoors on the third-floor veranda. It was an amazing feeling of freedom to sleep outside and count the millions of stars in the sky. We also would keep an eye on the thousands of pistachios our grandfather slowly dried on the roof.

Over the years, my sisters and I found our way into plenty of trouble when completing the daily housework. And truthfully, I cannot blame them for every problem we encountered.

In the kitchen, at the age of eight, I often enjoyed competitions between Vicky and me to see who could drag up the most water from a deep stone well built into our kitchen floor. The two buckets we used were tied to opposite ends of a long rope that was threaded through a small wheel. The wheel was secured to the mouth of the well and acted as a pulley to help distribute the weight of the water we had to drag up. Since I was two years older and obviously stronger than my younger sister, the rules of our daily contest only permitted Vicky to use the pulley. I had to stand on top of the well and drag up the water, hand over hand.

One morning, during our usual game, Vicky was able to pull up an unusually full bucket of water. Not wanting to concede defeat, I climbed carefully to the top of the well and straddled the opening for leverage. I lowered the bucket and waited until it was completely submerged so I could drag up a winning quantity of water. After drying my hands on my school dress, I pulled with my left and then my right, carefully, steadily maneuvering one hand over the other. I was thoroughly practiced in my winning technique.

Because of repeated use that morning, the rope was unusually slick, and the extra drops of water splattered on my straining arms, my feet, and the sides of the well on which I was standing. As I moved my feet slightly to get more leverage, they slid into a pool of moisture—and my legs suddenly shot out from under me. I instantly released the bucket before falling helplessly into the cold depths of the well.

When I was in mid-plunge, my face and torso scraped the jagged stones lining the well's interior. I reacted instinctively, springing my hands out and propelling my back into the other side of the well, from which I rebounded painfully into the frigid water. Dazed and on the cusp of unbridled panic, I finally caught some luck. My flailing legs landed directly into the bucket I had been retrieving. The added weight quickly propelled the bucket deeper into the cold water. A "ZZZZZZZZZZZ" and then a "BANG" echoed powerfully through the tight space—and with a violent jerk, I stopped moving.

It took me thirty seconds to realize I wasn't dead, and another two minutes to understand my situation. Apparently when I fell into the bucket I had been retrieving, my weight had quickly pulled the excess rope through the pulley until the second bucket had lodged into the pulley's wheel—halting my downward descent.

Considering I still couldn't swim, and the well was over three meters deep, I realized this had saved my life. Standing in a bucket suspended over the bottom of the well, up to my chin in water, I pulled tentatively at the rope running taut up to the pulley's wheel. It appeared to be holding fast. I yelled Vicky's name for a few minutes before I knew I was alone.

My vision adjusted to the dim light, and I searched for a foothold. I found one. I then found another, just a little higher, on the other side of the tight space. Using the rope, I balanced myself, swinging from one foothold to another, hoisting myself up a few centimeters at a time, until my shoulders and arms emerged from the well's mouth. Letting go of the rope, I jumped to the edge, managed a final, desperate pull up, and flopped onto the hard, unwelcoming tiles of our kitchen floor.

After composing myself, I went upstairs and found a cloth to wipe the blood off of my wounds. Before I began the painful process, I heard a big commotion in the kitchen. As I walked gingerly downstairs to investigate, I heard Mama crying hysterically.

"Oh, my poor Lucie drowned! Come quickly! Come quickly! Help me get my daughter! Help me get my daughter!"

I entered the kitchen and saw Mama, Vicky, and a few

neighbors peering down into the dark well. Victoria saw me first and gasped, my mother spun quickly around. After a few moments of non-comprehension, she ran over and enveloped me in her warm, loving arms. She carefully cleaned and bandaged my cuts and scrapes. Then she brought me up to her room, arranged some plump cushions around us, and reclined on a thick, soft Turkish rug with a burgundy border and an ivory center. I put my head in her lap and traced the carpet's detailed floral pattern with my finger until I fell into a deep, comfortable sleep.

Coffee Grounds

While Mama still had the money to employ them, my sisters and I shared our bedroom with two housekeepers: Yesenia, a Syrian, and Ani, an Armenian. During this period, there was widespread persecution of the Armenian people by the Ottoman Empire. Consequently, many Armenians fled the areas controlled by the Ottomans and settled in Aleppo as refugees or displaced persons. They lived together in barracks outside the city and many found employment at subsistence wages wherever they could. It was natural for young girls to work as housekeepers. They learned how to manage a home and saved a little money until it was time to find a husband, get married, and improve their desperate circumstances. Since my mother loved to play cards and socialize, as was the custom with ladies of her age, the responsibility of bringing up the young children was delegated in many instances to these kind, intelligent people. In our case, Mama luckily secured the assistance of the sixteen-year-old Ani.

Ani's straight ink-black hair, pastel-pink lips, and pale, immaculate skin the color of fresh goat cheese fashioned a perfect setting for her emerald-green eyes, which captivated all who were lucky enough to meet her. Her exceptionally beautiful face competed daily for attention only with her stunning figure. These attributes hampered our efforts whenever we had to go make a purchase in town. Every man, young or old, whom we passed focused all their attention on my lovely companion. At such a young age, I didn't understand the meaning of their stares, but I soon tired of their clandestine requests for introductions to my good friend. Their requests were futile. And the men knew, as well as I did, that Ani had her own people to go back to and would find a suitable husband from a family that her parents would choose.

Because of all the drama related to leaving the house with Ani, I much preferred staying home with her. There was so much work to be done—we often would be sweating side by side while cooking and cleaning. Due to the benefits of my small hands, my normal jobs were to clean out the oil lamps, wash the house's hard-to-reach places, and cut up the vegetables in extra fine pieces. As a reward for helping her with the housework, Ani would teach me how to read people's fortunes in Turkish coffee.

The theory behind this type of fortune-telling was that each coffee cup held a special message for the person who drank out of it. After one of our friends finished their coffee, the cup would be turned over on the saucer and rotated three times clockwise. This caused any liquid left to pool in the saucer below while leaving the sediment caked to the walls of the cup. Then the cup would be turned right side up, and the fortune of the coffee drinker could be clearly read. Ani taught me that small specks indicate good fortune, such as coming children, marriages, money, or family visitors. Large spots were bad luck, such as sickness, death, childlessness, or poverty. A thin brown line towards the bottom of the cup signified a coming trip. I soon found out that someone's fortune could be deviously manipulated by the coffee maker. The first coffees poured out of the pot usually had very little sediment. These were given to our favorite guests, who would be left with many small specks in their glasses. The middle pours usually contained small specks of sediment with a few bigger splotches mixed in. This would suggest that a mixture of good and bad luck was on its way. The last pours often held large amounts of sediment and would therefore tell a very disturbing tale. We would give these to our unwelcome guests.

I also treasured the company of Yesenia, an older Syrian lady with plump rosy cheeks who did most of the cooking for the house. Her long graying hair and longer black dress always smelled like the food she prepared that day. That was good when we had *kibe*, a cracked wheat or bulgur shell stuffed with meat, but not as good when we had only bread, cheese, and pickles to eat. She was like a genie in the kitchen, able to make a tasty meal using only a few ingredients. She had mastered the secret subtleties of Syrian cooking that have been passed down from mother to daughter for generations. Syrian women take great pride in and are highly appreciated for their skills in preparing food. Yesenia was quick with a smile, generous with her knowledge, and never hesitated to teach us any of her family's numerous delicious culinary secrets. So, with Yesenia, we had an "auntie" in the family who taught us culture through the preparation of food. She kept us from causing trouble by telling the usual Syrian fables that we loved to hear. The one that scared me the most was a story about a huge ink-black raven that would gobble up all the bad children. Whenever I made any of the adults angry, I watched the skies for days.

Through Yesenia and Ani, we began to learn the complex relationships of the various religious and ethnic groups that lived together in Syria. We would discuss our differences openly, but in the end, there was really very little difference between us. We agreed on almost everything, though each of us was bound to her own ethnic and religious group. Ani would marry a handsome Armenian youth and begin her family.

Yesenia was mother to children already grown and was soon to be a grandmother. And I had my own path to follow, perhaps, like Ani, to find a husband, and later on, like Yesenia, to go to work after my children had grown and left the house.

Chicken Bones

My mother, Seto, was always very social with the neighbors. She loved nothing more than to play cards all day and hear about the goings on in town. She was one of the most beautiful women I had ever seen, with striking turquoise eyes, high, rounded cheekbones, and chocolate brown hair. She stood out in public like a rose in the desert.

She always wanted the best for us, but being a woman in an Arab country did not give her many options as far as a career went. After my father died, she stayed in the house less and less. With my brothers all out working, and my sisters and I in school, she devoted more and more of her time to social activities.

During that time, though, I never felt ignored. We still had great days together. Some of my best memories are of when she would call the tailor over from town. It was around the time I was finishing my eleventh year, and as I was her eldest daughter and thus the closest to marrying age, she wanted me to look presentable at all times. She knew the neighbors always had their eyes on suitable matches for their sons. While I was always happy to have new clothing, I didn't truly understand why I was receiving so much of my mother's attention. We would buy fabric from the market, and the tailor would make me a dress. If my mother ordered a dress for me, I gave my old dress to Victoria. She didn't like wearing my old clothes, but her situation was not as bad as our younger sister Linda's. She had to wear the clothes that Victoria and I had both worn out.

Once I was helping Yesenia cook regularly, Mama, to show her approval, gave me the important job of buying the pita bread and fruits from local vendors. It was a good thing she only gave me enough money for one day's provisions, since the first time I failed miserably.

Often, olive-skinned gypsy women from the countryside would walk through our neighborhood on their way back from the market. Their worn leather sandals were covered by long, flowing, colorful skirts, paired with brightly colored cotton blouses. Their cascading black hair swung back and forth under vibrant, loosely wrapped scarves. As I was leaving the house, one such woman passed by. She spoke charismatically as I scanned her angular face, shimmering light-brown eyes, painted red lips, and gold-colored jewelry, which pulled my attention from the occasional smudge of dirt on her outfit.

"Would you like me to read your future?" she asked kindly.

"I don't have any money," I replied reluctantly, with a slight grin.

The woman sensed some indecision on my part, removed a basket of eggs balanced on her head, and placed it on the ground. "Come here," she invited with carefree enthusiasm. "Let me see if there is anything to tell. I will peer into your future, and we won't speak about money yet."

Reassured, I took a step closer to the woman, who took out an ancient drawstring pouch and sat on the floor. A few of the neighborhood girls, watching from the windows, came down to witness the sorcery. She pulled a bunch of loose chicken bones from her bag and tossed them suddenly on the ground.

"Ahhh... Very interesting... very interesting!" she exclaimed, her face glowing with mysticism. She looked at the pile of bones from the left, from the right, and squinted one eye. Seeing her audience increase with curious neighbors, she continued mysteriously.

"You will receive a beautiful present."

Her act was too enticing to ignore. "What will it be? What will it be?" I asked, jumping up and down with excitement.

She replied with bubbling confidence, "Someone will give you a beautiful new dress!" Her voice then lowered an octave and took on a raspy quality as she put an index finger to her cheek and tilted her head pensively. "But I see something else...something much more important! Yes... You will definitely need to know about this!"

"What is it? What is it?" I asked nervously.

"That, my daughter, I cannot tell you for free. I need to buy some bread for my children." She looked away slowly, giving me time to make my decision.

I took out the money Mama had given me and placed a coin in her hand.

Her forehead wrinkled as she looked at the bones once more. "Oh, yes... Oh, yes, I see..." she postured. "Congratulations are in order! You are to be married!"

"Really?!" I replied with a mixture of excitement and fear, rattling off a bunch of questions: "What is his name? Is he handsome? How old is he?"

She concentrated carefully and then relaxed her entire body. "I'm sorry," she apologized, shaking her head. "It is not so clear... Maybe if you give me another coin, it will help me answer those questions."

I pressed another coin into her hand and she drifted into a trance-like state. "Ah, yes!" She suddenly snapped to attention. "He is a handsome man but is quite a bit older than you are. You will give him children."

"Children?!?!" I exhaled in surprise. "How many? Boys or girls?"

It took less than five minutes to spend all the money mother gave me. I told her to wait, ran into the house, and gave her our last piece of bread to continue. After she dispensed a few more pearls of advice, she assured me, "Don't worry, my daughter! I will come back next week. Bring more money, and we will continue." She then moved on to someone else in the crowd.

I understood by the third or fourth victim that she was repeating the same story over and over again. She would throw the chicken bones for each new customer and weave an interesting tale until another pocket was empty. I was sent to bed that night not only with empty pockets but an empty stomach as well. I didn't make that mistake again.

I don't remember ever wondering where my next meal would come from, but I knew we didn't have a lot of money or food. Life was difficult for my brothers because they had to work and make a living. It was not as difficult for me because, even at twelve years old, I was not of working age yet.

What I did not realize was that, once I had reached twelve years of age, I was expected to get married very soon. The worst thing that could happen, according to some, was to be a girl no one wanted. That would destine you to a life of taking care of your mother. Adding to the urgency, my mother and brothers needed to marry my sisters and me off so they would not need to support us for the rest of our lives. This was not cruel—it was just the way things were. It was understood that if a girl was eighteen, she was already advanced in age and difficult to find a husband for. The fact that my father had died and I didn't have a dowry did not make things any easier on the family. It made finding a suitor even more of an immediate issue. Two assets that usually attracted a good husband were a big dowry and good looks. Luckily, I was good-looking.

Dancing and Dating

Yes, so I was good-looking. It's not as if I were aware of it at the time or flaunted it. Yet, it was an incentive to marry me, even though I came with no cash prize. More than anything, when the adults in our midst looked at me, they saw the promise of cute grandchildren.

At twelve years old, I was not thinking of marriage. I was happy just going to school, helping around the house, and playing with my friends. However, my mother had other plans...

Because Mama was a widow with three girls in the house, her first priority was to find us all suitable husbands. The tradition at the time dictated that when a man married, his wife moved in with his family. She, and later their children, would occupy his room in the family residence. This made it important to find a man with money because a poor husband may not have a room available. He would then either have to move-in with his wife's family or, worse yet, return the girl if he could not provide for her.

To notify all the eligible bachelors of Aleppo that I was available, Mama planned a small party for me in the Jewish Club. The Jewish Club was a one-story stone building on Djemaliyeh, overlooking a small outdoor area completely paved over with stones. The women would play cards and socialize on one side of the room, while the men played *towla* and discussed business on the other. Mama had brought me to the club previously, but my purpose there was merely to fetch the *nargileh*, a tobacco water pipe, from the coffee shop next door. I would be sure to tell the shopkeeper to wash the tobacco, as Mama directed, in order to cut the potency of the weed. The women would then take turns inhaling the harsh fumes, each from a different arm of the elaborately decorated water pipe.

The night of the party, Mama presented me with a pink taffeta dress that the tailor had made for the occasion. The long delicate sleeves, modest neckline, and fitted bodice flowed uninterrupted into a shining, fluttering, swirling skirt of rich, decadent fabric. Mama helped me paint pink nail polish on my toes and fingers, complementing my open-toed sandals. I twirled a few times, allowing the stiff material to swish around my ankles. To complete the outfit, Mama brushed my hair straight, tied it into a sophisticated bun, and sprinkled pink glitter all over my complicated hairstyle.

I didn't ask why she spent so much money and effort on my outfit, when we were always budgeting the available money for food. I already knew her philosophy: "Food no one will notice; a pretty dress everyone can see!"

In fact, my mother was demonstrating the business acumen she had developed at my father's side during their many years together. She knew that one can only get a good price for a product if there are multiple potential buyers. So she needed to have a party in order to stimulate interest in the merchandise. Once she had advertised sufficiently to determine the market for her goods, she would approach the most desirable customers and attempt to make a deal. A pool of five or six suitors would give her the upper hand in any negotiation. If more than one man met her requirements, she had two more models to sell—one named Victoria, the other Linda. And just to clarify, it was not only financial capital she was looking for in a son-in-law but good morals, a prestigious family history, friendly relatives, and good looks. Last but not least, the suitor had to overlook the dowry, since my mother had none to give.

In the soft light of the Jewish Club's oil lamps, Mama led me around the room and introduced me to every one of her friends. I was confused as to why we spent large amounts of time with women Mama had never expressed too much social interest in before. Years later, I realized that Mama was only interested in talking to the mothers, aunts, and grandmothers of potential husbands. As instructed, after saying hello as sweetly as possible, I kept my mouth shut!

Later in the evening, when the cookies and cakes we had prepared had almost entirely disappeared, a few young men set up a gramophone at an open window. The French music that started playing reverberated powerfully around the adjacent courtyard. A few younger married couples started to dance energetically—swaying, spinning, twisting, embracing, and stepping—mirroring the precise movements of their

partners. I sat down at a table with a full view of the spectacle, admiring their movements with jealousy, wishing to be
able to join them. An Italian girlfriend of mine had taught
me more than a few of the dances on display, but I didn't dare
demonstrate my familiarity with the activity. A few expressions of distaste directed at the participants from the older,
more religious members in attendance were sufficient to keep
me nailed to my seat.

It wasn't until a few months after my party at the Jewish
Club that I finally had a chance to join them. My Auntie Latife
and her husband, Halifa, also loved to dance and conveniently
lived next door to the infamous courtyard. My mother asked
Auntie Latife to take me to the club every month so that the
good families of Aleppo, with plenty of sons to spare, would
not have me too far from their minds.

Halifa's moves were smooth and polished, and after he
discovered my love for dancing, I became his partner for the
first few songs of the night. At the urging of my auntie, Halifa
screened all the eligible boys who asked me to join them for
the subsequent dances.

We had a few rules that could not be broken. It was absolutely impermissible to dance for two consecutive songs with
the same boy. This was tantamount to informing all of Aleppo
of your intention to marry. Second, I could only dance with
the boys whom my uncle and aunt considered good prospects.
We even had a system for communicating amongst ourselves
at that crucial time. When a boy approached the table, Halifa
would nod if he was acceptable and pass me a matchbox if he
wasn't. When I received the matchbox, I would apologize,
explaining that my feet were too tired to continue—although
the rejected boy would soon sadly watch me twirl across the
floor with another. Other rules forbid eye contact and required
an arm's length of distance between me and my dance partner. Every regulation was to preserve my pristine reputation,
which, without a dowry, was all I had to offer.

Of course, with some boys, there were ways to bend the rules. Raymond Mansour's neatly combed blond hair, fashionable clothing, perfect French, and proximity to my age assured that I would always reserve a song for him. Whenever he approached to ask my uncle's permission for a dance, Raymond had already made a few arrangements of his own. After Halifa's nod, I would get up, shyly place my right hand in his left and my left hand on his shoulder, and we would spin quickly around the floor, the music energizing our steps. When the song would start winding to a close, Raymond would wink at his friend operating the gramophone, who would restart the same song over again. Raymond would grip my hand tightly, so I had no choice but to stay on the dance floor. Often, he would play the same trick twice in a row so we could spend a full three songs together. An intense stare from my uncle would notify Raymond when his luck had run out. I never protested our extended sessions, since he was one of the only boys who could dance without counting his steps obsessively and he didn't step all over my feet. For nine minutes and one long, often interrupted, song, I felt like a French movie actress at a most luxurious and exclusive party.

Unbeknownst to my mother or brothers, I began visiting the Jewish Club on Sundays as well. My girlfriends and I would meet secretly and dance away the afternoon. My popularity grew fast since Moise and Rafoul would lend me all the newest music from the record shop. We would play the records and then return them in their original packaging to my brothers on Monday morning.

We listened to Maurice Chevalier and all the dance music we could find. The fox-trot, the tango—nothing was too difficult or off limits. Now, we almost always had female dance partners, so this was not as inappropriate as it sounds. But I would be lying to you if I said we never danced with boys. Even on the rare occasion when we did, though, we were all nervous enough to keep space between us.

We knew that getting caught dancing with boys was not a small thing. A poor girl's reputation was everything, and no one would marry you if they thought you had acted indecently. The Jewish quarter was very small and news spread at the speed of sound. This happened via a network of mothers and grandmothers with nothing more important to do than relate the virtues and vices of prospects for their sons. Even today's most advanced wireless telecommunication technology is a distant second to the effectiveness of these women with some time on their hands and a deck of cards.

Let me assure you that we all took our reputations very seriously. One misstep in this department would not only stain my honor but destroy many possibilities for Vicky and Linda as well. I knew that if I were even spotted walking side by side with the wrong boy, my sisters and I could all die husbandless and childless.

Lucky for me, as for most girls in Aleppo, we had a lot of help in avoiding anyone who could lead us down the wrong path. For most, it was a dominating father whose word was law. As my father had passed away, all four of my brothers did more than enough to instill fear and respectability into my heart.

Abraham fought with Mama constantly, yelling and screaming at her. "Why do you go play cards all day, leaving the girls alone in the house?" he'd bellow. "It is your responsibility to keep up the family's good name!"

It was always very scary to see them fight over how my sisters and I should be cared for. Obviously, there was nothing for me to say in the matter. My mother could not answer either.

Rafoul, who was closer to my age, had to take a more proactive stance to protect my future. He had a very good friend named Yitzchak who would come to the house often. Yitzchak was a good-looking Jewish boy, and while he came to see Rafoul, he started talking more and more to me. As I served them both coffee, he would ask me about my school classes and touch upon other light subjects.

All of this ended very quickly one afternoon when Mama was in the house and overheard us talking about my love for dancing. She called me into the kitchen, keeping me there until the guests had left, and afterwards approached Rafoul.

"Rafoul!" she scolded condescendingly, looking down her nose at him. "What is your friend's name?"

"Yitzchak," Rafoul answered obediently.

"And this Yitzchak..." my mother began analytically, "What does he do for a living?"

Rafoul, realizing his mistake, looked down at the floor and responded slowly. He recognized, only too well, the trap he was walking into. "Well... he tutors math and history."

My mother's face became redder and redder, but she fought semi-successfully to keep her voice calm. "And how much money does he make tutoring math and history?"

"I don't know, Mama," Rafoul responded, still looking at the floor, not daring to challenge her burning red glare.

Mother's patience shattered in a million pieces, like a windowpane dropped on the head of a spear. "Well, Rafoul!" she exploded. "Do you think he has enough money to support a family!?"

"No, Mama," Rafoul responded reticently, not daring to challenge her.

"So... if Lucie and this boy get married, and they move into our house, will you support them and their children?"

"No, Mama," Rafoul repeated sullenly.

"Then, you better tell this Yitzchak not to come to the house anymore." After getting these last words out, Mama calmed a bit and walked away to compose herself.

The next day, Yitzchak met Rafoul as usual and asked if he could come over. At that point, my brother looked his best friend in the eye. He told him the words he had rehearsed one hundred times since the night before. Furrows of determination and sorrow dug into his forehead and lowered the sun cracked corners of his lips. "You cannot come to the house anymore," he said solemnly.

Rafoul's relationship with his friend was never the same after that. His relationship with me changed as well, as he became more and more protective. A few weeks after this incident, I met my brother in the street one Sunday afternoon on my way to the Jewish Club. He was on his way home, but I was headed in the other direction. "Hello, Lucie," he said, surprised to see me. "Where are you going? Aren't you going to prepare the dinner?"

"Oh, hello, Rafoul," I answered quickly since I was already late: "I'm going to my girlfriend's house. A group of us are getting together for an hour or so."

"Don't you know it's dangerous to walk around here by yourself?" he warned in an eerily calm voice.

"Don't worry!" I fired back. "I will go quickly!"

"No, you will not!" Rafoul replied firmly. "You are coming back with me now!"

Annoyed that my plans were foiled, I replied callously, "You are not my father or my moth—"

He slapped me across the face in a sudden eruption, harder than I had ever been hit before. His usually pale cheeks turned crimson as he grabbed my arm and dragged me home. I shuffled my feet behind him in a halfhearted protest.

At any rate, one can say that I listened to my youngest brother after that. Years later, I really didn't harbor a grudge towards Mama or Rafoul for these events. First of all, I was not ready to get married anyway. I thought Yitzchak was a nice boy, but there is a gigantic chasm between enjoying someone's company and wanting to marry them. At the same time, the economic situation in Aleppo was only getting worse. Being poor did not mean living in a smaller house; it meant starving for the rest of your life. Of course, Yitzchak could have ended up a very rich man, but it is difficult to become successful if you are sixteen years old, your wife is thirteen years old, your baby is one year old, and you can barely scrape together enough francs[1] to buy food.

That is why, a few months later, my mother was only too happy to expedite my engagement.

Getting Your Goat

It would not be one hundred percent truthful to say that on the fateful day my mother took me to the coffee shop to marry me off, I had never heard Ezra's name mentioned before. It would also not be one hundred percent truthful to say that my mother had not dropped more than a few hints that he was my groom-to-be. In fact, my mother had been working on this priority-number-one project for more than ten years.

In romantic films, when a woman meets her future husband, their eyes meet, time stops, birds chirp, and they ride off on a white horse into the sunset. Our first meeting went quite differently, as my mother described it years later.

Ezra walked his mother, Farida, over to our house one morning. At the time, Ezra was nineteen years old and I was two. My mother, after the usual pleasantries, announced to Ezra with overflowing enthusiasm: "Allow me to introduce you to your future wife!" She was wearing a smile from ear to ear. He laughed nervously, and before he could say anything or run to the door, she plopped me into his arms. I instantly peed on him.

Now, this meeting did not happen by chance. Farida and Mama were good friends and played bridge together every day in a group of four. They would play from ten in the morning until late into the night, betting money on each game. Everyone knew, though, that the only person who could actually pay her bridge tab was Farida, who did so every time she lost. This was because Ezra was getting to be quite successful

---

1 Lucy remembers using francs as Syrian currency in her youth.

and would give her money every day. The rest of us were lucky to have food on the table, so it was politely ignored that many gambling debts were years overdue. The point was to inject some excitement into the day, not to become rich or poor.

Farida was always coming over for cards, coffee, or simply to talk with my mother. But every time I was in the room, it seemed like her blue, calculating eyes were fixed on me. There were many phrases which peppered our conversations in Aleppo, and *men nahasse* (made of copper or brass) was a good one to describe her intense mental and physical toughness—I made sure not to offend her. I was pretty good at determining the strengths and weaknesses of people around me and knew a battle with this woman would be a losing one. Although she was short even by Aleppo standards and slightly overweight, this belied her wiry strength. Her long, curly brown hair was blended with generous amounts of grey, which framed an extremely serious, rounded face. Her mouth was the feature that made her either approachable or *men nahasse*. When she was in a good mood her beautiful smile was contagious. When she was in a bad mood, her expression cast an ominous cloud over everyone. It seemed that I never got too many smiles thrown in my direction. I was always under observation, like a captured insect under a magnifying glass.

As Farida knew I had no dowry, she was constantly testing me to see if I were worthy of her only son. Her main concern was for Ezra to marry a strong, good-looking, compassionate, intelligent woman who could bear many strong male children for the family. In Aleppo, there were definitive ways of quantifying these attributes. The first test was for strength.

Each day of the week, the card game was moved to a different house to ensure each person was given the chance to be hospitable and share in the financial costs. During the summers, the game was often held at our house, and the ladies would sit outside.

Farida would say casually, "Have Lucie go get some milk for me." Mama would give me a stern glance, and I would ready myself for the task.

The goat and cow herder would come into town every morning around ten o'clock. He was a strong Arab man with a medium to large beard, depending on the season, and an unkempt hairstyle. He wore a shirt open at the neck and pants that were huge at the waist and tight at the ankles. His hands and clothes were always full of dirt and grime from looking after the goats, going back and forth from the city to his village, and sleeping under the stars. While the goats did most of their grazing out of town, the goat herder stopped very close to our house daily because there was also plenty of grass to eat there. He was a nice man but worked hard and was not about to do too much extra work if he had someone who could do it for him.

Approaching him, I would ask with a serious look, "Do you have any goat's milk left today?"

"Of course," he would say with a generous smile, "all that you and your house can drink!"

"Very good!" I would answer enthusiastically, returning the good cheer.

"Would you like milk from a white goat, a grey goat, a brown goat, or a black goat today?" he would respond, as if it were a question of profound importance.

"I would like half from a white goat and half from a brown goat, please."

"Excellent choice!" he would say. "Now go catch the goats you want so I can milk them for you!" Every day, approaching him, I was hoping for a different answer.

So the ladies playing cards would watch me run after the goats at full speed. The goats would run fast and swerve right or left, hoping to elude me. After a minute or two of sprinting as fast as I could, I would catch up with the goat, grab it high on its hind legs, and quickly move to the side to avoid any punishment. After a few unlucky occasions, I learned that the feeling of an animal kicking me in the chest was one that should be avoided at all costs.

After leading the goats to the man, I would tightly grab onto their furry coats. He would then hold a tin container under their nipples and expertly massage out the warm, fresh milk. His favorite trick was to hold the container far away from the nipples, creating a thick layer of foam on top of the milk. Then he would charge for a full cup, when one fourth of it would be filled with frothy, foamy air. We had a good relationship, though, and it would only take a little verbal prodding to get him to fill the container to the top.

"Will you be paying today?" he would always ask hopefully.

"Can we pay you at the end of the week?" I would plead.

"No problem, my child!" he would answer, smiling down at me. He would quickly draw a chalk line for each cup of milk we bought on the door of the house. At the end of the week, when we paid him, he would erase the lines.

Farida watched this entire process closely. It told her I was strong enough to catch some goats, a good enough negotiator to ask for a few extra squirts of milk at no extra charge, and that I could settle payment terms. In short, I could be entrusted with some shopping responsibility in the future.

The ladies loved to drink coffee when playing cards. Mama would want her coffee black with no sugar; Farida would want hers with milk and a lot of sugar; Zarife would want hers black with a lot of sugar; and Nour would want hers black with a little sugar. It was no accident that everyone ordered their coffee a different way. It was a test of intelligence.

I picked up our ancient *doleh* (brass coffee pot) which looked somewhat like a medium-sized, wide-bottomed genie bottle with Hebrew letters etched artistically onto the rounded sides and a straight metal handle which projected out from just below the lip. I measured out the cold water, added four large spoonfuls of coffee, stirred the mixture, and placed the pot over the fire. After a few minutes the dark, delicious foam started to form and I spooned some into each elaborately decorated, small porcelain cup. I returned the pot to the fire until it boiled and quickly filled each cup halfway with the unsweetened coffee. I then returned the pot to the fire and, when it boiled again, poured more unsweetened coffee into the cups needing little or no sugar. I then added a few spoonfuls of sugar to what remained in the pot, stirred quickly, brought it back to a boil, and filled the remaining cups. I added the milk where needed, placed a small plate of cookies on the brass tray, and arranged the cups in the same orientation as the guests.

Etiquette required that I serve them in order of their age and my mother last. So, I served Farida first, then Zarife, then Nour, and then my mother. Farida watched every move closely until the last of her friends was served. At first, I shivered nervously, afraid that I would make a mistake. Later, my confidence grew, and I was just unhappy to be in the kitchen with the coffee, instead of out playing with my friends. No one would complain in front of my mother if I prepared their coffee incorrectly, but by all reports I passed the test. They were all impressed: first by the strength of my memory, second by my politeness in serving the eldest first, and last that I made a great cup of coffee.

The tests kept coming. I understood that they were tests of my abilities and moral fiber. Intuitively, in the recesses of my mind, I knew that these women wanted me to marry their sons. However, it never occurred to me to sabotage my opportunities with certain suitors by purposely failing a test—by occasionally serving a cold, acrid cup of coffee to an unwelcome visitor. I only tried to do everything asked of me to please my mother. Many mothers, including mine, considered Ezra a good catch. He was twenty-nine years old with a kind yet strong angular face; light-blue eyes full of intelligence; and a medium-sized, well-proportioned nose. His

muscular frame easily supported a one-hundred-sixty-centi-
meter height—which is not tall in any country. However, in
Syria there were many short people, so he did not stand out.
He habitually combed his straight light-brown hair with a
precise part on the left side, which made him look the consummate businessman. He always took pride in his clothing, wearing many nice western suits that emitted an aura of
respectability and confidence with every step he took. To the
mothers of Aleppo with daughters to marry, there was one
detail that mattered more than all the others.

Ezra had a good career. He had been working for a
Christian man named Asouad for many years. Their main
business was importing fabrics from Italy in large quantities
and selling them by the meter to the local Arab community.
It was good for their livelihoods that the dress code for Syrian
Muslim women required covering almost every centimeter of
skin with fabric. It meant that each dress made would require
a large fabric purchase. Over the years, he had become an
excellent salesman and would travel to many places throughout Syria to sell the stock they had imported. However, the
fabric imported from Italy would constantly increase in price.
Asouad started buying low priced fabric from other countries through a dishonest middleman, which put them at a
disadvantage. The fabric quality and deliveries were unpre-
dictable. To solve this problem, Asouad made Ezra a business
proposition. Before accepting, it was important that Ezra get
engaged. If not, his mother would never agree to the terms.

As Ezra was already twenty-nine years old, Farida acted
quickly, and chose me for her son. This was no small decision. She was the third wife of Ezra's father, who had passed
away shortly after the birth of her only child. Ezra was all
that she had.

The Insect

While Ezra and his mother started to think about marriage, I slowly became more of a focus in their lives. I started receiving small presents but didn't realize my life was expected in return.

Because Ezra sold textiles, he always had a lot of samples around the shop. At the urging of both my mother and his, he would give me some of this extra material. Farida would bring it over and present it to Mama, who would, in turn, present it to me. The first time this happened, I was caught completely off guard.

"What a beautiful green fabric!" Mama exclaimed loudly to Farida. I was in the kitchen, and they were in the living room, but she spoke so loudly I jumped in surprise. "Come into the living room quickly, Lucie, and see what Ezra sent for you."

There were a few questions sprinting through my mind as I walked slowly into the other room, but I wasn't brave enough to ask them. Why was my mother so excited about the gift? What was the occasion? I had really never spoken to Ezra, so why had he sent me something?

Mama met me at the door to the living room and mouthed, "Say, 'Thank you very much,' to *Um* Ezra." *Um* Ezra, literally, "the mother of Ezra," was a respectful way of addressing Farida.

Looking over Mama's shoulder, I could see Ezra's mother smiling and holding a dark green fabric. Although green was one of my least favorite colors, I walked over to her, avoided eye contact, and thanked her shyly with a big false smile on my face.

Mama didn't waste any time and started barking orders at me: "Lucie, you must call the tailor over. Have him cut the material for you and then get some needles and thread from upstairs."

"Yes," I said obediently, knowing better than to argue.

I brought the tailor back to the house. When he was halfway through cutting the material, I sat where Mama told me to, near Farida, and started working on the hem of the dress. My help was not needed by the dressmaker, but we always did some of the easier jobs to save money. Mama also needed to demonstrate that I was a good homemaker, and not lazy or spoiled. Later, after the guests had left, the tailor helped me finish the dress. Mama wanted to make sure it looked good on me.

When I viewed the finished product in the mirror, I gasped in horror—I looked like a huge grasshopper! The long-sleeved, green top fit tightly around my arms, making them appear long, thin, and gangly. The material then puffed out at my shoulders and the conservative neck line before it tightened at my ribs, ballooned out over my stomach, and re-tightened at my waist. The alternating tight and poufy bodice made my torso look segmented and the large, gaudy bow on my lower back looked like bug wings. I ran away from Mama as fast as the movement of the dress would allow, tears flowing down my cheeks. What really hurt was not my dislike for the dress, because that could have been remedied by leaving it in the closet. I cringed at the thought of having to give my beautiful pink taffeta dress to Vicky and add this to my wardrobe instead. We did not have enough money to do this any other way, as Linda's dress was already tattered.

The result was an embarrassing night out in my insect dress. We walked by the coffee shop so that Ezra, Farida, and everyone else could witness the spectacle. The good citizens of Aleppo knew quite well why a twelve-year-old girl, skin pink with embarrassment, was parading around town showing off an ill-fitting garment. I think I was the only one in the city who didn't know that an engagement was approaching. Nevertheless, we did achieve a goal of sorts. Ezra remarked, after Farida's hard glances across the table and possibly a kick under it, that I looked very nice. Mama, while ignoring my pleas to stay home, did redeem herself by telling Ezra that I looked even nicer in blue.

One thing that was appreciated much more than the fabric was Farida's cooking as we never had enough food in the house. Farida had the opposite problem—only one person to cook for. And as Ezra grew more successful in the textile business, she received more money for her daily expenses. The money was spent on the best lamb, chicken, eggplant, rice, lentils, onions, pistachios, and anything else that warmed the stomach or tickled the taste buds. *Kibe*, hummus, *babagannuge, sambusak*, stuffed grape leaves with apricot sauce, fried filo dough with spiced meats, and *baklawa* were just some of the daily offerings.

Lucky for us, the more successful Ezra became, the more time he spent at the office. He often was too busy to eat with her. She was too good a mother, though, to ever serve her son leftovers. Farida would bring the food over and we'd salivate as she described how she had cooked that day. When she made *zeroa,* we sat through the account of the buying, the boiling, the spicing, and finally the roasting of the lamb. Like every good Syrian woman, she would leave out a few ingredients—as one didn't need too much competition in town. By the time she had finished her story, we were ready to grab the food out of her hands. But we had enough self-control to wait; every tortuous second of delay was well worth it. Each new dish she brought over was better than the last.

After we finished, it was my job to bring the serving plates back to Farida. It was not polite to bring them back empty, so we filled up the plates with pickles. This was one thing we always had plenty of, since they lasted for a long time and required no preparation. It was a trifle compared to the food she gave us, but she always politely thanked me for them.

Mama and *Um* Ezra worked slowly but diligently towards joining our families. My personal relationship with Ezra's mother was forced to grow when I returned her plates or paraded around in my newest dress. The ultimate goal of all this posturing was to get Ezra and me closer together. Ironically, my sisters and I were always thrilled when he didn't appear at his mother's for dinner. We never ate better in our lives.

The Naked Truth

On the night of the engagement and during the days that followed, I felt like a tortured prisoner. I had no choice but to sit in my cell, as each minute brought me closer to my ultimate punishment. I cried and cried in my room, mourning all I had imagined for my life that was suddenly swept away like dust. Now there was a plan set in motion that I had no power to delay. Mama had bought me a one-way ticket on a train that never stopped, and never reached a destination. My life would never be the same as it was before. I hated her for it, and could not even look at her.

In the schoolyard, we would tease each other about who liked whom, but all of us were fourteen years old or younger. Now I was promised to marry someone who was almost thirty! What could we possibly have in common? What could we possibly talk about? What could we possibly do together? I mean—he was even older than my school teachers!

My face got bright red and my blood boiled with anger whenever I even thought of Mama. I didn't want to get married yet! I didn't want to leave Abraham, Moise, David, Rafoul, Linda, and Vicky! I didn't want to leave school! I didn't want to stop playing with my friends and become an old, proper woman!

At the same time, I felt small, lonely, and insecure about the frayed bond between Mama and me. Every question I had was like a bee sting to my heart. Why was she in such a hurry to get rid of me? Why did she hate me so much? Why was I so difficult to be around? Was I such a bad person?

Auntie Latife was the only one who listened when I complained. For many nights, I lay in her arms and cried, pouring out my anguish onto her blouse.

Where marriage and my mother were concerned, Auntie Latife also harbored a little bit of a grudge. When Mama was getting married, over twenty years earlier, Auntie developed a small boil on the left side of her face. With all the festivities, no one had the time to take proper care of it. Following a neighbor's recommendation, they put some plaster on the infection, hoping that it would be a fast cure. After weeks of applying and reapplying the plaster it was obvious that, instead of helping her, it was distorting her face badly. The boil not only grew, but the plaster also pulled some of the skin around her left eye in a downward direction. By the time a doctor was contacted to fix the problem, she had a permanent scar and mild disfigurement on the left side of her face. Now she realized this was hardly Mama's fault, but she resented the fact that not enough attention was paid to her when she desperately needed it. And she was left with a constant reminder of her sister's marriage, staining her otherwise beautiful face.

We became a lot closer following the engagement. She helped me in any way that she could to take my mind off of the situation. On our weekend trips to the country, she would play the *oud* accompanying her husband's violin, coaxing my mind to drift to happier places. She also would take me around town with her, creating some needed space between Mama and me.

My favorite activity was spending time with her at the public bathhouse. The bathhouse (*ḥammām*) in Aleppo was for men half the week and for women the other half. I did not go there often, as it cost money, and money was in short supply. Our routine was that, upon reaching the front of the line, I would bend my knees and hunch over a little. This got me in for the ten-year-old's price. The jovial fat lady behind the counter was very friendly and never argued about my age. We would spend hours washing in the hot water, sitting in the steam, and listening to the news of the town. I was proud to go with my auntie, as her body was so beautiful that the other women would stare in envy.

One morning, while we were nearing the front of the line

to enter the bathhouse, a small scandal erupted. There was a boy who went to my school in the lower grades. His mother would regularly take him to the bathhouse on the day for women, as she did not have any male relatives who could accompany him. I would always scurry out of any bathing room he occupied, since I didn't want him to see me naked. He was almost ten years old, but looked eight, so the fat lady always let him in without too much argument. Her thinking was that an eight-year-old would not pay too much attention to what was going on around him. Apparently, those two years between eight and ten made quite a difference.

Word had spread in the wrong circles about the boy's ability to go where no man dared. Some older men of various backgrounds, who enjoyed cultivating trouble, were sitting at the coffee shop one day when he walked by.

"Hey boy!" they called with welcoming smiles on their faces, "You come here!"

He walked slowly over to them, slightly fearful, not knowing what they wanted.

"Hey boy, you were in the bathhouse with the women yesterday! Yes?"

The boy cracked a slight smile, which gave him away immediately, and the group of men started chuckling amongst themselves. They knew an opportunity when presented with one.

"So, did you see any women naked?" they asked slowly and deliberately.

"Yes," he answered, a little proud but wary.

"Well, who did you see?" a brave one among them pressed.

The boy was young but not stupid. In a strict Muslim society you don't just talk about seeing peoples' wives, sisters, and mothers sans clothing. This indiscretion could damage your reputation for life or get you excommunicated or killed.

"I ca—ca—ca—can't say," he stammered, blushing.

"Yes you can! Yes you can! Yes you can!" they all chorused emphatically.

All it took was a little time, some more cajoling, a few francs, and a bar of chocolate for him to spew out the contents of his memory for all to hear. It wasn't that the boy was devoid of honor, just that the rowdy mob's pressure was too great. He went into detail about every naked woman he had seen.

"This one has a fat behind!" "That one is hairy everywhere!" "This one has plenty of loose skin!" "Mrs. So and So has huge breasts!"

An explosion of laughter would follow each blow-by-blow account of their neighbors' assets and liabilities.

After the sordid affair, the adults made him swear to secrecy. They were all good about keeping their secret. The men gave him names of women to watch and the promise of more riches and chocolate in his immediate future. A few days later, the boy went again to the bathhouse, this time taking mental notes of all he saw. All the happenings of the day were recounted in a similar fashion. He went a third time, and the crowd grew and grew. Instead of one chocolate bar, he started coming away with five or six and pocketed a good amount of money.

Alas, the secret was too good to keep! The men would start whispering and laughing each time a woman went by who had been studied by their spy.

"Imagine how hairy she is under that dress!" some would erupt with laughter. "Look at how her behind sags, just as he said!" they would joke.

The husbands of these women were also ridiculed as soon as they passed from sight. "Can you imagine being so unlucky as to have to look at that woman every night?"

Pretty soon, all the women's carefully guarded secrets circulated all over town, and it was not difficult to divine who was responsible.

Auntie Latife and I returned to the bath on the morning under description. The fat lady jumped up from behind the counter and ran at the boy and his mother. "What do you think you are doing?" she screamed. "You both can never, ever come back here again! Your son has been telling all of Aleppo what my customers look like naked! No one wants to come to the bath anymore!" she shrieked.

"What???" she shouted at her son. "Is that true???" He didn't answer, but he didn't have to. His skin was as pale as bleached linen, and his knees were shuddering so violently they were hitting each other. She slapped him hard across the face multiple times and dragged him away as he cried hysterically.

After these events, the boy did not have an easy life for a few years, but people eventually forgave him, and he led a respectable, honorable life.

Personally, I was always very happy to visit the bath despite the risks. It meant that Auntie Latife and I could spend the entire day together. One such day, at the end of one of our long discussions, she told me something I could not repeat to my mother or anyone else. It gave me hope and made the next three years of my life bearable.

We were speaking normally and washing our hair, until the rest of the ladies were out of earshot. "Lucie, I have some news of great importance!" she whispered with subdued excitement on her face.

"What is it?" I replied apprehensively, unable to imagine any possibility of good news.

"Ezra is leaving for Japan in two days! He first will get settled and start his business, and... only *then* does he plan to come back and marry you!"

"Oh," I said, thoroughly dejected. "why should I be excited about that?"

Auntie Latife shook her head, as if I knew nothing of the world, and sighed. "You don't realize it Lucie, but this may be good news for you. If you really don't want to marry him, you have to realize that now there is a chance it may never happen!"

"What do you mean?" I replied intrigued, now fully focused on the conversation.

"Well... Japan is very far away, and he will probably be gone for years. Also, there are pretty girls in Japan, and other girls here who may try to steal him from you. What I am saying is that time changes people and could change what is planned for you. So don't worry as life is full of surprises—some good, some bad. The best advice I can give you is to eat while you can... dance while you can... sleep while you can... and laugh while you can... You never know what tomorrow will bring."

Auntie's news provided a spark of hope that, when spoken with her words of comfort, kindled a warm fire within me. It melted away my despair and gave me a reason to believe that my life could still be saved. The bath, the walk home, and this new development put me in a resilient mood.

Auntie and I walked into the house with bright faces. Right after we entered, Mama came in from the kitchen and announced sternly, "Ezra is leaving for Japan in two days. He will be here tomorrow to speak with us. Get ready to receive him."

"Oh really? So soon?" I answered with as much concern as I could summon.

"I will go ready my outfit."

As I skipped to the staircase, I flashed a big smile at my mother. After my enlightenment, there was absolutely no reason to argue.

Lending My Hand

The next day, I did my best to look nice because Mama would be hypersensitive to any subtle effort on my part to sabotage all of her hard work.

Ezra arrived as promised that morning. Dressed in a nice black suit, he looked very professional, and very different from any of my thirteen-year-old male school friends. His hair was recently combed and freshly parted on the left side.

I was glad my mother, Farida, and Auntie Latife were around so I didn't have to talk too much.

They were glad they were around too, and interpreted our every movement as if we were the main characters in the latest French movie to hit the theatre. They would need to watch closely to answer all the important questions the neighbors would ask later:

Were they getting along? What were they talking about? Were they smiling at each other? How many sons do you think Lucie will give him?

After Auntie disappeared into the kitchen, Farida and Mama immediately started working like a team to get us both into the correct position and frame of mind. Ezra and Farida sat in the salon on two wooden chairs next to the faded blue couch. Farida took the chair farthest from the couch, forcing Ezra to sit directly next to it. Then Mama guided me with a firm shove on the waist to the seat on the couch adjacent to his chair.

We were dangerously close together. My face blushed, my fingers fidgeted, and my mind was racing as fast as a spooked horse. I needed to do something—anything—to rope it under semi-control. I started quickly counting the holes in the white wall opposite to us. My mind repeated this two or three times until I was sure my number was right. After the holes were counted, I started on the hats and coats. Then I tried to figure out the number I would get by dividing the total number of holes in the wall by the hats and coats in the room.

All of this was to prevent something more terrifying to me than anything I had yet experienced in life. I did not want to catch his eyes and be forced to look into them for any length of time. This was not only because I was scared to death of having any interaction with him but also because it could be interpreted as brazen or immodest by the others in the room.

The mothers, once getting us correctly situated, started weaving a web of conversation designed to bring us together.

Even though Ezra was Farida's only son, and I was Mama's first daughter eligible for marriage, they acted like veteran match-makers, together pairing up their most promising clients.

"So, Ezra," Farida prompted, "Why don't you tell Lucie about your upcoming trip?"

At this point, I had no choice but to look at him or face an equally terrifying proposition—a slap from my mother. The pallor in his face and the beads of sweat on his fore-head betrayed that I was not the only one who felt extremely uncomfortable with the situation. Since Syrian society iso-lated the sexes from one another, neither man nor woman could act with any degree of composure when thrust into each other's company. The redness of my face was in stark contrast to the whiteness of his. Anyone who had mistakenly entered the room unannounced at that moment would have thought that we were both deathly ill.

He said slowly and clearly, as if it were a line he had prac-ticed a few hundred times, "I will depart to Japan tomorrow where I will get settled. When I have finished making some money so we can start a life together, I will come back and marry you."

What could I say? What could I do? I blurted out the only answer that came to mind: "Can I get you some coffee?" Halfway through springing up off the couch, Mama pulled down hard on my upper leg. I fell involuntarily, helplessly back down into my seat.

They were all way too clever for me.

"Oh, Lucie," my mother projected loudly, "you are always so polite! Don't be silly. I will get the coffee for you! Ezra, what would you like?"

"Black with sugar, please," he responded obediently.

At that point, Farida piped up, "Oh, Seto, let me help you."

Before either of us knew what had happened, Ezra and I were alone in the room. We knew our mothers were not coming back with coffee.

We were silent for about two hundred and forty interminable half seconds. I would look quickly at him. He would glance quickly at me. The silence grew and grew until it was like a big, hungry tiger thrashing around the salon. Ezra was aware of it; I was aware of it; our mothers in the next room were well aware of it. The silence became scarier to me than the prospect of marrying a man twice my age whom I hardly knew. I had to break it just to end the suffering on both of our parts.

"So... what are you going to do in Japan?" I asked with more than a little hesitation in my voice.

"Work," he answered matter-of-factly.

Another forty-two half seconds passed, and the tiger started pouncing around the room again. I could feel Ezra looking at me more intensely now, so I made a bold move.

My photo album happened to be on a dresser in the room. I went to retrieve it, placed the album on my lap, flipped through the pages nervously with my right hand, and trying to appear relaxed, rigidly placed my left hand on the couch's armrest. I then started showing him the pictures one by one.

"This is my friend Sarine and my sisters Vicky and Linda," I began. I went through the pictures in the book and talked about how I liked playing jump rope, hide and go seek, and other games with my friends. I continued for another three to four minutes about my poetry teacher and how much I liked to write. From time to time, quick, furtive glances that could barely pass for eye contact were made on my part.

Suddenly, in the middle of a story about how I didn't like my math class, without word or warning, he extended his hand and rested it on top of mine. My heart immediately dove into my stomach, and my skin blistered with apprehension.

My gut reaction was to jerk it away, but somehow I overpowered my instincts and left it on the couch's armrest. My face got even redder than before, but I stopped speaking only for an instant before I continued my math story. Now I couldn't look at him but felt his gaze even more intensely than before. I had to keep talking about something to occupy my mind so that my body would not run out the front door. My hand went numb under his lukewarm touch as, for another few minutes, I discussed the finer points of school life.

Before I ran out of stories to tell, he unexpectedly and quickly got up. "Lucie, I must meet with a customer and make some last-minute arrangements for my trip," he said quickly. "I will see you soon."

With that, he left out the front door before my mother or his could delay his escape.

Farida, Mama, and Auntie Latife came in from the kitchen and looked me up and down.

"What happened?" Auntie Latife asked, surprised at his sudden departure.

"Did he touch you?" my mother asked inquisitively.

"Where did he go?" Farida asked, a little shocked.

Relieved at his departure, I answered calmly, "He touched my hand."

"Why did he leave?" Farida pushed again.

"He said he had a meeting with a customer," I responded curtly.

"What did you talk to him about?" Auntie Latife pestered.

"I showed him pictures of my friends and talked about my poetry and math class," I replied innocently.

"Next time, you should talk to him about something more interesting!" my mother half scolded, probably more for the benefit of the audience than for me.

"Yes, mother!" I answered automatically and ran up to my room. I escaped the cross-examination before anyone else could get a comment in. A sigh of relief was pushed out of my lungs and through my lips as I crashed down on my mattress and fell sound asleep from exhaustion.

Love Letters

I felt like a prisoner released from jail and given a second chance at life when Ezra left for Japan. Going to school, playing with friends, eating with family, and even doing chores were not just day-to-day activities anymore. They were each cherished events to be enjoyed like ice cream, *choux a la crème*, or Friday night dinner. I understood too well that any day, with very little warning, my family could ship me off to another part of the world. There the people, the language, the culture, and the food would all be foreign to me. Anything would be better than that!

There was only one daily reminder of my incarceration. Ezra's mother: my parole officer. I thought she made an effort to come around the house a lot before Ezra's departure, but it was nothing compared to afterwards! She would come over every day and ask my mother, "Where is Lucie? What is she doing? Who is she with?"

When I was in the house, she would come see for herself. She would look carefully at me, not in a nice way, but in the way my brother looked when he was inspecting a fabric: head tilted to one side, with intense concentration, to see if any defect or flaw could be discovered before purchase. Actually, it was exactly the same thing. She was just observing and protecting her investment.

If I was doing nothing wrong, my reward would be a sideways, stone-faced glance and a swift departure by my new monitor. I never understood why she was so worried because there was really no choice but to behave.

Everyone who lived around us knew that Ezra was supposed to marry me. I knew that if anyone even suspected I had walked home with another boy it would bring great shame to my family. Even though marriage was the last thing I wanted, to rebel against my mother and give my family a bad name was unfathomable.

Let me clarify, though, that just because running away with a good-looking classmate was not an option, it did not mean that I was going to give up. Accepting my mother's plans for me without complaint was not an option either. She approached me in the kitchen, two weeks after Ezra's departure, and gave me a way to fight back.

"Lucie," she oozed with manufactured excitement, "Farida is coming over today, and we are going to write a letter to Ezra in Japan."

"What?" I shouted in surprise.

"You heard me, Lucie," she repeated sternly, "Today we will write a letter to your future husband."

"Why should I write him?" I replied evenly, standing my ground. "I'm not going to marry him!"

Now, this created a slight problem for Mama, as neither she nor Farida could write. Being my mother, though, she knew how to motivate me.

"All right, Lucie," she began again in a softer tone, "what do you want?"

"I want to not get married," I replied defiantly.

"That's not what I meant, and you know it." She massaged me vocally with the same soothing tone: "What do you want in return for writing the letter?" She looked at me convincingly with soft eyes.

"Ten francs!" I demanded—not because I wanted the money, but because I didn't want to write the letter.

Her eyes froze into a steely gray as the patience trickled out of them. She countered, "I'll give you one franc."

I acquiesced with my head down.

Farida arrived later that afternoon looking like a poor merchant who had just been swindled out of every material possession. Her usual self-confident appearance had melted away, and only worry was left embossed into her face. After reaching the salon, she collapsed on the sofa and started to cry uncontrollably. "Oh, Seto!" she cried, tearing at her hair.

"I have not heard from Ezra! Maybe he is sick—or worse—dead!!! Wwwaaaaaaaaaaaaaaaa!!!" She screamed in agony.

My mother sat beside her and put an arm around her but said nothing.

"My poor boy. Who can take care of him in Japan? My poor boy... My poor boy... My poor boy," she repeated over and over to herself, sobbing with her head in her hands.

My mother and I were completely silent for what seemed like a few years. When Farida's sobs became less frequent, Mama took over. "I know he is fine," she said with soft confidence. "It has been only two weeks, and a letter from Japan must take at least one month to arrive. He may not even be there yet."

"Oh, my poor boy... Wwwaaaaaaaaa!!!" Farida exploded again, tearing more clumps of brittle hair out of her scalp. "He may be in a storm at sea, or what if there is a fire on the boat..."

"There is no storm, and there is no fire!" my mother answered with forceful conviction. "He is doing very well, and we will hear from him soon! We will write a letter to him today, so he knows that you are doing well and waiting for his return."

"Lucie," Mama demanded abruptly, "get a pen and paper so we can write that letter."

I returned quickly with the writing tools and sat down obediently. "What should I write?" I asked seriously.

Farida stopped crying and began dictating in between shallow, pained breaths. Without saying a word nor adding nor subtracting anything, I wrote as neatly as I could:

Dear Ezra:

I am here visiting Seto Esses. Your uncle is in good health. I am in good health. I cooked some ejjeh b' jibneh today and then started crying because you are not here.

After a few lines, Mama interjected and ordered me to write about my day as well. She didn't want Ezra to forget about me, and ruin all of her hard work.

"What am I supposed to say to him?" I questioned petulantly. Despite all the drama of the morning, my feelings towards him had not changed.

"Tell him how you are doing in school!" she fumed and delivered a hard stare that made the hair on the back of my neck stand up.

It was much easier to placate my mother than cause a bigger problem, so I added one sentence about me, and kept writing for Farida:

> *Lucie did well on her math test and is on the honor board at school.*
> *Are you eating well?*
> *Are you sleeping well?*
> *Are you wearing your long underwear?*
> *Who are your friends?*
> *Who is cooking for you?*
> *Are you going with any Jewish or Japanese girls?*

This line shocked me. She wanted me to ask my fiancé if he was going out with any Jewish or Japanese girls. I didn't change her words because if he said yes, the wedding would be cancelled, which was just fine with me. Ultimately, it was her way of telling my mother, and especially me, that we better behave if we wanted the privilege of marrying her son.

When we finished the letter, I quickly volunteered to deliver it. I couldn't wait to get out of the house! Luckily, Mama accepted with no argument. She even gave me some money to take a carriage and pay the postage. Of course, I pocketed the money instead of taking the carriage and took a long walk away from my crazy new life.

The Threat and the Response

Mama, Farida, and I would write letters together often. As the days became weeks and the weeks became months, Farida became more and more depressed. The writing sessions became absolutely unbearable as there was crying and shouting the entire time.

She would scream, "Waaaaaaaaa!" and rip out her hair in agony. In between fits of anguish, she muttered, "Where is my boy??? What could have happened??? How could I leave him all alone with no one to take care of him??? Maybe he's dead? Maybe he's sick or injured? My poor boy... My poor boy..."

We did our best to comfort her. There was not much we could say besides, "I'm sure he's fine," and, "Don't worry," but after a while, our words sounded like lies, not only to her but to us as well.

Mama, as usual, acted ingeniously. She had not forgotten Farida's veiled threat in our letter: asking Ezra if he had any Japanese or Jewish girlfriends. She was not going to sit by idly and leave my future to chance.

She called me into her room one morning and told me to sit down next to the mirror. She spent hours carefully styling my hair into marcels. Afterwards, she smiled at me and applied makeup carefully all over my face. When she was done, I did not even recognize myself. She nodded with approval at her work and sent me downstairs to wait.

Farida came over, depressed as usual, and we all went into town. I had no idea what my mother was planning until we arrived at the photography shop. We did not have a lot of money, so taking a professional picture was no small thing. I was pleasantly surprised to get the chance to be photographed.

Being in front of the flashbulbs and camera, posing in different positions, and having everyone focus on every detail of my appearance was a very special, novel experience; I felt like a movie star. When we received the black and white pictures a few days later, I was overjoyed that they made me look like a glamorous model. When we wrote Ezra's next letter, Mama put the picture inside the envelope.

The event had a calming effect on all of us for a few weeks. Deciding which picture to send and wondering if her son would like it relaxed Farida. When she relaxed, we were finally given a small dose of peace and quiet.

A few months after Ezra had left for Japan, Farida finally received a letter. She came immediately to our house, eager for me to read it to her. My mother and I were very happy, relieved we would not have to endure any more crying sessions. I thought life would go back to normal for a while. When I read it, I found out how wrong I was.

Sitting in front of the couch on one of our wooden chairs, I began reading the letter to my audience. Both Mama and Farida, in ecstatic joy over the great event, hung on my every word.

Dear Mother:

I am in the boarding house in Kobe, Japan, and sharing a room with Alfred Shoah from Beirut and Peppo Harrari from Argentina.

"Thank God he is well," Mama and Farida exhaled together joyfully.

We are each paying a few yen and sharing the cooking and the grocery shopping.

The moment the full sentence had left my mouth, Farida's mood soured. "What!!! My son cooking and grocery shopping!!!!" she exclaimed. "What is this??? My poor boy has no one to take care of him... What does he know about cooking??? He is not going to be healthy... He might get sick... My

poor boy!!! What have I done sending him there all alone???"
She immediately started crying and tearing at her hair again.

I didn't really know what to do, so I just sat silently with
my mother until she got quiet.

"Continue," Farida glumly whispered between sobs, getting control of herself. "Continue."

> *I am looking for materials and samples to send to Asouad in
> Aleppo. When I have enough money, I will come back and see
> you. Today Cohab cooked the jedrah for us, but it was watery
> and the samak was burned.*

The weeping suddenly began again. "How can my son work
if he has nothing to eat? What if he starves? How could I leave
him there all by himself? My son is not used to eating such
garbage! My poor boy! Waaaaaaaaaa!" she wailed in agony.

Five minutes later, I continued again.

> *We take turns washing the clothes and cleaning the d—*

I didn't even get through the sentence before she
screamed, "My son doing laundry and dishes!!?? He does not
know how to do this!!! How can he make money if the whole
day he is cooking, washing clothes and dishes??? Why did I
agree to let him go??? What should I do??? Why did I leave
him with no support??? My poor boy!!!"

Again, I waited until she calmed down.

"Continue," Farida urged tearfully. "Continue."

> *Your son,*
> *Ezra*

Once I finished, I immediately excused myself and escaped
to my room before she started crying again. I was happy for
her that Ezra was alive. At the same time, I had patiently sat

through plenty of crying during the past few months. This was the first good news she had received. I sympathized with her and understood why she was crazy with grief, but there was only so much sadness I could absorb. In the recesses of my mind, I also understood that I would be the one doing the laundry, cooking, cleaning, and living on the other side of the world if things progressed as planned.

Working Girl

At home, I was beginning to feel like a lamb being prepared for slaughter, with all the attention people paid to where I was and what I was doing. This, in addition to the periodic visits by Farida in her depression, made home life uncomfortable at best. These were minor inconveniences, though, compared to the other drama in our lives.

Abraham and David, overcoming the business disadvantages of youth and inexperience, had managed to run my father's textile business for nine years. We were all fiercely proud of their efforts, since no other people we knew were responsible for an entire business from such a young age. However, like cracks in an exquisite ceramic dish, problems began to emerge.

My brothers had sold merchandise on credit to a few long-term customers but had not yet been paid back. In addition, they had imported a large shipment of European fabric using virtually all of their remaining capital. Before they could sell the merchandise to recover their investment, a large financial crisis hit Aleppo. In 1934, Japanese fabric began appearing in the marketplace with increasing frequency. What cost one hundred francs from Europe cost only fifty francs from Japan. Many Syrian businessmen, like Asouad and Ezra, began importing large quantities of fabric from East Asia.

Suddenly, all the Aleppo vendors who had imported their material from Europe immediately lost half the value of their stocked goods. Whereas before the sale price was ten or twenty francs, now it was only five or ten francs. Almost all Middle Eastern customers, the majority of whom were not affluent, preferred the lower-priced goods—which were of only slightly lesser quality. Most Aleppo fabric merchants needed to halve the cost of their goods and absorb the price difference, merely to make a sale. The larger companies had money to recover from such a loss. But the smaller companies, like the businesses my brothers had lent merchandise to, went bankrupt. The loss of the money expected from these associates, coupled with the huge decrease in the value of their own inventory, threatened the survival of my brothers' business. There was only one thing that could save it.

My father had left my mother an extra house when he passed. Although it was only of modest size, it did provide a small monthly rental income to our family. We could sell the house and save the business, or keep the house and let the business fail. Mama and Abraham were the unlucky ones who had to make this crucial decision. Unfortunately, the only two possible options each led to immediate negative consequences.

If mother didn't sell, the business would fail, leaving Abraham and David without work. It was also very probable that they would need to leave the country to find employment. The positive aspect would be that she, Rafoul, and her young daughters could survive on the income. If she did sell the house to keep the business going, we would lose our only other source of funds. The family would be able to stay together, but there was no guarantee the business would succeed—or be able to generate enough income for everyone. It would also probably be necessary for one of my brothers to move to Japan, as Ezra had done.

Abraham and Mama argued, discussed, and deliberated loudly for a few weeks before the decision was reached. They intelligently concluded that due to the unstable business environment present in the country, and the many newly poor people driving down the price of assets, the best decision was to keep the property. It offered a guaranteed income that would secure the safety of us younger children for years to come.

I was deeply moved by their decision. And while it provided for our safety, it did not make it any easier to say goodbye to Abraham and David who both left for Palestine the next morning in search of a better livelihood. A few months later, Moise left to Haifa. Rafoul was left to run the record store and become the man of the house.

That left my mother with three girls, one boy, and very little money. My brothers in Palestine were able to help sporadically by sending almost everything they could earn. However, it just wasn't enough to support us. Palestine was not a big commercial center like Aleppo. It was a developing country with few resources and many poor people. After I finished the school year, there was only one thing to do: Mama told me I needed to get a summer job.

I was thrilled! Ecstatic! Excited! This was my ticket out of the house, where Farida's daily inspections were getting too stressful for me to handle. The only problem was that it was not so easy for a fourteen-year-old girl to find a job. Who would hire me? So the search began.

Auntie Latife finally had a breakthrough. She asked her neighbor, Lieutenant Compagnon of the French Army, if he knew of any job openings for civilians. He said that he needed someone for secretarial work, and Auntie promised him that I would fill the position nicely. She happily instructed me to arrive at the *Parc de Réparacion* at six-thirty the following morning for an interview with the Captain. Despite the early hour and the two kilometer walk, I was thrilled. The job was a way for me to be independent and get out of the house for a while.

After bread and jam for breakfast, I sprinted through the darkness toward the interview. When the sky lightened, I slowed to a run until the *Parc de Réparacion* came into view. It was the only way to calm the swarm of bees whirring around in my stomach and pacify the stampede of thoughts running around in my head. What if I didn't get the job? Could I survive all summer being watched by my mother and Farida? How were we going to get the extra money we needed? Could I find another job that could keep me safe?

Another story crept into my mind as well, giving me something else to worry about. It was well-known that a few weeks earlier a man from the family Shalmeh was walking near the French Captain's house. The Captain was by his wife's bedside, accompanied by a doctor, while she was giving birth. A few overzealous soldiers were standing guard outside when the man walked by. The soldiers informed him that he would have to take another route since no one was permitted near the building. Mr. Shalmeh didn't understand French and kept walking, unaware the soldiers were even talking to him. After a loud warning, he was shot dead.

I tried to disregard this incident since I knew that the French in Aleppo were generally friendly with the Jews. Furthermore, I knew that working in a military compound would be much safer than working in a regular Syrian company—if a Syrian company would even hire a woman. In many respects, it was the perfect place for me. That is, if I didn't trip myself up! I decided that I needed to get the job, whatever the cost.

As the *Parc de Réparacion* came into view, I slowed down to collect myself, brushed my hair, and straightened my dress. The sun was coming up over the large compound. Behind a high iron fence were many types of Jeeps, trucks, and cars, all in various states of disrepair. The morning sunlight danced on the green vehicles and leapt off the chrome into my eyes.

As I approached the main gate, I carefully studied the French soldier guarding it. He was by far the tallest man I had ever seen, muscular, with skin black as midnight. Reviewing the story of poor Mr. Shalmeh over and over in my head, I focused most of my attention on the brown rifle resting on the shoulder of his drab green uniform. His eyes studied me as I approached closer and closer. I had just about expended all my courage when I was within a mere meter of the gate. The guard suddenly sprang into action, swinging his rifle to the other side of his body and smashing his heels together violently.

I crumpled to the ground, put my hands over my head, and cried out in terror, "Noooooo!"

I waited to be shot or killed, but instead I heard a deep voice deliver a cheerful, "Good morning, Mademoiselle!"

I looked slowly up from the ground and saw the soldier's hand extended over his forehead in a salute. A transient smile danced quickly across his otherwise serious face.

I stood up quickly, very embarrassed, and informed the soldier, in a very small voice, that I had an appointment.

After briefly apologizing for scaring me and flashing another warm smile, he opened the gate. I walked through the courtyard, littered with broken-down automobiles, and up to the main building. It was a functional concrete struc-ture, otherwise unremarkable. The inside was equally plain, but there was plenty of movement. There were three rows of five oversized desks with black and white soldiers, in full uni-form and very short haircuts, sitting at each. Each soldier was battling a formidable stack of papers on his desk with a bulky typewriter. They seemed very busy and professional even at that early hour. A uniformed man directed me to sit next to the door and wait for the Captain.

The Captain emerged quickly from his office in the back. Everyone redoubled their work efforts, and an uncoordinated symphony of keystrokes filled the room. The Captain's big, black leather boots pounded the stone floor and boomed like oversized drums, complementing the orchestra of typewrit-ers. The tremendous noise was barely sufficient to mask my heart beating one thousand times a second in nervousness and fear. As he marched efficiently towards me, I had just enough time to process his tall, muscular frame, shaved head, and rigid posture. My eyes rested on the large horsewhip he carried in his muscular right hand.

"Mademoiselle," he said respectfully and gestured with the horsewhip in the direction of his office, "Please follow me."

After entering a Spartan room, I sat carefully in a hard, wooden chair built for men three times my size. He sat quickly on the other side of a large table and momentarily glanced at me with hawk-like eyes. As he efficiently arranged his immediate area, placing a pad of paper he needed for the interview in front of him, I gathered all the remaining courage I had.

"What is your name?" he asked, beginning to write on his pad. This man did not look or sound as though he had ever wasted a second of his day.

"Polissa Esses," I answered.

He scribbled some notes without looking up. "What is your age?" he asked.

"What age do I need to be?" I replied confidently.

He raised his head, a little startled, then glared and remarked in a matter-of-fact tone, "We will not employ anyone here under the age of seventeen."

"Very good." I smiled cheerfully, pretending to be relieved. "I turned seventeen late last year." I was not happy about lying to him, but it was the only way possible for me to have a chance at this job. While lying was a sin, it was better than starving.

Inspecting me up and down slowly, as if trying to determine my age by sight, he replied, "You really don't look seventeen."

"Many people say that to me," I remarked with a casual smile. "I suppose I should take it as a compliment. The truth is my mother is small, my sisters are small, and my brothers are small, too. I would like to be more mature-looking, but I'm not."

He looked me up and down again, maintaining his serious expression. "*Bon*," he conceded. "When is your birth date?"

I didn't really know the answer to the question. Mama only knew that I was born before the snow. But I didn't have a birth certificate, as I was born at home. So, I chose November 11, since I learned in school it was Armistice Day, which celebrated the end of World War 1. I then quickly subtracted three years from my actual birth year. "November eleventh, 1916," I replied, without pausing enough to raise his suspicions again.

"Can you read and write in the French language?" he asked.

"Yes!" I said with more confidence. Because Syria had been controlled by the French since before my birth, I attended a French school.

"We need a stenographer," he said without looking up. "Can you type and take shorthand?"

I knew there was no way to lie about this. I couldn't type, and I didn't know the first thing about shorthand. Instead of answering in the negative, I simply loaded my voice with all the seriousness I could muster and announced, "I will learn!"

"What?" he countered in surprise and annoyance. "You don't know how to type or take shorthand?"

Instead of saying no, conceding defeat and ending the interview, I said the only thing that came to mind: "Let me work for you for one month." I didn't beg but tried hard to sound confident in my ability. "If, at the end of the month, I cannot type and write shorthand fast enough for you, you don't have to pay me."

I looked right at him with total sincerity, and he looked back at me for what could have been ten seconds, one thousand years, or any amount of time in between.

"*Bon*," he replied unemotionally. "I will give you one month here. If you perform well, you will be paid. If not, I will get someone else."

"Thank you very much!" I blurted out, having trouble controlling my tremendous excitement. "You will not be disappointed!"

"Please report here tomorrow morning at six-thirty," he replied. He immediately proceeded to his next task and dismissed me from the office with a wave of his horse whip.

The Romanoff Way

When Mama and Auntie heard that the Captain had given me the job, they were absolutely thrilled. They also knew that if I didn't perform, I would be fired. So, Auntie Latife gave me a solution that day. She had a friend named Mr. Romanoff, whom she told of my needs, and instructed me to go see him.

Terrified I would lose my invaluable job, I went to see him immediately. I arrived at his building, trekked up three flights of stairs to his door, and readied myself to enter. My heart pounded like a drum as I ran through everything that could possibly go wrong. After making sure my dress and hair were presentable, I knocked firmly on the door twice. From somewhere on the other side of the wall a tired male voice shouted, "Come in! Come in!"

I opened the oversized, creaking, heavy wooden door, and my senses were immediately slammed by a front of stale, musty air. At the same time, my eyes had to adjust to the darkness in the apartment, so I was momentarily paralyzed. Fighting every feeling to turn around and run in the other direction, I kept my feet fixed to the ground and waited for my sight to adjust. Once it did, my eyes rested on an old, emaciated man engulfed in a large bed at the left corner of the room. On the right side of the bed was a small desk with a typewriter on it. The curtains, the floor, the bed, the typewriter, and the man all appeared to be covered with a fine layer of dust.

"Come closer, come closer, and have a seat," he said, motioning to the desk. Swallowing my apprehension for the good of the family, I listened and shut the door behind me, cutting off my only escape route. As I got nearer to the bed, some dim light emanating from a shrouded window permitted me to get a better look at Mr. Romanoff. He was a very thin old man, with cracked skin, a long aquiline nose, bony face, big bushy eyebrows, thin lips, and a pair of very thick glasses.

"You must be Lucie," he said, trying to be friendly and hospitable.

"Yes," I answered cautiously, sitting down next to his bed at the typewriter.

"What can I do for you today?" he continued with a slight smile, trying hard to relax me.

"Well, I need to learn how to type quickly, because I just received a job with the French military. I need to type and take shorthand, but I don't know how to do either. If I don't learn quickly, I will be dismissed without payment."

"No problem," he said calmly, before combating a fit of violent coughing for a few seconds. Every cough was accompanied by the tremendous vertical movement of his prodigious eyebrows. "I can teach you how to type quickly, but you must pay me."

"How much do you usually get paid?" I asked sensitively.

The number that came out of his mouth was more money than I had ever possessed in my life. He wasn't trying to cheat me. It was just how the bedridden man made his living. Despite the cost, I decided that I couldn't let money get in my way of success.

"All right," I said firmly, "but I don't have any money now. I must pay you thirty percent of my salary the first month, thirty percent of my salary the second month, and so on until the amount is paid in full. The main point is that I must learn quickly, or I will not be paid at all."

"Agreed!" he replied. Then his friendly demeanor evaporated as we got down to business. "If you are to learn quickly, you must do as I say," he warned gruffly while coughing and quivering his eyebrows again. "If not, it is a waste of both my time and yours, and I would rather not even begin."

Mr. Romanoff suddenly sat up straight in his bed, pulled out a wooden ruler like the type used by Directrice Penso at school, and began the instruction. He first gestured energetically with the ruler, indicating which line of the typewriter my fingers should be resting on. He then loudly enunciated each letter while pointing to the corresponding typewriter key. Third, he indicated which finger was supposed to type each letter by tapping my thumb, index finger, middle finger, ring finger, or pinkie finger with the ruler each time he announced a new letter. He then explained that no matter how slowly I was typing with two hands, in the beginning, it was unacceptable to type any other way. After an hour of instruction, he gave me a paper and had me write down the first line of the typewriter keys.

"Go home and memorize it!" he ordered firmly. "Then come back tomorrow after work, and I will test you. Oh, and I hope I don't have to use this ruler to give out any punishments," he warned with no malice in his voice. It was understood that he just didn't have any patience for little girls who didn't want to learn.

My Just Desserts

I arrived at work the next morning at six instead of the required six-thirty. One of the soldiers, who had arrived at the office even earlier, showed me the desk where I would be working. Not wasting any time, I started typing the first line slowly, trying to remember each letter without looking.

At six-thirty, the rest of the soldiers arrived at the office and started working right away. They each took the time, in between keystrokes, to shoot each other smiles concerning their new colleague. Their condescending grins seemed to ask the question, "I wonder how she got this position?"

The Chief, who looked like all the rest of them but with

more stripes and patches on his uniform, called me into his office. He explained to me that this was an automobile repair yard for the French military. My job was to help him with correspondence: requesting automobile parts, filling out forms, and typing letters to his colleagues in other areas of the country. He gave me a handwritten note and asked me to type it up at once.

I quickly returned to my desk, determined to retype the letter perfectly. After reviewing the Chief's note, I realized that the second line was full of grammatical errors. My teachers at school would have never allowed me to write like this.

So I waited until the Chief concluded a meeting and knocked on his office door. Apprehension pooled in my legs, making them heavy and difficult to move. If I typed as he dictated, his colleagues would think he was stupid. However, if I changed his words around, he might fire me. I was also sure he didn't want a little girl telling him what to do when he commanded a large team of soldiers.

"Come in," he barked from inside his office. When he saw it was me, he let out a large sigh to show me that he didn't appreciate the interruption. "What is it?" he fired impatiently.

"I recommend we change some of the words in your letter. They need to better communicate the high rank and intelligence of the author. Is this acceptable?"

"Yes!" he answered with even more impatience. "Don't come into my office every five minutes and ask me about every sentence! Your job is to make the letter sound good by yourself, so I can focus on more important things!"

"Yes, Chief!" I replied respectfully and scurried back to my desk. It was easy to comprehend that the less the boss saw of me, the better my chances were of staying employed.

The soldiers ate breakfast in the cafeteria from seven-thirty to seven-forty-five. Not me. I practiced feverishly on the first line of the typewriter. At lunch, when everyone returned to the cafeteria, I had a snack and stayed with my typewriter. Upon everyone's return, I heard one soldier grumble to another, "Don't give her any trouble—she was recommended by the Lieutenant."

When work finished for the day, I went straight to Mr. Romanoff's apartment and kept practicing. He yelled out the letters, "E, R, T," and so on and made sure I typed them without looking at the keys. He made sure my hands were in the right place and my posture was correct.

This routine continued day after day for three weeks. I typed diligently, determined to vindicate Lieutenant Compagnon for recommending me and determined to keep my employment. After memorizing the first line, I started with the second and then the third. Mr. Romanoff became more and more demanding as my typing quickened. Occasionally, he would slap my hands with the ruler when the result was less than perfect. In all, though, he was a very good teacher, and I learned very quickly. After the three weeks were up, Mr. Romanoff simply advised, "Good. You don't need to come back anymore. Just keep practicing, and you will be fine. Remember, you owe me thirty percent of your salary for the first three months."

I assured him that our deal was still in place.

He answered, "If you have any friends that want to learn to type as well, I am available."

That was actually the best compliment I could have received.

I don't know why, but it took me a few days to realize that all the soldiers at work typed with two fingers instead of ten. So, after a short time, I was by far the fastest typist in the office. The Chief kept giving me more and more work every day. I welcomed it, as the more valuable I became to him, the more I could ensure my payment.

When the end of the month came, my efforts were substantially rewarded. My first paycheck contained more money than I had ever seen before. It was an extraordinary feeling to finally be able to help my mother and my sisters. After running all the way home, I gave the entire amount to Mama. She lit up with happiness, since we now had more money for food and clothing. We gave thirty percent to Mr. Romanoff as promised, and Mama gave me five percent for myself. Even five percent of the paycheck was more spending money than I had ever possessed. Rather than use it for a noble cause, I have to admit that most of it went directly to buy *choux a la crème* and chocolate ice cream.

Although the money was very important, perhaps my greatest reward came when the Lieutenant visited the office one Friday, as was his custom. I always treated him with the greatest respect because I knew he had recommended me at great risk to his reputation. I was not aware of the gossip he had been subject to for his act of charity, but after my second month at the *Parc de Réparacion*, he came for his revenge.

He instructed everyone in our office, besides the Chief and Captain, to clear off our desks, except for five invoices each. He passed out five blank pieces of paper to every person and announced that, on his signal, we had ten minutes to finish all the work possible. He then produced a silver pocket watch from his shirt pocket and signaled us to begin by rapping his fist powerfully on an empty table. My typewriter hummed like a car engine as I copied the papers in front of me, one after another. As my eyes scanned the pages, the letters seemed to appear magically on the blank sheets in front of me. The only interruption was a loud clank as I reset the ribbon every few moments. When Lieutenant Compagnon called, *"Fini,"* everyone stopped and waited in silence.

He walked directly over to the first desk, reviewed the finished work, and shouted, "One invoice completed!" He moved to the second desk, reviewed the completed work, and shouted, "Three invoices completed!" He continued shouting as he moved around the office, checking each soldier's completed work— "One invoice completed... One invoice completed... Two invoices... One invoice... One invoice"—until he arrived at my desk. He paused for a second, then shouted, "Five invoices completed!" and proceeded announcing the test results. After visiting the last desk, he resumed his position at the front of the room.

He allowed everyone to simmer in silence for one minute before shouting, "Would you agree that Mademoiselle Lucie can type just as fast as a grown soldier!?"

"Yes, sir!" everyone shouted back.

"Would you agree that the woman I recommended is competent enough to occupy a desk at the *Parc de Réparacion*!?" he bellowed.

"Yes, sir!" everyone repeated.

"*Bon!*" he said, lowering his voice. Point made, he strode quickly down my aisle, delivered a quick personal wink, and disappeared out the door.

A Girl Among Men

I loved working! Just loved it! It gave me the freedom to get out of the house, the respect of my relatives, and a little pocket money after helping with the monthly expenses. I soon found out that once someone starts working all the time, there is rarely time to spend anything. I was too busy making money to worry about the trivial point of what to do with it. When time came to go to school again, Mama told me simply that school had taught me enough; now it was time to work. I was sad to leave my friends and teachers. However, I was happy that my efforts were contributing to the family and not leaching from our limited resources.

The Chief would give me more and more work every day. I did my best to complete it, and my typing kept improving. After a few months, I was doing the work of five or six soldiers. I was proud of my accomplishments and kept trying to improve myself every day. As this was my first job, it did not even enter into my mind that fifteen big, strong soldiers would feel threatened by a young girl. It was then that I received my first lesson in politics.

Since I was the only girl in the entire office, everyone went out of their way to be nice, polite, and helpful. I soon found out that I was not necessarily returning the favor. One of the soldiers approached me during the lunch hour one day and said sensitively, "May I please have a word with you, Mademoiselle Lucie?"

"Certainly!" I replied enthusiastically.

"Well, we can all see, Mademoiselle Lucie, that you are typing faster and faster every day!"

I was proud that someone had noticed I was doing a good job and blushed. "Yes," I answered happily, "well, a neighbor of mine was teaching me, and I practice in my free time."

He smiled politely, "We have all noticed your great improvement." Then he paused, a sly look slowly transformed his face. "You see, the problem is that before it required fifteen soldiers to do the work here. Now you are doing the work of five people, so there are four of us who have nothing to do."

"Oh," I responded, a bit confused. My forehead wrinkled involuntarily. "I didn't think about that."

His face got more relaxed, and his delicate smile grew as he kept talking. "It would help us a lot if, instead of working faster and faster every day, you could slow down. Maybe you can look busy most of the day but actually not do a lot of work. That way, we will all have a better chance of keeping our jobs and supporting our families."

"Oh..." I repeated, too shocked to say more.

"Just think about it," he pressed, "and do your best to help us."

For the next few days, I struggled with this moral dilemma. On the one hand, I owed it to the Chief, the Capitan, and Lieutenant Compagnon to do the best job I could for them. They were paying me a lot of money to help them. If I didn't do my best, wasn't that stealing? On the other hand, these soldiers relied on their jobs to survive. If I took a large portion of the work from them, they might be reassigned or fired. It is a great *mitzvah*, or good deed, to teach a man how to make a living. If so, how big of a sin is it to take his livelihood away?

As my brain twisted itself in knots to arrive at the correct course of action, my typing slowed. I felt thirty eyes tracking each of my key strokes, watching to see if I would eventually adopt their practices of self-preservation.

When I reached home after the second day of deliberation, my mind became clear. As I looked around the house at what our lives had become without my three brothers, I realized we genuinely needed this money. My loyalty needed to be placed with the people who were paying me, and from that point on, I was determined to do the best possible job for them.

The next few weeks in the office, I pushed myself to work at an extraordinary pace. My boss seemed happier, but I felt thirty eyes following me around the room, cursing every completed assignment. The soldiers were still very polite and courteous with me. They never brought up the issue again, but they did get even.

Around one month later, the Chief called me into his office. "Mademoiselle Esses," he began unemotionally, "You have been doing a good job for us here at the *Parc de Réparacion*."

"Thank you," I answered proudly. I thought he was going to congratulate me on improving the office's productivity.

"In fact," he continued confidently, "I think we are not correctly utilizing your talents. So, I am going to transfer you to our main office, which is not far away from here. You will receive a salary increase and a promotion."

"Thank you, sir," I responded slowly, not knowing if the move was good or bad.

"So you accept then?" he asked with a slight grin.

"Yes... yes, Chief!" I replied slowly, delivering my best false smile.

Something didn't feel right about the whole situation. The Chief's self-assured tone said one thing, but his subdued body language communicated quite another.

I was transferred within the week. While I made more money, which was better for the family, the walk was over one and a half hours each way. That, combined with longer working hours, made this new position much more physically demanding than the first. I left every morning before dawn and returned just before dusk. All my free time was spent either eating or sleeping. I didn't give up, though.

I later discovered that I had been transferred because the French soldiers had complained about me to their superiors. It was a good lesson for me overall. I realized that, while it was in my best interest to work as hard as I could, it was probably in the military's best interest to have enough work to support the troops that were required to maintain a military presence in Syria. I may have been the best typist of the lot, but I could not help at all in a battle.

I learned that sometimes right and wrong is confusing and relative. I understood that my moral decision to work hard for my employer and thereby earn an honest day's wage had led directly to my dismissal. And it became clear that sometimes it would be better to compromise my moral principles for the good of the people around me.

While this political situation at the *Parc de Réparacion* was one of the few that were within my limited ability to influence, most were not. The next one took me completely by surprise—and pulled me back into the part of my life that I was trying to escape.

Unexpected Alliances,
Unexpected Complications

Until the day I received a most interesting letter, I thought everyone agreed that Ezra was the perfect choice for my future husband. The letter explained that if I wished to escape my obligation to marry, I had an open invitation to live in Palestine with my brothers. Of course, I was ready to go, but I would have to tell my mother first. Any option that would prevent my marriage and allow for the possibility of a new life was acceptable to me.

My regular routine was slowly making me crazy. I dreaded our weekly letter writing sessions, where Farida and Mama would cry for hours about how difficult Ezra's life was. On top of all this, at my fiancé's request, I now had to take English classes every day after working a full-time job. He had written that people in Japan spoke only Japanese and English and, therefore, I would not get very far speaking French and Arabic there. Even though the language came to me rather easily, there were one million things that I would have rather been doing. While my friends were in school, I was in a perpetual cycle of work and study.

As I was soon to learn, even though my brothers had left Syria with troubles of their own, they had not stopped at a simple invitation in their efforts to help me find happiness. They had secretly sent letters to Ezra in Japan, saying that they did not support a marriage between us. Despite my ignorance regarding their communications with Ezra, I immensely appreciated my brothers for gallantly taking the precarious position of siding with me over our mother with regards to the marriage.

Although everyone in my family knew exactly what action he or she supported, Ezra was thrown into a deep confusion. He was getting letters every week from Mama, his mother, and me saying how we missed him. He had even started sending us money to pay for my English classes. Concurrently, he was receiving letters from my brothers saying he was not welcome to marry me. In short, he was investing emotionally and financially in a fiancé who would possibly never be his.

As long as Ezra was out of the country, we were all able to coexist and avoid confrontation. However, three years after he had left for Japan, Mama became impatient. She made me write that if he was still interested in marrying me, he needed to come back right away and do it. Otherwise, we would look for someone else. When we received notice that Ezra would be back in one month, I knew that nothing would remain hidden for too much longer.

I thought the battle would begin with a resounding boom the second he arrived in Aleppo. Instead it began in complete, uncomfortable, painful silence when Ezra decided not to leave his mother's house once he had arrived.

Fighting for My Life

No one needed to tell me that Ezra had arrived in Aleppo that Friday as planned. Mama's beaming smile, the fresh rosy hue on her cheeks, her carefully styled hair, and her obsessive attention to every detail in the house alerted everyone that an expected guest could burst through the front door at any second.

I did my best to stay out of her way and looked increasingly pale and withdrawn. Worrying about the weeks to come robbed me of precious sleep and left black splotches under my eyes. I could not imagine a happy ending to my predicament. What would happen? In two weeks, would I be married and departing for Japan? Unmarried and struggling with my brothers in Palestine? Alone and renting a room in Aleppo? Truthfully, none of my available options sounded appealing.

We did not receive any guests that Friday. The following day, Mama's smile had disappeared. Although she didn't voice any disappointment, the lines that formed at the corners of her mouth and on her forehead expressed everything we needed to know. She still busied herself as much as the Sabbath would allow, keeping the house clean and her face made up just in case.

We did not receive any guests that Saturday either.

The next day, Mama did not even try to mask her frown. "Where was Ezra? Why had he not come to see them? What had changed?" were thoughts that accented each of her movements with a subconscious tremor. My mother was not the kind of person to sit around and do nothing. She knew something was out of the ordinary, and the news she heard from the neighbors later that day only confirmed her suspicions: Ezra had moved up his plans and was leaving the following week.

She could not wait any longer and shouted up to me, "Lucie, put on your nice dress. We are going to Farida's house."

I knew she was gravely serious, exasperated, and stressed. But I also knew that if I were going to say anything to shape my future, now was the time.

"I am not going!" I shouted downstairs. "I am not going to marry him!"

Instead of a verbal reply, I heard what sounded like a freight train with a screaming whistle and a deafening rumble shoot up the stairs. The door to my room was thrown open. Before I could think, the crazed spirit that possessed my mother unleashed a violent slap with her right hand. My cheek caught the brunt of the force, and my head whipped around violently. Before a sob or even a gasp could escape from my lungs, her body whirred in the other direction. A left hand crashed into my other cheek, pushing my face to the left side of my body. I stared at the wild woman in front of me, too stunned to breathe. She stared back at me unflinchingly, her wild eyes daring me to say something else.

"You will put your nice dress on NOW!" she thundered suddenly, the last word reverberating violently around the room.

I spun around slowly toward my closet to put some space in between me and my attacker. When eye contact had been broken, my senses returned.

"This is it," I thought. "This will determine my whole life. If I don't say anything now, it is very possible I will never get another chance."

"Mama," I repeated again softly but firmly, not daring to turn around. "I am not going to marry him." After the last word escaped from my quivering mouth, I shrank into the corner of the room and covered my head to shield it from a new barrage of blows.

None came.

Her eyebrows raised, her mouth widened, her eyes scrunched up, and a scowl formed on her face. Her tough façade transformed into a look filled with contempt and disgust. "Who do you think you are?" she spat. "You have no dowry, you are not beautiful, you have no father, and you have no money! Are you also so stupid that you cannot see that you are lucky to have a man like Ezra? He is a successful man from a good family. He is not asking for any dowry. In fact, he is not asking for anything. What other option can there possibly be for a poor, ugly girl like you?"

Not wanting to earn another slap, I answered quickly in a subservient tone. I did not dare stop staring at the floor, as it helped avoid dangerous eye contact. "I will go to live with Abraham and David. We can all live together. They want me to come stay with them."

"And what will you do for them!?" she countered with condescending repulsion in her voice. "Prepare their dinner, shine their shoes, and clean their apartment? They barely have enough money to support themselves. How will they feed you?"

Her temper rose again. She began to yell with so much passion that her hot breath moistened the back of my neck.

If I had been brave enough to look up from the floor, she probably would have hit me again.

"And what about you?" she screamed. "You want to be a maid for your brothers the rest of your life and remain unmarried? Is that what you want?"

"No, Mama, that's not what I want." At that point, my strength ebbed, and I broke down sobbing. "I don't want to be a burden on my brothers and I... I... I... don't want to never get married. I just don't want to get married now."

"You need to get married now!!!" She exploded, "I cannot take care of you anymore!"

With my last bit of strength, I turned around, looked her in the eyes and begged in between fits of crying, "I can take care of myself... If my brothers can't take care of me... I can rent a room in Aleppo and keep working for the French military." After those words left my mouth, I crumpled down in a heap and stewed in an uncontrollable fit of agony. I felt as if I were just going to die right there, my insides ached so much from the unrelenting emotional torture.

My vision was obscured both by dense tears and by my arms—which I had clumsily thrown over my face in hopes of deflecting the next slap—but I glimpsed a flash of sudden movement when a figure dashed in from the door and forced its way in between my mother and me. Mama jumped a few steps back in surprise. Auntie knelt down next to me and put my aching head on her cool lap.

She was not there to take sides, since Mama was obviously the stronger of the two. Furthermore, she never said a word to Mama about how to raise me, as she knew it was not her place. Mama understood she was there only to diffuse the argument, and the fact that Auntie Latife didn't speak out against her generated a calming sensation in the room.

Mama looked at Auntie and me angrily but firmly in control of herself. "If you want to move out, that is fine," she announced bluntly. "You will see that the amount of money you make is not enough to live on. Also, I want you to realize that at your age I had a husband and two children. You are sixteen years old and not young anymore. You must get married as soon as possible. I also want you to remember that you have two younger sisters. They cannot get married until you do! So, all of your selfish, childish behavior is not only hurting your chances of success, it is hurting your sisters' chances as well. I want to know in one hour if you will go with me to Ezra's or not. If the answer is no, you can leave the house, and don't come back. I have done all that I can do for you."

I was going to answer right then and there! Luckily, Auntie pinched me hard and looked lovingly straight at me. The knowing expression on her face communicated that there was something she wanted to discuss in a way that only she knew how. The fact that she appeared to have hope gave me hope as well for that instant and somehow kept me silent. Mama departed the room quickly and quietly.

The Decision

I did not give up the safety of Auntie's lap when Mama left the room. Burying my head in the coarse fabric of her dress, I wept until all of my tears had been spent. When my body stopped shuddering and convulsing, Auntie pushed my shoulders back gently so I was sitting up facing her. She removed the yellow shawl from around her head and used it to clean up my face. Her kind, watery green eyes focused lovingly on mine, while her pale, anemic skin tone attested to the pain numbing her body on my behalf.

"What is your choice then, child? You need to make one," she whispered softly.

"What should I do?" I whimpered, breaking eye contact and staring sullenly at a defect in the carpet we were sitting on.

She broke out of her whisper and began in her softest

speaking voice: "I can't tell you what to do. I am not your mother. But I can tell you that you definitely cannot go out and live on your own. There is no place for a sixteen-year-old girl to live alone in this country."

"So, you think I should either marry him or go live with my brothers?" I answered slowly, not looking up.

"Yes," she responded confidently but kindly. "It's just a question of where you can do the best for yourself and your family."

I didn't respond for over ten minutes, as my brain slowly worked its way through the problem. That was the simple question that needed to be answered. What *was* best for me and my family? As much as I hated to admit it, even to myself, the best path did not lie with my brothers. They did not know many people in their new country and were making very little money. What kind of husband could they find for me? What kind of life could we live? I had no problem with working and cleaning the house. However, there was a very large possibility that, instead of helping them, I would be a burden on them. They would not only have to feed me but also find me a husband. Marrying would not get any easier with them, as they could not afford a dowry either.

So, the only path that remained was to marry Ezra. Why would I do that? Was there any good reason I could give myself to go through with it? After thinking for only one minute, two reasons came to mind. The most important one was that I didn't want to be responsible for my sisters' remaining unmarried. Victoria and Linda could not marry until I did. Marrying Ezra would make it possible for them to begin looking for husbands of their own.

The second reason had just been made as obvious and painful to me as a butcher's knife plunging into a goat's head. I was not welcome in my own house anymore. Was I that much of a nuisance? Was I that difficult to take care of, that I needed to be given away to the first acceptable suitor? Was I such a bad person? Well—if I was not wanted in the house,

I definitely needed to leave as soon as possible. I did not need my mother's help anymore, and it was obvious that she felt she did not need mine.

I slowly raised my head and met Auntie Latife's soft gaze. I spoke with resigned acceptance: "The best decision for the family is for me to marry Ezra." As the words left me, I began to lose control again, but I continued, "It will clear the way for Linda and Vicky so they can..." I could not get the rest of the words out as my throat tightened, my stomach churned, my eyes watered, and my body collapsed into Auntie's lap for another bout of misery.

Auntie Latife ran her fingers through my hair and repeated softly, "Shhhhhh... Shhhhhhhh... Everything will be just fine. Trust me. Everything will be just fine."

After a few minutes passed, she tried to help reinforce my decision. "Lucie... Lucie... it won't be so bad. Ezra's mother is a great cook. She will teach you her recipes, and you will eat well every night."

I kept crying just as loudly as before.

She tried again a few minutes later. "You know, there are many Jewish bachelors in Japan. You can bring pictures of your sisters with you and help them find suitable husbands."

My crying softened. That had planted a seed of hope. It made me see even more clearly that my decision was the right one.

It took a very long time for me to calm down that night, and she stayed with me for its entirety. When control of all my faculties had returned, I got up from Auntie's lap, cleaned my face in the wash basin, and went straight to Mama's room. I opened the door as quickly as I could. I saw her sitting up in bed, her face and blouse soaked with tears. Her hair was a mess, her eyes were red, and her nose was running. I looked straight at her and said, "Tomorrow morning I will go with you to see Ezra."

"All right," she answered.

I closed the door just as fast as I had opened it. But the walls were not thick enough to prevent me from hearing her weep as I returned to my room.

Like a Leg of Lamb

All of the skin blemishes remaining from the night before were buried beneath a delicate layer of color. Mama expertly applied cosmetics on the both of us so our fight was invisible to the hyper-perceptive, well-trained eyes of the town gossipers. Unfortunately, they had not yet invented something to smooth over the emotional wounds we had both suffered the evening before.

We left early to go to Ezra's house, but we headed down a dirt road in the opposite direction. Mama was walking briskly, trying to stay ahead, while I was walking slowly, trying to stay six steps behind. I didn't ask her why we were going the wrong way, and she did not tell. She was obviously still angry, as was I, but this marriage had nothing to do with our personal feelings; it was the business at hand. She kept looking back at me, making clicking sounds with her mouth, and repeatedly gesturing with her hands for me to keep up. But no words were spoken.

After a short walk, we arrived at an area with many small shops. Mama went directly toward the one I knew best—the chocolate shop. To my surprise, she went inside, and I sped up to join her. Without looking at me, she exchanged pleasantries with the shopkeeper, and placed the most extravagant order I had ever seen. A kilo box of chocolates was soon being packed in front of us with caramel chocolates, nougat, chocolate with almonds, chocolate with hazelnuts, solid milk chocolates, and solid dark chocolates. When the man finished filling the box with sweets, he placed a piece of wax paper over the merchandise, carefully wrapped the container in a shiny black piece of paper, and expertly manipulated a sparkling gold ribbon into a crown-like bow proudly adorning the top. The shopkeeper gave me the box with a generous smile, and after Mama paid, we left as quickly as we had come.

She was the first to break the silence between us. "Don't even think about eating those chocolates," she said casually. "They are not for you; they are for Ezra."

"Can I have just one?" I asked as nicely as I could under the circumstances.

"No," she replied calmly, expecting the follow-up question.

I eyed the beautiful ribbon and out of habit asked, "Mama, may I have the gold ribbon for my hair?"

"No, you may not. Hurry up, or we'll be late!" she half-scolded, more focused on the conversation she would have with Ezra than on anything I was doing.

I knew they weren't expecting us, and I knew we didn't have an invitation. But I did not press the issue. Mama knew something was wrong and did not announce our coming in fear of being told we were not welcome. She knew that if there was anything to be resolved, it needed to be resolved in person.

On our walk to Ezra's house, Mama started barking advice at me like a drill sergeant in the French army:

"If they offer you any chocolate, you are to say, 'No, thank you,' politely.

"If they insist on your taking one, you may take one but no more.

"Eat it slowly—do not act like a hungry person.

"Actually, just put it in your pocket and eat it later.

"If they give you anything to drink, like coffee or juice, finish only half. We don't want them to think you are starving and difficult to support.

"Do you understand everything I am telling you?"

"Yes, mother," I answered obediently.

Mama and I climbed the steps to Farida's apartment, which

was on the second floor of a building quite close to our house. We knocked on the decrepit wooden door twice, and Ezra's aunt opened it. She looked surprised and asked us to return later, but mother would not be dissuaded. We were let into a one-room apartment where Ezra was lying on a bed in the corner.

He sat up with a jolt and yanked the covers up over his waist. He was obviously very surprised to see us. His uncombed hair was pointing every which way on his head, and he was in an undershirt used for sleeping. His face looked tired and older than I remembered it.

"Hello," he said uncomfortably, growing red from embarrassment. He paused for a second and, after seeing the determination to stay on Mama's face, reluctantly invited us to sit down. "Please have a seat and make yourself comfortable. I apologize for not being able to entertain you correctly, but I have a fever. I have been sick for a little over two days."

Ezra's aunt pushed some chairs up to a table next to the bed, and we sat down.

"No problem," Mama replied, anxious to get to the point. "It is just that we have an urgent subject to discuss with you."

"Can we get you a juice or a coffee?" he asked politely.

"No, thank you," Mama replied, very businesslike.

"Oh, but we have some very good Jaffa oranges," Ezra insisted. "My aunt can make you an orange juice."

"That would be wonderful. Thank you very much," she relented graciously.

"Lucie," Mama ordered semi-sweetly, "Please give Ezra the present you bought for him."

Shyly, I got up and held the chocolates out to him. I didn't really know where to look but made a point not to look straight at him. I also tried not to look at the bed where he was lying, so my gaze rested on the ground. Knowing I was watched closely, I managed a thin smile.

"Thank you very much," he beamed. The happiness displayed on receipt of this gift was genuine, but he was still self-conscious about the fact that he was in his pajamas and we were dressed up in our finest. He managed an agreeable smile, which put us at ease. He must have really loved chocolates, because he tore open the wrapping paper in front of us and tossed the gold ribbon on the bed. Before anything else was said, he dispatched three chocolates, one after the other.

After the third chocolate was eaten, he offered one to my mother and me.

"No, thank you," I said politely. I was still afraid to look directly at him and kept my attention focused on the floor.

"Please have one," he pressed again amiably.

That was the only opening I needed. In one fluid motion, I got up, leaned toward the bed, and picked up the biggest chocolate in the box. As I relaxed in the chair, I got a strong pinch from Mama on the back of my arm, refreshing my memory concerning our earlier conversation. I quickly complied and put the chocolate in my pocket. "Thank you very much," I said as sweetly as I could.

When the orange juice arrived in front of us, it really was tempting for me to down the whole thing at one time. The juice was undiluted, and Ezra's aunt had even put ice in the glass. Aware that I was still under close scrutiny, I took only a small sip.

Mama did not waste any more time with niceties.

"So, Ezra," she began, staring straight at him. "I hear you are planning on returning to Japan next week."

Looking away and getting red, he answered, "Yes, I am planning on leaving for Japan next Sunday."

"No, you're not!" Mama shot back, raising her voice. "You are not going anywhere without my daughter!"

We all fell into a very awkward silence, and Ezra got redder. I wanted to run out the door but was so shocked my muscles did not respond to the orders of my brain.

After an eternal pause, he answered, treading carefully, "Look, I don't want to have problems with your family."

"What are you talking about?" Mama answered incredulously. "There is no problem from my family. You are engaged to my daughter and you need to honor your commitment. She has waited three years for you to return from Japan."

"Yes. That is true. But I received many letters from your sons telling me not to marry her. I don't want to cause problems. There are many girls I can marry. My uncle has three daughters, and he wants me to marry his eldest. My friend in Egypt is getting married this week, and he wants me to meet his sister. If your family does not want me, I can find another wife."

Mama was silent for a few seconds while she overcame the surprise news. It was completely transparent to Ezra and his aunt that this was the first time she had heard of the mixed messages he was receiving. His words were a surprise to me as well. My brothers had said they were trying to assist me, but this was the first evidence I had received of their actions. I was inwardly very proud that they had tried to help me, but if I had shown any joy in this, I would have been killed on the spot.

She answered him with anger—not anger towards him, but anger towards my brothers. "I am Lucie's mother. My sons are not in the country, and they have no idea what is best for my daughter. I do. I do not need the permission of my sons to offer my daughter to you in marriage. Are you still interested in marrying her? Yes or no?"

"Of course I want to marry her!" he exclaimed, matching her energy without hesitation. "Why would I give my promise if I did not intend to go through with it?"

"So, you still want her?" Mama confirmed aggressively.

"Yes," he replied confidently.

"So, let's do the wedding this week. Then you take her and go to Japan," Mama pushed. Once she had the confirmation, she was not going to stop until the deal was done.

"Good," he answered agreeably.

"You do the wedding," Mama pushed again.

"Of course," he confirmed. "We can do it at my uncle's."

"You take my daughter to get the dress. You are the fabric professional," Mama pushed a third time, understanding the negotiation was at an end.

"Here is some money." Ezra fumbled around in the folds of his sheets and pulled out some bills. "You take her and get the dress. It is better that you get what you like."

"Thank you very much. We will see you at the wedding. When your mother returns, tell her to come over and see me." Mama smiled nicely at him and bid him goodbye.

I was still frozen from listening to my entire life being planned out before me when Mama yanked me off the chair on her way out the door. During their conversation, my self-esteem was reduced to nothing, but the love for my brothers increased greatly. I was very moved that they had tried hard to help me marry the man of my choice—whenever I might meet him. At the same time, I felt like a leg of lamb being haggled over by a butcher and an aggressive customer. The leg of lamb doesn't decide whether to stay with the butcher or go with the customer. It's just a dead piece of meat.

Inspecting the Merchandise

Farida came to the house early the next morning with two gifts: a basket of white flowers for Mama and a day plan of pain and suffering for me. Since the wedding was going to take place that week, Farida wanted to take me to the *mikveh* right away. Mama never went to the bathhouse, and I did *not* want to go alone with Ezra's mother. Luckily, Auntie Latife agreed to accompany us and prevented any argument before it began.

They will tell you that one goes to the *mikveh* before a wedding to purify one's body in a religious ceremony. In reality, it is a chance for the future mother-in-law to do some due diligence before the transaction. It is very comparable to a real estate evaluation during the inspection period. If the future owner finds anything wrong with the apartment or house to be acquired, she can call off the acquisition of the property before any money changes hands. This was Farida's chance to make sure that everything was in order with the merchandise.

At the bathhouse, I was very surprised when Ezra's mother paid the *chasale* to give me a treatment. No one had ever paid to have my hair washed before. It was simply too expensive and a waste of money. The *chasale* was a thin, strong woman with dark-brown hair tied in a bun. She was naked from the waist up and breastfeeding when I sat down in the chair in front of her. She did not stop breastfeeding to put soap on my hair. With her baby in one hand, she stood up and massaged soap and water all over my scalp. Then she put her child down to sleep behind us, and the real work began. Using both hands, she tripled her efforts by pushing, pulling, and scrubbing my hair. It felt as if she were trying to pull out every strand! I wanted to scream but didn't want to look like a child in front of Farida and Auntie. Instead, I just bit my lip.

When the *chasale* had finished washing my hair, and had hurt me sufficiently, she massaged *belun*, sweet-smelling earth, into my hair. Next, she rubbed a yellow, terrible-smelling paste on my arms, underarms, and legs. When she removed the paste, my hair was removed with it.

After that, the three of us went and bathed in hot water before visiting the *mikveh*. Ezra's mother asked me to scrub her back, which I did quickly and inefficiently. She then asked to scrub mine. While she washed, I could feel her eyes inspecting me from the top of my head to the bottom of my feet for any sign of a defect. She was like an eagle, and I the mouse that was her prey.

After I was prepared for the ceremony, Auntie led me down many steps into a pool of freezing cold, neck-deep water. I immediately started shivering and turning a light shade of violet. Ezra's mother threw some white flowers into the water and then told me to dunk my head under. She told me to do it once, twice, three times, again, and again... Then once for good luck... And then again for good luck... A group of women gathered around the pool, smiling, commenting, and enjoying themselves, while I was turning into an icicle.

After I had immersed myself seven times and said a Hebrew prayer, Farida yelled, "Lelelelelelelele!" All the other ladies in the bathhouse joined in the chorus, and the noise could probably be heard from Damascus. With everyone leering and yelling at my naked body in the *mikveh*, I wanted to shrink into the freezing cold water and never come up. I was extremely embarrassed, but the big commotion just meant that I had passed inspection. The apartment was acceptable, the money could change hands, and the contract could be closed.

Wedding "Necessities"

These days, most modern weddings cannot take place without a bare minimum of necessities. One needs only to look at any corner newsstand and pick up any of twenty different bridal magazines. At my wedding, we didn't have a guide to tell us what was needed, but we did our best with what was available.

I did not want to speak with Mama, and she did not want to speak with me. So, we walked to the market together in awkward silence and bought some white velvet. After the tailor had made the bodice and skirt, we realized that we would not have enough fabric left for the arms, which would leave my shoulders inappropriately revealed. It was not considered proper to wear a sleeveless dress, and any religious person in town would likely refuse to give the service. So, we had to go home and think of a way to come up with the extra money. I gave Mama three thin gold bracelets, out of five that I owned, that had been my presents for Purim various years before. She sold them, took the money, bought more velvet, and made a shawl to go around my arms. In this way, my skin was covered, and the dress was deemed suitable for the ceremony.

The shoes were easier since we didn't have any money left. I had some silver shoes with small heels that I had owned for several years. They had fairly narrow straps in the front and back, with a silver bow embellishing the top. Most importantly, the shoe was open in front. This was not just for the sake of fashion. As my feet grew, the shoes would still fit—my toes would just push further out of the front openings.

When Farida took me to buy the wedding ring, we discovered that all the rings in stock were too big for my skinny fingers. They had to take some of the silver out of the ring in order to fit it correctly. We received a twenty percent discount, so I could not be blamed for causing any money problems.

The banquet hall was a tricky situation. Ezra's uncle had the house with the biggest common area, so it was a logical choice for us to have the wedding there. He also was part owner of the coffee shop down the street, which gave him many extra tables and chairs at his disposal. While it was the best choice for us, approaching Ezra's uncle for this favor was a delicate matter. He had been trying for many years to arrange a wedding between Ezra and his eldest daughter, Dina. Farida, however, did not want Dina as a daughter-in-law because she was Ezra's first cousin and, thus, too closely related. In Aleppo, if you had a cousin who was exceedingly beautiful or exceedingly wealthy, marriage was a possibility. But in the absence of these factors, you were encouraged to look for a wife elsewhere. Although Farida recognized that Dina would have made an excellent daughter-in-law, for the health of her grandchildren she wanted to look outside the family. The situation was resolved without any problem, though, since Ezra's uncle and his wife, Sarah, were very generous people. They agreed to the arrangement because of their love for Ezra, whom they had helped raise, and with that we had a venue for the reception.

There was no money for invitations on sophisticated paper, but in Aleppo these things were done a bit differently. If anyone wanted to have a big party, it was necessary to hire a well-known old woman named Leah to do the inviting. Leah came over in the middle of the day and asked Mama to get some dried chickpeas from the kitchen. We counted out forty or fifty dried chickpeas and gave them to her. Leah, Farida, and Mama went over the invitation list, and she separated one chickpea for every name mentioned: one chickpea for the Choueke family, one for the Cohen family, one for the Sultan family, one for the Chammah family, one for the Sassoon family, and so on. We needed a system like this, as most people could not read nor write.

After reviewing the list a few times by memory with the party hosts, Leah would go around town and invite the families. Upon arriving at the first house, she would knock on the door, and yell, "Lelelelelele!" It was well understood that the more noise she made, the better luck the occasion would enjoy. She proclaimed loudly and musically, "You are invited to the wedding of Ezra Choueke, son of Farida Choueke, and Polissa Esses, daughter of Seto Esses, at six o'clock in the evening this coming Sunday. Join me in wishing them the best of luck." She would spend some time in the house, discussing the upcoming wedding in gruesome detail, and then go to the next family. Before leaving, she would take one chickpea and throw it on the ground beside the doorpost. During the day, she would check how many peas she had remaining in her purse, so she would know how many more families needed to be advised. If she was unsure if she had visited a certain house already, she only needed to check the doorpost for a chickpea. At the end of the first day, she returned to our house with five chickpeas. Mama, Farida, and Leah had to go through the entire list again to see who had been forgotten. The following afternoon, when Leah finished inviting the entire group, she was paid. She always came to the weddings to give good luck speeches and drum up new business.

In any wedding preparation there are hiccups, and ours came while arranging the food. The main meal of the festivities was to be a lamb barbequed on a spit. My grandmother and Farida were in charge of preparing the rice and vegetables to stuff inside the unfortunate animal. As the lamb roasted, the fats and juices would be absorbed into these foods, adding a meaty, greasy, and smoky flavor to them.

The principal ingredient, the lamb, was entrusted to Ezra. The butcher arrived at his uncle's house with the ill-fated beast on the morning of the wedding dinner. Ezra met the butcher and the *shochet* there to coordinate the proceedings. A *shochet* is a Jewish man who is in charge of inspecting and slaughtering an animal in a distinct way so it can be certified kosher. The *shochet* inspected the animal carefully and then slit the lamb's throat with a razor-sharp knife, spilling its blood in the courtyard. Once the blood and life had departed from the animal, the *shochet* conducted his final inspection. To Ezra's surprise, he found an abnormality in the right lung of the lamb and declared it non-kosher.

This was a big problem! Ezra had planned to spend money on only one lamb. But now, the purchased lamb could not be served at the wedding. Ezra was angry with the butcher for bringing a sick animal and with the *shochet* for recognizing the malady only after the animal's death. The butcher expressed no sympathy for Ezra's situation. The only way the inflexible man offered to help was to take the old lamb and bring a new one. Of course, the second lamb would have to be paid for, and no discount would be given for the free meat the butcher had received. The butcher had many customers from three or four other religious backgrounds who visited his shop daily, and he could resell the lamb without a problem. Only the Muslim and Jewish customers had stringent religious requirements when it came to mutton. The Christians and liberal followers of other religions would be able to purchase it.

Ezra tried to negotiate with the butcher and began a heated

discussion with him. The *shochet* pulled Ezra away before any fight erupted or any unpardonable insults were exchanged. He told him a story involving the very same butcher and a different *shochet*.

The butcher was of Arab descent and was constantly fighting with a certain *shochet*. He needed the *shochet* to come to his shop and certify an animal kosher before any Jew could buy it. It was a difficult, daily conflict, as the butcher wanted to sell as much meat as possible to the Jews. They argued constantly because the meat the Arab butcher wanted to sell was not the meat the Jewish *shochet* was ready to stamp.

Two weeks before our wedding, they had had their final disagreement. The butcher brought in a sick animal that had yellow eyes, a growth on its leg, and trouble breathing. He needed to kill the animal right away and wanted it to be certified kosher. The *shochet* argued as usual, but this time the butcher put him in a choke hold, grabbed a big knife, put it to his neck, and threatened menacingly: "Kosher this animal, or I will kosher you!"

The *shochet*, to preserve his life, certified the meat kosher, as the butcher demanded. However, the *shochet* was not going to allow the butcher to get away with this serious offense. He visited each Jewish household in town and told them not to buy lamb for at least one week. He explained to them how he had been forced to stamp a non-kosher animal.

The butcher was surprised that no one came to buy his kosher meat, for which he received a higher price. Eventually, he discovered the reason. He arranged for a mob to find the *shochet* and kill him. Luckily, the *shochet* heard what was about to transpire and escaped the country just in time.

The *shochet* who had arrived the day of our wedding reception was his replacement. After hearing of the events that took place, Ezra realized there was no negotiating with the butcher. The dinner was that night, the people were coming, and the cooking was already behind schedule. He paid for the new lamb, the butcher brought it over, the *shochet* killed and certified it, and then Farida quickly started the food preparation. The lamb fiasco leached us of extra money earmarked for the wedding dinner. Ezra's friends had already paid for the entertainment, but all other wedding "necessities" had to be cast aside.

"Yes We Do!"

The religious ceremony, which made the marriage official, was on a Friday afternoon, two days before the lamb incident. The same man who sealed the engagement, Meyer Shebetai, performed the service for two reasons. One was that Meyer was a good friend of Ezra's and religiously capable of performing it. The second was that the money for the wedding had run out, and we could not afford to pay a rabbi. The ceremony was in the salon of our house at two in the afternoon. Mama, my sisters, and I worked together to prepare for the occasion. We dusted the couch, octagonal table, and armoire. We brought down a deep burgundy woven carpet and chairs. Finally, we worked in the kitchen to make fresh orange juice, coffee, cakes, and cookies for the occasion. The chairs and couch were arranged around the edge of the room, and the table, with the food on top, was placed beside them. The wedding would take place on the carpet, in the center of the room.

Mama personally helped me get ready for the event by preparing my bath and carefully applying my makeup. Under her supervision, I put on my new dress and straightened my freshly washed, frizzy hair so it was falling over my shoulders. The supervision was more to make sure I didn't run away rather than for any cosmetic benefit. We still were not speaking to each other.

Only one problem emerged before the religious ceremony. Since Ezra and I both did not have living fathers and three of my brothers were out of the country, we did not have the required number of men to perform the service. Ezra's uncle quickly went to the coffee shop and lured in a few more with the promise of coffee and almonds covered in sugar.

When Ezra arrived from the office of Asouad, wearing a navy blue suit and tie, we started right away. Four of the newly arrived men each held up a corner of a large *talet* (prayer shawl) over our heads. Mama stood with me, facing Meyer on the left side, and Farida stood with Ezra on the right side. Meyer, in a jovial but serious mood, said the prayers in Hebrew and then paused.

He then switched to Arabic, so everyone could understand, and looked directly at me. "Polissa Esses, do you accept Ezra Choueke, son of the Honored Yaoub and Farida Choueke, as your husband?" he asked loudly.

I froze, and my heart stopped beating momentarily. However, Mama was there to make sure the transaction went through.

"Yes we do!" she said confidently, while smiling and nodding agreeably.

Meyer did not continue, as he was waiting for me to answer.

"Yes I do," I said without emotion, spurred into action with a pinch on the arm and a quick scowl, courtesy of Mama.

Meyer grinned kindly at me and then directed his attention to Ezra. "Do you, Ezra Choueke, accept Polissa Esses, daughter of the Honored *Hacham* Simantov and Seto Esses, as your wife?"

"Yes, I do!" he proclaimed, beaming with enthusiasm.

Farida nodded vigorously and ad-libbed, echoing the sentiment: "Yes we do!"

Meyer then asked us to exchange rings. He took them slowly out of his pocket and presented them to us. Ezra carefully placed mine on my left ring finger. I then slid a ring on his, keeping my gaze fixed on the floor. I understood that struggling or protesting at this point would only make everything more difficult. We were getting married. I needed to understand that and go along with it. I saw no point in acting out in front of our guests, as it would only add to my embarrassment.

Meyer then asked us to join hands as he finished the service in Hebrew. I don't know if it was mostly from Ezra or me, but there was a lake of sweat between our palms. It made me realize that we were both nervous, albeit probably for different reasons.

Meyer concluded by proclaiming, "I now pronounce you man and wife!"

There was no kiss or hug or any other romantic display of affection. Ezra looked at me with joyful, shimmering eyes, smiled widely, and gave me a silver coin with his right hand. Then he slowly relaxed his grip on my sweaty left hand and declared loudly to everyone, "I have to meet a customer at work, so I must go. I will see you all at dinner on Sunday. Thank you very much for coming!" Before anyone could stop him, he was out the door.

Following Ezra's lead, Meyer, Ezra's uncle, and all the men from the coffee shop filed out of the house. The only ones left were Mama, Farida, and my two sisters. Farida, who had tears in her eyes, excused herself and went home. Mama, also crying, went to her room. My sisters and I were thrilled that everyone had left without taking any of the extra food. We heartily ate all the remaining cakes and happily drank all the orange juice.

Later, I lay in my bed pondering my depressing future, but I was happy about one thing. Lucky for me, at these Jewish religious ceremonies, the husband makes the commitment but doesn't get to take the bride home afterwards. So, I was still safe at home and tried to enjoy my final nights of freedom with my sisters.

The Camellia

We didn't have any bridal magazines to explain to us how a wedding should be, but nevertheless, I knew that mine fell far short of the ideal. Mama and I started arguing on Saturday night, about twenty-four hours before the wedding party, and our fight carried all the way up to the festivities.

On Saturday night, Mama insisted that I give my sisters the majority of my clothes and shoes, my two remaining gold bangles, and everything else not given to me by Ezra. Since I had a husband now, she lectured, he would buy me those things. Mama was in a bad financial situation, and she needed help to take care of the remaining people in the house. If that had been the only thing required of me, it probably would not have developed into a big fight, but she did not stop there. She sat me down and painfully injected words I had never thought that I would hear from her.

She warned, "Get it into your head that you cannot come back to us. Ezra is your family now. You need to do what he says. You must take care of him, and he will take care of you. If you have difficult times in Japan, don't think that you can come back and stay with us. Your place is with him."

I didn't even talk back. I just started crying, too hurt to do anything. A fact that compounded the sadness for me was that I did not know Ezra that well. If he didn't want me after one or two years, I would have no one. I would be welcome nowhere. I felt terrible. I felt worthless. I felt unloved. I felt abandoned. I felt thrown out. I couldn't eat. I couldn't drink. I couldn't even talk. I walked around in a daze all Sunday.

When it came time to get ready for the wedding, I did so in silence. I put on my dress, shawl, and silver shoes, brushed my hair back, and walked alone to Ezra's uncle's house.

A big buffet outside in the courtyard greeted the guests at the front of the house. Farida, Sarah, and many others worked tirelessly to put the last-minute touches on all the

delicious food. At exactly six o'clock, the guests started
arriving. A big line formed where the skewered lamb was
being roasted above glowing hot charcoal. The meat's juices
made hissing sounds as they dripped every few seconds on
the coals. Happy guests loaded their plates with the choicest
pieces of lamb, cooked to perfection. They then migrated
over to fill the remaining space on their plates with *kibe*,
hummus, tahini, rice with chickpeas and pine nuts, *yebra*
(stuffed grape leaves), and hot, homemade pita bread. For
dessert, they had watermelon, dates, oranges, nuts, and
almond-flavored gelatin. Multiple bottles of Arak and wine
were being passed around, getting everyone drunk. The
smells intermingled, lifting everybody's spirits. Their plates
packed with food, the guests began filtering into the two
large adjacent rooms.

The two rooms where the party was held were not luxurious but comfortable. The tables and chairs, on loan from
the coffee shop, were made of stained dark-brown wood and
remained uncovered. Oil lamps, made of glass and bronze,
hung from the ceiling, one above each table, bathing the bare
room in a warm, golden light. The only flower in the room
was a white camellia I had taken from a bush in our house
and tucked behind my ear.

I chose the most remote table, as far from the courtyard
as I could get. I had not taken anything to eat or drink all
day because I was still very angry. As the aromas from the
food drifted into the house, it was difficult to abstain due
to anger alone. But I had also been warned one thousand
times not to look like a hungry girl and eat in front of all
the guests. My mind, filled with its worries about manners,
won the battle with my stomach and left a festering ball of
anger in my abdomen, which prevented me from devouring
everything at the buffet. Nonetheless, there was nothing
that could prevent me from getting more and more light-
headed as the night progressed.

One hour into the event, I realized something that depressed me even more. I realized, after looking around, that I knew hardly anyone at my own wedding. Mama was as angry with me as I with her and had become ill. Upon her arrival at the wedding, she went upstairs and fell asleep instead of joining the party. My sisters could not yet fit into the dresses that I had given them. They had to wear their school uniforms to the wedding and were so embarrassed, they hid the entire night. Auntie Latife's husband had been relocated a few days before to work for Syria's new electric company. They were so far away they could not return for the wedding. Rafoul, who had maintained a respectful distance from Mama and me during the past two weeks, was saddened by the entire argument and could not bring himself to attend the party. Farida and Sarah were in the kitchen cooking for the guests. Strangely enough, I realized that Ezra was the only person I knew at the entire wedding. And even I did not know him very well. If one counted every second we had spent together in my entire life, including our religious ceremony, they would not add up to more than one hour.

I sat at an out-of-the-way table, watching all of Ezra's friends and relatives. There were Jews, Muslims, and Armenian Christians all joking and laughing together. Most were men who knew each other from the souk. They were dressed in their best Western suits: nice slacks, long sleeved-shirts, and dark jackets. The Jewish and Christian women wore long dark dresses with long sleeves that covered their bodies, while their necks and faces remained uncovered. The Muslim women had their faces covered as well.

Even though I tried to stay away from the activities, the activities came to me. As I was in the only corner of the room not choking with people, the musicians and dancer set up right in front of me to begin the entertainment—a gift from Ezra's friends. The three musicians started playing the oud, the violin, and the tambourine, electrifying the room with Arabic music.

The dancer got up and started gyrating to the music less than one meter away from me, the finger cymbals on each of her hands chattering and orbiting suavely around her waist. As the music picked up in pace, so did her movements. Her long red cloak pushed a gust of air by my face, almost knocking my camellia to the floor every time she twirled around. Something about her act made it different from any other dancing I had ever seen. I noticed some of the red-faced men moving closer, posturing with palpable raw enthusiasm. They began clapping their hands and stomping their feet to the music.

Suddenly, the woman dropped her red coat, revealing only a flashy red and gold sequined brassiere and a matching very, very, very short skirt. Simultaneously, a roar went up from the crowd of men, and they pushed closer. The dancer shaked, jiggled, and jerked more feverishly to the music, whipping the audience into a frenzy. The men, brave with drink, started throwing money at her or putting it in her brassiere. Responding to the enthusiasm, she danced faster and faster, in an increasingly sexual manner. At the start, she kept chattering her finger cymbals in front of her body, but as the money kept falling, she raised them higher and higher above her head.

Every man in the drooling mob wanted my seat, since I was right next to her. Her body parts kept flying past my face at a dizzying speed, and I desperately wanted to get out of the room. The group had moved so close together, though, there was no way to leave. Fear paralyzed me; I had never before seen grown men act like a crazy pack of animals. I thought about running home or leaving, but I knew that was not allowed. I would not be invited back in the house if it was without my husband. I had to wait in my seat and eventually go home with Ezra. So, I sat there, closed my eyes, faced the other direction, and listened to the music. The only thing I was thankful for was that Ezra was not a participant in the melee I was witnessing.

Until two o'clock in the morning, I sat next to the energetic musicians. Everybody, especially me, was more relaxed after the dancer got tired and left. The guests did a few toasts, wishing us success in Japan, many sons, a long life, along with other best wishes. The band continued playing until Ezra and I were the only people remaining in the two large rooms.

The Wedding Present

I did not know where we were supposed to go after the wedding. Ezra was very shy, and although we were the only people left at the party, we still had a healthy distance between us. Finally, although I was reticent as well, I got tired of waiting. It felt as if morning were going to arrive at any minute. I walked up to him and said respectfully, "I'm tired. I am going to my house."

"Fine," he replied slowly, "I will go too."

I walked back home, and Ezra followed a few meters behind. He was obviously very drunk but in control. I hadn't eaten in thirty-six hours but couldn't distinguish between the anger and hunger still gnawing repeatedly at my insides. Only one other thing occupied my thoughts. I revisited a story in my mind that had been worrying me for the past few days.

An acquaintance of mine had pursued the affections of a certain woman for a very long time. Whenever she would walk by his shop, he would present her with flowers. At first, she just ignored him, so he found bigger and better flowers, hoping to win her affections. One day he gave her a jasmine, which she accepted—then quickly threw on the floor and stomped on mercilessly. She wanted him to understand that she had no desire to marry him.

After several years, she had not received a better marriage proposal. The parents rapidly arranged the *busra* between them, performed the ceremony, and had a meal with many guests in their home, after which everything seemed to be in good order. At the conclusion of the night's events they both entered the bedroom, where he paid her in full for the humiliation suffered long before. He slapped her twice across the face and tore the dangling earrings from her earlobes. She cried the entire night and cowered fearfully in the corner of their bedroom.

My acquaintance explained to her the following morning that his hostility was meant to repay her for the shame she had caused him. Now, he was happy that they were married but warned her never to forget that he was the boss.

When we arrived at my house and entered the salon, I was surprised to see two mattresses lying side by side. There was a sheet covering both mattresses, so they could not be separated. I hesitated for a fraction of a second as I considered my available options. I then escaped into the kitchen, replaying Auntie Latife's earlier advice in my head. "On your wedding night," she had said softly, "just do whatever your husband wants."

No one had ever taken the time to give me more detailed instructions. While I didn't know what to do, I knew enough to know that I didn't want to do it. I ate some bread, cheese, pickles, nuts, and rice that were sitting on the counter. I took my time chewing and digesting my food. When my stomach had quieted somewhat, I began to think about what waited for me in the salon. After stalling for another half an hour, I walked timidly into the room with the mattresses.

Ezra's clothes were tossed on the couch, and he was in bed fast asleep, snoring as loudly as a bear. I curled up as far away from him as the mattresses would allow and faced the other direction. I did not undress and just used my tiny velvet shawl as a blanket.

The next morning, Ezra woke up at dawn. I kept my eyes closed and pretended to be asleep as he dressed. When he was finished, I opened my eyes a crack, and he was looking down at me. "I am going to work," he said kindly. "This afternoon, I will come back and see you, but tonight I will stay with my uncle."

"All right," I answered and forced a quick smile. After he had left, I got under the covers and fell asleep for a long time.

For a few consecutive days, Ezra would come over in the afternoon, talk with my mother, and then excuse himself to go sleep at his uncle's. Mama forced me to be in the house while he visited, but I didn't go out of my way to make any small talk. I liked the new arrangement better than the alternative, but Mama and Farida would not let it continue.

Farida came over one morning and sat down for a coffee with my mother. They talked civilly over the strange behavior of their children. I was in the room but didn't dare say a word.

"What is happening with your daughter? What is she doing? Ezra is not sleeping here. He is sleeping at his uncle's house. People are beginning to talk!" she complained accusingly, jerking her head in my direction.

"What do you mean?" Mama countered. She raised her voice a little and gestured with her hands for effect. "Your son comes over here for five minutes and then leaves! He runs off to work and then goes to sleep somewhere else! What is supposed to happen if he is always working?"

"I only have one son," Farida responded in a lower voice, trying to keep the discussion amicable. "If they keep on going like this, I will never have any grandchildren!"

"What shall we do then?" Mama asked, throwing up her hands.

"Well," Farida advised, "Beirut is beautiful this time of year. What if we send them there for three days? If they share a room for all that time, something is bound to happen." She shot me a look as if to say, "After three days, something *better* happen!"

Mama did not hesitate. "That is a wonderful idea. You talk to Ezra, and I will get Lucie ready." She made a point not to look in my direction, as she already knew my feelings on the subject.

"You know, Farida?" Mama said, smiling as our important guest got up to leave. "When Ezra and Lucie go to Japan, we will be able to play cards together every day!"

Farida looked at Mama and frowned. "Ezra is my only son. My place is with him. From now on, whenever he and Lucie make a step, I will step together with them." Mama was visibly disappointed but kept quiet.

I was even more disappointed. "What a wedding present!" I thought. "She will be watching me like an eagle until the day I die!"

Ezra and I were on the train to Beirut the next morning. Beirut was known as the Paris of the Middle East. Yet since we were still in a state of awkward non-communication, the city's majesty was lost on us. On our return, we were no closer than when we had left. Mama and Farida did not use any more tricks to get us together. They knew we were leaving for Japan in only two days. I suppose they decided just to let nature take its course.

Exodus and Reconciliation

Farida and I fixed our papers, and soon everything was in place for our journey. A car arrived to take us all to the train station, and it was time to say goodbye. Leaving Vicky and Linda in Aleppo made me feel as if part of my heart were being ripped out of my body. All three of us cried and embraced in a triangle of sorrow. I had a few copies of their pictures with me and assured them it would be my first priority to show them to all the handsome, eligible bachelors of Kobe, Japan. If I found them a suitable match, we could possibly see each other again in the future. We didn't really need to say anything else. The love and anguish were carved onto our faces.

I gave Mama a hug but didn't look her in the eyes. I couldn't. I didn't understand why her main goal in life was to be rid of me. I just left some tears on her blouse and hurried into the car without looking back.

We took the train from Aleppo to Damascus and a car from Damascus to Palestine. We stopped near the city of Jaffa.

"Why are we stopping here?" Farida asked Ezra in surprise.

"I have something I need to do," Ezra explained vaguely. "Lucie and Yamo," he said, using his nickname for his mother, "come with me!"

Ezra held a printed envelope in his hand, and he walked the neighborhood, searching for the sender's return address. I assumed he was looking for a business associate when we turned into a shop full of wooden crates overflowing with vegetables. I immediately grabbed Farida's arm in fear when I recognized my brother Abraham at the back of the shop, taking money from a customer after weighing produce with a balance.

As soon as Abraham finished with the customer, Ezra quickly closed the distance between them, grabbed his hand and shook it hard. "Hello, Abraham!" Ezra said energetically. "It is very good to see you! I married your sister last week, and I came to visit—specifically, to ask for your blessing!"

Abraham's whole body initially tightened as if he were ready to throw a punch but then relaxed. He answered warmly, and a grin slowly expanded across his face. "Ezra, I was never against you," Abraham explained. "I thought that my sister was too young to marry. I know that you are a good and honorable man. What's done is done, and I wish you both a long life together."

At that moment, I breathed a sigh of relief, and relaxed my rigid grip on Farida's arm. Moise and David ran out of the back and stood together laughing, and through my joyful tears I realized my brothers were all struggling. They were still wearing the same shoes and clothes they had left Aleppo in.

We all went to dinner at an outdoor restaurant that served falafel, hummus, and pita. Ezra sat next to Abraham in order to make sure he eliminated all animosity between them. When they were relaxed, he said, "Abraham, it is sad for me to see you selling vegetables in the market like this. In Aleppo, you and your father were one of the biggest clothing merchants in the souk."

Abraham answered softly but unashamed, "Well, it is not my first choice, but I have very little money, so it is the only business I can do."

Ezra replied hopefully, "What if I sent you some material from Japan? You could sell the material or finished goods in your store and do some good business."

Abraham looked straight at Ezra and became serious. "I would love to do it, but I don't have the money to buy a shipment of goods."

Ezra slapped his hand enthusiastically on the table. "Never mind that! Let me send you the goods. After you sell them, you can send me the money. Tell me what sold, and I will send you more. In this way, you can start to do your old business again."

Abraham nodded his head and answered cheerfully: "We have an agreement!"

The visit to see my brothers was a priceless gift. I was too embarrassed to say anything to Ezra, but I immensely appreciated his taking the time to solve the problems between them. In addition, offering to help Abraham restart his textile business was a wonderful gesture. For the first time, I saw in Ezra what my mother saw in him, even if it was only for a brief moment. I still couldn't imagine having a romantic relationship with him, but I understood he was a good person.

The next morning, Moise drove us to the Egyptian border. At that time, it was easy to exit Syria and Lebanon. However, it was not easy to enter Egypt. The officials at the border checked our boat ticket reservations directly with the port before we were permitted to enter the country.

Conte Verde

The most awe-inspiring aspect of the eight hundred-kilometer journey from Aleppo, Syria, to Port Said, Egypt, via modern-day Israel, was the ocean. I had never imagined the ocean could be so vast, that it could extend to such great distances. And I had always found it hard to believe that it was possible to sail across it in safety. I could not fathom the kind of boat that must be built to take us all the way to Japan. When I saw the *Conte Verde* for the first time, sitting in Port Said, I had my answer.

The shiny, white *Conte Verde* was as long as two city blocks and taller than almost any building I had ever seen. The boat had over three levels and was sprinkled with lifeboats and portholes at regular intervals. The lower levels of the boat, where we were staying, were for the tourist-class cabins. The middle level of the boat was home to the dining room and the dance floor. The top level was for the first-class cabins, but we knew we would not be spending any time up there.

We gave our luggage to the porter and followed him up a swaying bridge to the lower deck of the giant ship. The porter did not have such a difficult job because all of our belongings fit into one suitcase. I had only brought two changes of clothes for our new life in Japan. He led us first to Farida's room and next to the room I would be sharing with Ezra. When we entered, I was happy to see bunk beds. That meant I did not have to share a bed and, better yet, did not have to sleep on the floor either.

We stayed in our rooms until it was time for the boat to leave. At the departure time, they called everyone to the middle deck and gave us colored streamers to throw over the sides. As the boat pulled away, the sun began to set on the glass-like sea. This was the first ocean sunset I had ever witnessed, and I still remember the shades of red, orange, and pink vividly.

That evening, when we stepped into the dining room for dinner, I was speechless at the opulence and luxury on display. There were white tablecloths on every round table, each accented with a red rose centerpiece. Crystal chandeliers hung from the ceiling, filling the room with a soft, delicate light. A small orchestra was complemented by an Italian singer, completing the perfect ambiance. And in the adjoining room, people glided across a parquet dance floor.

The first night on the ship, we sat at the Captain's table, as we were among the newest passengers on board. I sat next to the Captain, while Ezra and Farida sat across the table. The quantity of food they served was astounding. Never in my life had I eaten so much. First, the white-gloved waiter served a pasta in a bolognese sauce. We were given two forks, two spoons, two knives, and two plates. In Aleppo, we had eaten only with spoons, so I watched Ezra carefully. He stuck a fork in the pasta, twirled it slowly over a spoon, and put the ball of spaghetti in his mouth. I watched him do it once, twice, and then I was ready. Five minutes later, I was performing as if I had been using a fork all of my life. I was very surprised when they came with a chicken soup for the second course. I thought the pasta was all they would give us. The soup was not very tasty, but I was happy to have food in my stomach. I was ready to get up when they brought beef steak for the main course. "Aiiiiii!!!!" I thought. This was like a dream. I watched how the Captain ate with a knife and fork, cutting the beef carefully and putting it delicately in his mouth. I did the same and succeeded in blending in with everyone else. Then dessert came, with a choice of cake or ice cream. I was bursting and could not eat another morsel of food. Furthermore, to adhere a little more closely to the kosher laws, we could not eat milk after meat, so I stopped there.

The Captain took the opportunity to start talking to me. He was about forty years old, with a handsome, rigid face;

very light-brown hair; tortoise-shell spectacles; and a professional, spotless white uniform with stripes on the arms. He explained the workings of the ship, and I responded politely to his explanations. I really was genuinely interested in the multitudes of engines, propellers, levers, and buttons that powered such a large machine. Out of nowhere, he abandoned his discussion about the boat and lowered his voice.

"Do you see that couple over there?" he said, gesturing with a sideways glance.

"Yes," I answered politely, "what about them?"

"Every night, they eat with their hands. They have extremely disgusting manners, and they do not bathe before coming to the dining room. Not only that, but they are very picky about the food and do not come to the on-board church on Sunday. Those people are Jewish. You should watch out for them."

"Oh," I answered, narrowing my eyes and speaking more aggressively. "And what religion do I look like I am?"

"I would guess Protestant, but you may be Catholic," he declared with a smile.

"Actually," I replied in a low but malicious tone, "I am from Aleppo, Syria, and I am Jewish also. If you are going to watch out for them, at the same time, you should watch out for me."

The Captain's face became beet red. I did not raise my voice. I only excused myself from the table and went to my room. Later, when I told Ezra what had happened, he said that I had acted correctly. He advised me not to do anything about it, but just to keep my distance. He was not angry at breakfast the next morning when we were seated at the worst table in the room. We were happy; it was the table farthest away from the Captain.

I did not take the incident too seriously because I had been in more difficult situations in Syria. I knew that from time to time there were kidnappings of Jewish girls who were walking in the wrong part of town. We also knew never to walk alone after dark outside of the Jewish quarter. Plenty of stones had been thrown at me by overzealous local youths when I did not have my hair and face covered "properly." We had to be careful all the time but especially during Ramadan. During Ramadan, the population fasted for approximately forty days, and many were in a sensitive mood. The neighbors who were friendly towards us stayed friendly towards us, but the individuals who were unfriendly became more aggressive. The Captain did not scare me but only put a small black stain on an otherwise pristine ship. It was ironic to be in such a luxurious setting yet encounter the same problems that I had seen everywhere else.

Unkosher Food and Relationships

The next day, after an exceedingly large breakfast, Ezra and I were walking on the middle deck. The *Conte Verde* had an exercise path around the boat bordered by a row of lounge chairs. To my surprise, a few meters in the distance I saw an acquaintance of mine named Asher reclining on one of the lounge chairs with a friend.

"Ezra!" I gushed with excitement. "That is Asher Saad from Beirut. He is a colleague of my cousin's. Let's go talk to him!"

Ezra's face soured instantly, his upper lip twitching in anger. "You are not going to say one word to him!" With a mountain of controlled rage rumbling in his voice, he wagged his finger slowly from side to side and ordered, "You are not going to look at him! You are not going to talk to him for the entire trip!"

I was shocked. I walked right past Asher, and instead of greeting him, I peered out to sea. Ezra had never been angry at me before, and it scared me. We didn't speak. Both of us marinated in anger and disappointment for about five

minutes while making another lap of the boat. Then Ezra, in a state of calm agitation, broadened and clarified his point: "You are not to speak to any men who are not my friends. You may speak to women, and you may be friendly with them. You don't need to be friendly with any men. It can lead to no good."

"Very well," I shot back quickly, placating him in hope of ending the lecture. Tears welled up in my eyes. I broke away in a run and hurried down to the room. I sat there for a long time, contemplating my new life.

Asher spotted me the very next morning. I turned my face, stayed silent, and walked on by. He repeatedly tried to get my attention but soon understood we would be ignoring each other uncomfortably for the remainder of the thirty-day voyage.

The day only became worse. For lunch, they served another feast with four courses and dessert. Halfway through the soup, nausea began to creep into my bones. I became dizzy, sick, and had to run out of the dining hall in order to vomit over the side of the boat. I felt terrible as my first bout with seasickness set in. It was torture to finally be able to eat whatever I wanted, for the first time in my life, but forced to throw all of it back up. For the rest of the day, I alternated between spending time in the room and vomiting outside.

My seasickness did not go away. Nonetheless, I didn't know if I would ever get the opportunity to eat so much great food again and tried my best to be present at most meals. It was about once a day that I would have to dash away from the table to empty the contents of my stomach over the side. The ice cream, cake, pasta, soup, meat, and fish made all the pain worthwhile, though. I regretted my bad luck. When I finally had the opportunity to eat everything possible, I was in no condition to enjoy it. The kilo I had gained over the entire trip, despite the vomiting, was more a reflection of how little I had eaten in Aleppo, instead of the amount of food I was able to keep in my sensitive stomach.

Ezra's mother was going in the opposite direction: she was losing weight. She did not suffer from seasickness, but she did suffer for her religion. Technically, no food on the boat was kosher, since it was cooked in a kitchen where pork and shellfish were being prepared. Farida dealt with the problem by eating only pasta with butter and rejecting all other food she was offered. I followed Ezra's example by eating everything except pork and shellfish.

Farida also had trouble sleeping and chain-smoked for most of the night. Every morning, she woke Ezra and me up at the crack of dawn with a loud knock on the door. One benefit of not particularly enjoying my mother-in-law's company was that she didn't particularly enjoy mine either. She demanded that Ezra walk with her, and I was able to sleep in. I even began skipping breakfast and joining them for an early lunch at eleven-thirty. After adopting this schedule for a few days, we pushed Ezra too far.

Ezra, Farida, and I sat down for lunch, and they brought us the usual cornucopia of offerings. Ezra was tired from being up at six o'clock every morning despite his wishes. Farida was eating her pasta with butter when Ezra noticed for the first time that she had lost a considerable amount of weight. "What are you doing?" he sneered at his mother.

"I am eating," she replied defensively, surprised by his hostile reaction.

"I know that! But why are you eating pasta with butter every day?" he interrogated, his voice a level above the background chatter in the room.

"The food on the boat is not kosher," she replied meekly, apologetically lowering her voice so as not to anger her son.

But the last couple of days had taken a toll on him, and he let her have it. He raised his voice and I nearly fainted. The entire dining room stopped what they were doing, became completely silent, and focused their full attention on us.

"THERE IS NO KOSHER HERE!!!!!" he screamed.

"THERE IS NO KOSHER IN JAPAN!!!!!" he shouted.

Releasing some of his rage, his voice lowered a few octaves but still maintained enough intensity so everyone could hear. "*You* wanted to come with us to Japan! I have no time to take care of you if you get sick for no reason! I need to focus on the business because we are almost out of money! You will start eating at once, or I will talk to the Captain and send you back to Aleppo on the next boat that passes! There you can eat all the kosher food you want!"

Farida stayed silent and looked down in her lap. I stayed silent as well, but Ezra was not finished. It was my turn next.

"AND YOU!!!!!" he shouted. "WHERE DID YOU LEARN TO EAT PASTA WITH A FORK AND SPOON AND MEAT WITH A FORK AND KNIFE????? HOW MANY BOYFRIENDS COULD YOU HAVE POSSIBLY HAD TO TEACH YOU SUCH MANNERS?????!!!!!"

I could not leave that accusation unanswered, so I answered as subserviently as I could. "Where did *I* learn to eat with a fork, knife, and spoon? I learned it by looking at you. As you ate your pasta, that is how I ate my pasta. As you ate your meat, that is how I ate my meat." Like I copied Ezra with his eating habits, I copied Farida in her response. I looked down into my lap and started to cry.

We sat in awkward silence for the rest of the meal, eating nothing else, as the rest of the dining hall whispered and pointed in our general direction. Farida made an effort to eat some fish, and I had to make an early exit to vomit over the side of the boat.

A Day in Bombay

The *Conte Verde* made its first stop in Bombay, India, after more than one week at sea. Ezra was happier since his mother had started eating more and feeling better. I was still seasick but was happy that his suspicions regarding my rendezvous with other men had ebbed. He asked if we would like to take a tour. Farida wanted to stay on the boat, but I was only too willing to get off of it. Not only did I want to see Bombay, but I also wanted a reprieve from my seasickness.

A middle-aged man wearing a long white robe and matching turban energetically introduced himself as our tour guide. As he walked us to a waiting automobile, I admired how his darkly tanned skin, jet-black hair, and thick mustache stood out handsomely against his clean white garments. He drove us to different parts of the city and walked us by various houses of worship and government buildings, intelligently explaining the interesting history of each. Along the way, I noticed many men chewing beetle nut, which made their tongues and saliva run red. A few haphazardly spit out the red juice without regard for their surroundings, scaring me whenever a choice glob landed close by.

At the conclusion of the tour, the driver showed us an area with countless gigantic birds. Some of these birds were bigger than me, with huge wings, big bulging eyes, sharp black beans, and large, sharp talons. He explained that one of the city's religious sects cared for their dead in a unique way. They placed the deceased in a field for a few days and these birds stripped the flesh from bone. When the birds finished, relatives buried the body. I could not believe that these people allowed frightening birds to eat their parents and grandparents.

Although I thought aspects of Bombay were extremely beautiful, I was more than happy to return to the swaying deck of the *Conte Verde*. After we had rounded the tip of India, the weather changed for the worse. There were a few storms that rocked and pitched the boat violently. It was even difficult for me to make the one-meter trip to the bathroom. More than once, I thought we were going to die, but the truth was that I didn't care. If we didn't make it to Japan, my sad, insignificant life would simply end prematurely.

Death on the ship was a real possibility. Ezra and I often walked around the boat after sunset. One evening, we strolled past a group of the crew, dressed in white, all saying a solemn prayer. At the prayer's conclusion, they tossed a body wrapped in a white cloth overboard. We saw this ritual repeated a few nights later.

The first time I witnessed the event, I pestered Ezra, "What are they doing?"

"It is better you don't know right now," he answered sadly. "I'll tell you when we get to Kobe."

When I saw he was in a mood to field my questions, I asked another one that had been bothering me for a while: "Ezra, we have milk and eggs every morning for breakfast. Where do they keep the cows and the chickens?"

At that, he laughed for a full minute and replied with a straight face, "I'll show you before we leave the boat. Now it is too late. The animals are probably fast asleep."

He put his hand on my shoulder, and we continued walking.

Shanghaied—with No Possibility of Return

As the *Conte Verde*'s propellers churned through the Port of Shanghai's calm waters, I was amazed by the large number of giant ships with foreign-sounding names and delighted by the strangely shaped Chinese boats called junks. I was still seasick on that thirtieth day of our journey, when we finally arrived in China. I was hoping to be cured the instant my foot touched the shore, but it felt as though the ground still rocked beneath my feet for our entire stay.

The next day was December thirty-first and freezing cold. A friend of Ezra's took us to a furrier to get coats made for Farida and me. While Ezra had warm clothing, neither of us did, and the temperature was not going to get any higher than ten degrees Celsius. Ezra assured us that the weather in Japan would be similar and insisted we both buy nice coats. It did not take us a long time to pick one out. Every animal skin was out of our price range except for one from a beige-colored sheep. We chose a beige leather trim and a dark cotton lining. Farida and I both were fitted by the tailor and returned later to pick up our matching coats. We were pleasantly surprised that they were very warm and well made.

We wore them that night to a New Year's party on the top floor of a luxurious Chinese hotel. We had never celebrated the Christian New Year before, but in China most of the expatriates spent time together. Because there were not many foreigners and most spoke common languages, it made sense for them to take advantage of the occasions they could celebrate together. There were Americans, Europeans, Chinese with foreign educations, and a few Jews from different parts of the globe, all drinking and dancing at the party. They had a seven-man Chinese band playing great international music from the US, France, and other countries.

One of Ezra's friends from Brooklyn was sitting at the table with us. His name was also Ezra, and he was close to forty years old. He spoke to me about his wife and three daughters in New York for a good portion of the night. More than anything, I wanted to get out on the dance floor and enjoy myself with the crowd that had gathered there. I managed to keep myself in my chair for a while, but my hands were moving to the rhythm of the music, advertising my desires. When Ezra's friend asked me to dance, I was only too happy to say yes. We danced the foxtrot, among other steps, before the band took a break. I loved gliding around the room in the festive atmosphere and was out of breath by the time we returned to the table. Not long after that, we all left to go home, as it was already late.

When we got into the room, Ezra slammed the door with a tremendous bang.

"Why did you do that?" I asked in surprise.

He didn't answer, removed his clothes, got in bed, and turned his back to me. I knew he had been drinking, so I didn't press the issue. The next morning, he was still not speaking to me, so I knew something was wrong. Confused, I asked softly, "Are you ignoring me?"

He answered with only silence. Then I knew he was angry, but I didn't know why.

"Are you upset with me?" I probed timidly, afraid of what the answer might be.

"Of course I am upset with you!" he roared.

I kept silent for a few minutes until my courage returned. "Why are you angry?" I asked again, in an even quieter voice.

"Why do you think I'm angry!?" he bellowed.

"I don't know," I responded hopelessly.

"You were dancing with that man last night! What kind of wife are you? Dancing with other men!" His face became blood-red. The intensity of his penetrating gaze made me flinch and turn my head.

I pleaded, almost crying, while staring at the wall, "But he is a good friend of yours."

I received silence as my only reply.

"He is married with three daughters," I explained innocently. Dressing quickly was his response.

"Why don't you ever dance with me?" I asked sadly.

He left the room without saying goodbye and shut the door loudly behind him. A few minutes later, Farida knocked, and we went down to breakfast together. Ezra did not appear for a long time, and when he did, a friend accompanied him—so the issue did not have to be addressed immediately.

Later, Ezra talked about my immodesty with his mother. Since I was still at the table with them, I considered this our first family discussion. The conclusion was to make *my* moral instruction *their* new project.

"You know, Ezra," my mother-in-law explained philosophically, "the first education of a girl is from her parents. The next education she gets is from her husband and in-laws. So, from time to time, we must tell her how to behave correctly. You tell her what you want her to do, and she will do it."

That night, he ignored me again. Before sleeping, I approached him defiantly.

"I want to go back to Syria!" I demanded, looking him straight in the eye and shattering the silence between us. I didn't care if Mama would not take me back. I would try to get another secretarial position with the French army or move to Palestine and live with my brothers. "Anything would be better than this!" I thought.

"You are not going back to Syria!" he countered strongly but less angrily than before. "From now on, you will not dance with anyone, and we will finish with this issue."

I didn't respond but understood that I had no say in the matter. My future was firmly in his control.

BOOK TWO

A Partnership

First Impressions

The voyage from Shanghai, China to Kobe, Japan lasted fewer than four days. The trip was largely uneventful, except for the afternoon the Captain brought our attention to some whales swimming nearby. I had never imagined that an animal could be so enormous. We knew the journey was coming to an end when the waters calmed down and we passed increasing numbers of small fishing boats, dragging nets or fishing lines behind them. Soon, the industrious Port of Kobe stretched out before us. Nestled in between serene green mountains and the blue sea, was a mix of traditional Japanese buildings unlike any that I had ever seen. Hugging the coastline were numerous long, squat wooden shipping warehouses. At a slightly higher elevation, countless jagged triangular tiled roofs crowned groups of simple wooden houses. The houses were interrupted occasionally by large grey, multi-story factory buildings, spouting various chemicals into the frigid air. The bustling city was in stark contrast to the dead calm of the spacious, mostly empty bay. Ten or twelve huge ships sat on the water, like ducks on a pond, as goods were loaded into their ample cargo holds. Even from a distance, I could see many opportunities in this dynamic city.

Our ship pulled into the dock, and I was very happy that our voyage had finally ended. From the gigantic smile on Ezra's face, I could tell he was also thrilled to be back. It was the first time I saw him genuinely happy. Ezra introduced us to a large group of international young men, who were waiting to meet us on the pier. There was also an older, married man in the crowd named Faraj Cohab, who was contracted to help one of the group open a buying office.

Each man gallantly paid his respects to Farida by kissing her hand. "*Um* Ezra," they complimented, "we have heard about your legendary abilities in the kitchen. It has been so long since we have tasted good Syrian food, we have been counting the days until your arrival. We have barely been surviving on the cooking of Cohab and whoever else takes their turn in the kitchen." Farida laughed warmly but flashed me a troubled look as if to say, "I am *not* going to cook for twelve people two times a day!"

Then it was my turn. "Lucie, you are more beautiful than your picture. We tried to set Ezra up with some of our sisters and cousins, but he kept telling us that he had already found a wife. Once he showed us your picture, we knew why he was waiting for you. We now see that even a camera cannot capture the full essence of your beauty." Ezra, Farida, and I smiled at the excessive compliments. I was happy and touched that Ezra had showed them my picture. For a split second, I thought maybe everything here would be different, but then reality came crashing back.

"Let's go to the house!" the group chorused.

Ezra took his mother by the hand and gave me an order casually over his shoulder: "Lucie, make sure you stay with the luggage. Cohab will accompany you, and we will meet at the house."

I was a little frightened because I had never been by myself in a foreign country. I also spoke no Japanese. But most of all, I was strangely undecided on whether I should be happy or sad for the chance to spend some time alone.

I walked cautiously by two very tough-looking Japanese soldiers waiting on either side of the immigration queue, wearing olive green canvas uniforms with red stripes on the collars, matching hats, and one-meter swords carried in brown sheaths hanging from their waists.

Cohab quickly proved to be a good companion, and stayed by my side the entire time. I tried my best to communicate with the government agents using only hand gestures and common sense. Before receiving instructions from the customs man, I opened our suitcase on the floor in front of him. Instead of inspecting our luggage, he seemed to get angry and waved me outside. For immigration, they gave me a Japanese stamp on my travel papers. I didn't know what the artistic characters meant.

Cohab hired a taxi and gave me a brief overview of the area. He explained that Japan is a collection of islands. The four main islands, running north to south, are Hokkaido, Honshu, Shikoku, and Kyushu, and these account for over ninety-five percent of the country's usable land. The Port of Kobe, in Osaka Bay, is located on the southwestern part of Honshu Island. Kobe's uniquely calm waters are protected from the east and west by Honshu, and from the Southwest, by Shikoku.

On our way to the house, I first admired a main thoroughfare flanked by large brick or stone buildings with large windows, and small wooden houses with traditional tiled roofs curved out at the corners. We then passed a colorful shrine guarded by large grey stone lamps and orange, free-standing wooden arches towering over everyone's head. There was a long line of people waiting at the house of worship to vigorously pull a stout rope, ring a large bell, throw a coin into an ample wooden donation chest, and pray for future happy events.

The road started out paved, but, as we got closer to the house, it became flattened earth. The people walking beside it had wheat-colored skin, beautiful straight black hair, almond-shaped eyes, high cheekbones, nice, rounded faces, and noses in perfect proportion. They were mostly thin and athletic-looking and wore very unusual bathrobe-like garments called *kimono*. The women combined these with uncomfortable-looking wooden platform shoes, called *geta*, that made

a hollow "clack, clack, clack" when hitting the ground. The
men wore *zori*, flat sandals with no tops or sides and only two
thin straps running across the wearers' toes to hold them on.
Many younger men and women wore uniforms consisting of
matching jackets, long pants, and hats with an embroidered
insignia on the front. Cohab explained that the insignia identified where they worked or the school they attended. Other
individuals we passed simply wore work pants, long shirts,
and Western shoes.

I saw one individual who looked very unusual. A man
wearing a kimono and a pair of *zori* was walking down the
street with an upside-down thatch basket covering his entire
head, a wooden flute in his mouth, and a sign on his chest.
Curiosity got the better of me, and I had to ask what he was
doing. Cohab explained that this was a religious man who
collected money for the temple. The basket on his head was
obstructing his eyesight and made him anonymous, so that a
potential donor would not be embarrassed in the event that
he could not afford to contribute to the temple.

After a fifteen-minute drive, the car stopped in front
of a small wooden Japanese-style house. A cheerful, overweight man named Michael left the group of Ezra's friends,
who were laughing and carrying on outside, and came over
to get the luggage. He joked that we were kicking him out
of the house he had shared with Ezra. He was moving into a
boarding house with a large group of bachelors, where twelve
young men occupied three rooms.

Michael took me on a tour of our new home. It was
small but surprisingly nice. We had to take our shoes off and
put slippers on before entering, as was the style in Japan. I
thought this was a good custom since it would reduce the
housecleaning. The downstairs had three small rooms: the
living room, dining room, and kitchen. The living room and
dining room were separated by a thick paper screen door
mounted on a wooden frame. Called a *shoji* in Japanese, this

kind of door could slide back and forth, making one big room or two small ones. The kitchen was a few steps lower than the dining room and made completely of grey stones. This was so the house wouldn't burn down in case of a cooking accident. I was surprised to see a gas stove, as we had never had one in Aleppo. Upstairs were two bedrooms and a bathroom with a flushing porcelain toilet—an amazing convenience. In Syria, we had had to leave our home to use the outhouse. On cold Aleppan nights, we had made use of containers in our room instead of bumping around outside in the dark.

Ezra and I were to share a room, and Farida was to have her own. Michael explained that beds were expensive in Japan and considered a luxurious item. We were lucky to have a large one in each room. The local Japanese slept on *futon*, thin mattresses, placed directly on the *tatami*—nice-smelling, tightly woven straw mats that covered the floors of their houses.

By far, the best aspect of the house was the electricity. In Aleppo, any time I had wanted to turn on the light, it had been necessary to prepare the oil lamp and go through a long process. Here, light instantly appeared whenever I pulled a string. It was truly magical.

The Perils of Preparing a Meal

Early the next morning, Farida and I went to the market to buy the needed ingredients for lunch and dinner. We left at seven a.m., as it would take us over three hours to do the cooking. Ezra went to the office but would be back in the afternoon to taste our progress. I only knew the Japanese words that Ezra had taught me: *niku* ("meat"), *sato* ("sugar"), and *takai* ("expensive"). Therefore, the only way to communicate at the market was by exchanging crude hand signals and facial expressions with the non-English speaking housekeeper, a very pretty, petite, long-haired young woman named Sakura.

Sakura was as careful with her dress as she was with her light skin. Her immaculate black kimono, *geta*, and snow-white apron were always paired with a colorful red parasol. Even when it wasn't raining, she would carry the parasol to protect her beautiful skin from the tanning rays of the sun.

We walked twenty minutes on a dirt road bordered by many one-story wooden houses, each expelling the powerful odor of fried fish, and arrived at a small, clean, well-organized market. We wandered down two thirty-meter rows of wooden stands covered by a large overhang. The stands were attended by short-haired men in work uniforms of pants and shirts, and women in nice blue kimonos. Everyone wore large, white aprons to advertise the cleanliness of their goods.

Since Ezra's friends had said they wanted *mechshi*, we went first to buy the meat. On a wooden slab, the old butcher had many types of meat I had never seen before. He bowed low to us when we arrived and welcomed us to his stall by saying, "*Irashaimase*." Farida and I normally ate lamb, but they didn't have any. We gestured with our hands for the shopkeeper to show us what each animal was.

He took us into a cool wooden back room where there were three animal carcasses hanging on big metal hooks. One was obviously a pig, one was a big cow, and one was a small cow with lightly colored meat. We assumed the last was veal. In Syria, we didn't eat cow, but it was better than pork. Farida, obviously practiced in the art of procuring food, quickly gestured that we wanted one eighth of the small cow's ribs and plenty of meat from the leg.

We understood that the butcher did not normally specially prepare the veal for his customers, but Ezra's mother showed him how to wash it, salt it, and mince it. He also had blocks of beef fat on the side, which Farida had him mince as well. At this request, he gave us an incredulous look and warned Sakura that we would ruin the taste of his fresh meat by mixing in the fat.

He wrapped up our purchases in large plant leaves, and we

put them in Sakura's wicker basket. When we paid, he bowed low again and thanked us with the words "*Domo arigato.*"

Next was the easier task of buying the eggplant, string beans, onion, garlic, and other vegetables. The shopkeeper was a nice woman but looked at us with incomprehension when we tried to bargain. "*Takai, takai,*" we complained, but she just smiled and pointed at the price. We gestured to the lady to find out whether the vegetables were selling by piece or by kilogram. The eggplant was selling by piece, so naturally, we picked all of the biggest ones. The green beans were charged by weight, so all three of us picked the choicest pieces one by one, making sure we didn't waste money on spoiled vegetables.

Sakura and I carried everything back to the house and began preparing the lunch. While Farida instructed us how to make the food, I scribbled notes furiously with a pen and paper in between each step. First, we cut off all the eggplant stems. Next, we hand drilled a deep hole lengthwise through the eggplant with a *mawara*, a carving tool from Aleppo. Third, we mixed the fat together with the minced meat—ignoring the butchers advise. I then mixed the spices together, putting a pinch of this and half a handful of that into the mixture according to my mother-in-law's orders. To help me replicate the recipe, I first placed each ingredient separately into a measuring cup and wrote down the exact amount I added. Farida did not like this, but there was no other way I could remember it, so I kept doing it anyway. Next, we mixed the spices, washed rice, and meat in a bowl. Since we were behind schedule, Farida quickly stuffed the chunky mixture into each eggplant.

We started getting a little nervous, as the men were going to arrive in less than two hours and the recipe needed more than two hours to fully cook. To save time, Farida asked me to pour oil in a pan and sauté the onion and garlic. I had never used a gas stove before, but it seemed relatively simple. So,

I turned on the gas and grabbed a match. In Syria, matches were very expensive and I had always lit them after everything else was completely prepared. When I struck the match against the sandpaper on the side of the box, it broke in two. One expensive match wasted. I tried again, applying less pressure, but the tip broke off. Another expensive match wasted. I grabbed a third match, determined to do it right, and struck it perfectly over the stove.

WHOOOSH!!! A big ball of orange-blue flame shot up, instantly engulfing my upper body and face. Sakura sprang from her seat, grabbed a bucket of water, and dumped it over me. I didn't have the time or the presence of mind to scream. I knew only that my forehead was burning and stinging as if my skin had been ripped off. Panicking, I stumbled around with my eyes closed, trying to find more water. Sakura grabbed my arm, lead me to the sink, and guided my head under the faucet. The searing pain was quickly numbed to a dull ache by the gentle caresses of both the cool water and Sakura's encouraging voice. After calming down, I took stock of the damage in the mirror. My eyebrows were completely gone, my bangs were singed, and my forehead was bright red, but surprisingly, nothing else was amiss. I was amazed with my luck.

Since this was my first day assisting in the kitchen, I didn't want to disappoint my new teacher. I didn't waste any time on my appearance but walked purposefully back to the stove. When Farida saw that I was alright, the concern on her face melted away, and she quickly finished the lesson. We sautéed the garlic and onion, put all the *mechshi* in a large pot, and cooked the mixture for two hours over a low flame. While the eggplants were cooking, we made the *riz halabieh* by first briefly frying uncooked rice kernels in vegetable oil and then adding water to boil them to completion. We left the rice on the stove for over an hour to make certain the desired golden crispy crust formed on the bottom of the pot.

"When a blind wife cooks..."

When the last eggplant disappeared off of the serving plate, it was clear that the meal was a resounding success. The bachelors threw plenty of compliments at Farida and me. The conversation during the meal was a bit embarrassing, as everyone gave me advice on how to light the stove, and Cohab continually reassured me that my eyebrows would grow back quickly.

At the conclusion of the meal, the men politely put in their order for the next day. They hinted: "This lunch was really unbelievable. Just imagine if we had *caque* and *mahmoul* for dessert."

That afternoon we went to find the flour, pine seeds, sugar, cinnamon, and nuts that were necessary for the pastries they wanted. Farida and I cooked together daily for our first few weeks in Japan. We rarely made the same meal twice. My suspicions were confirmed later, one afternoon, when Ezra's friends put in their usual "suggestions" for the foods they craved.

"Ezra," they prodded amiably, "we heard that your mother makes the best *kibe hamda* in all of Aleppo! When are we going to have the pleasure of tasting it?"

Farida had been relatively patient with them but had had enough. Before he could answer, she interjected, "My son is married now. I have already cooked for my whole life. Now, I will not enter the kitchen nor touch another pan or dish. It is his wife's turn to take care of our distinguished guests."

Instead of responding verbally, I just blushed uncontrollably. I really couldn't imagine cooking twice daily for over ten people.

Ezra looked a little surprised by his mother's statement but just smiled and reassured his friends: "No problem, Lucie will make the *kibe hamda* tomorrow."

Sakura and I went to buy the ingredients, and we started cooking later that day. We were missing some spices that were not available in Japan, but we improvised where needed.

I was pleasantly surprised when Ezra's mother started telling me, step by step, how to prepare the meal—although, true to her words, she did not touch a pan or dish. Her help was invaluable, but she was impatient and produced a colorful phrase for every mistake I made.

While the bachelors ate the following afternoon, they heartily sang my praises: "You can really taste the lemon!"

"The *kibe* is perfectly spiced!"

"We feel like we are back home!"

I knew they were lying, but I enjoyed their encouragement.

My mother-in-law was not shy, though, and wanted everyone to hear what she thought about my first effort. "The broth is much too salty," she complained with a look of distaste.

Ezra and his friends stayed silent for a few awkward moments and then changed the subject.

This was repeated for the next few weeks. Sakura and I would make the lunch with the help of my mother-in-law, and the bachelors would extol my efforts. Then Farida would proceed to complain in front of everyone at the table that the food was too sweet, too sour, or the completely wrong taste. I soon found out that this was only the beginning of our rivalry and that she was just warming up. I knew that the compliments I was receiving were compliments that ultimately belonged to her. Despite the fact that it wasn't my fault, all my newfound popularity cultivated my mother-in-law's distrust, distaste, and displeasure with respect to all of my activities.

After we had been in our new home a few weeks, my voracious appetite returned. However, my hunger was difficult to appease because I had to serve everyone during the meal, which left me with no time to finish my food. Furthermore, it demonstrated a total lack of hospitality or feminine charm to remain at the table and eat when the men had already finished their meals.

So one afternoon, when I was cleaning the dishes with Sakura, I put some leftovers on my plate for later. Once everyone left, I sat down to finish my lunch. However, Farida was never too far away.

"What are you doing?" she reproached with her nose up in the air. "We just finished eating less than two hours ago! You are eating again???"

"I'm still hungry," I answered self-consciously, embarrassed by my appetite.

"You should only eat lunch at the same time as everyone else! That way, the kitchen will not be open the entire day. If you are not finished, don't get up from the table!"

"Yes, Yamo," I agreed, to escape further criticism. Nonetheless, I knew perfectly well I was not permitted to sit at the table and eat by myself when the guests were still in the house.

My first solution was to wait until my mother-in-law was asleep after lunch or dinner. I would then sneak downstairs and eat my fill. This saved me for about one week, but she astutely noticed food missing from the icebox. One day, she pretended to doze off after lunch, and when I snuck downstairs, she followed quietly behind.

She caught me, spoon in hand, eating a full plate of rice and string beans. "What are you doing!?" she shouted menacingly. "I told you not to eat in between meals!"

"But I'm hungry," I answered back, annoyed and hurt.

Her eyes narrowed, and she shot a verbal arrow into my heart: "You came from your house hungry, and you will always be hungry!"

That night, she started complaining to Ezra as soon as the guests left. "This girl, your wife, cannot stop eating. We cook for noon and night at the same time, but she eats, eats, and eats until all the food is gone."

Ezra, intelligently, did not want to get in the middle of a fight between his mother and wife. He answered the question in his own way: "I'm tired." He yawned. "I'm going to sleep."

Farida did not forget, though. The next day, she tried

to embarrass me in front of everyone. When I brought the food to the table, she brought some bread and jam from the kitchen. "I cannot eat your food!" she obsessed. "It has no taste! I will eat this instead!" She then asked everyone deviously, "Does anyone want some bread and jam?"

The men could see that a fight was brewing and wisely did not answer. Ezra took my side in the only way that he could. He took the serving spoon, scooped a healthy portion of the *bizeh b' jurah* (rice with mixed vegetables and meat) I had made, and dumped it on his plate. The bachelors followed his lead.

My mother-in-law, never at a loss for words, quickly delivered a choice phrase for the occasion: "Even if a blind wife cooks, the husband will eat it happily!"

No one said anything for a few moments as they slowly chewed their food. The mood was eventually restored with a business discussion used to diplomatically change the subject.

That night, I snuck into the kitchen at midnight to make myself a bread and cheese sandwich, but she crept down the stairs after me.

"People do not eat all the time like this! Only animals do!" she criticized vehemently. "You are behaving like an animal!"

Animals, like the one my mother-in-law compared me to, often solve life-threatening problems with strength, speed, or intelligence. Since I didn't possess an overabundance of the first two, the last would have to be my salvation. Michael, Ezra's former housemate and an ally of mine, unknowingly came to my rescue. He was overweight and ate with us daily, which made him an ideal accomplice.

The next afternoon, after all the bachelors had finished their lunches, I enlisted his help. "Michael," I asked, grinning, "are you still hungry?"

"No," he answered politely, looking away in embarrassment. "You gave me just the right amount."

I pushed hopefully: "The reason I'm asking is because we

have some extra food right here, and I was wondering if you would like to share some with me."

"Yes!" he acquiesced, studying the plate of food I was holding. "I would be happy to!"

I took all the leftovers, gave half of them to Michael, and left half of them on my plate. Both of us stayed together at the table and finished every last morsel of food. My plan was perfect! I looked polite by not leaving the table until everyone had finished, I had enough time to finish my lunch, and I wasn't accused of flirting with anyone.

Although it solved one problem, this plan did not liberate me from the wrath of my persecutor. She still complained about how much I ate whenever anyone would listen and stepped up her assault by including more embarrassing subjects in her repertoire. I was speechless when she started inspecting the sheets in my room every morning. Farida wanted proof that we were sleeping together and, when she didn't find any, became increasingly nervous. She started crying hysterically and regularly pulled out her hair in fits of anguish.

"Waaaaaaa. I only have one son, and his wife doesn't want to have any children. What am I going to do? When am I going to have grandchildren? My poor son... My poor son..."

The abuse was getting to be too much, so I looked for ways to occupy my mind in the afternoons. I found a Franco-Japanese library and borrowed books. I read in the French language about *Romeo and Juliet*, the Kings of France, the Royal Palace, the Seine River, and many other subjects about faraway places.

A month or so later, Farida tired of tormenting me daily with small annoyances and gave me something to really worry about. "You know, Lucie," she grumbled one morning, after looking me up and down critically. "Did I ever tell you the story of my friend in Aleppo?" Farida paused for effect but not long enough for an answer. "Like me, she had only one son. And her son was also a great man like mine. His stingy wife was not giving him any children. Do you know what my friend did?"

"No," I replied, only half listening but expecting another empty threat.

She smiled slyly and continued with nonchalance. "She found him a second wife, of course. The second wife got pregnant right away, and the first wife got pregnant soon afterwards. Don't think that this is not an option for me as well. If no children come from you, my son can get another wife. If she has children, then you will be the second wife, and have to clean up after them every day—until the day you die."

The frightening part of her speech was that she was not joking. I knew this was a real possibility, and I didn't want to clean up after another woman.

With that possible outcome now firmly lodged in my consciousness, I luckily was offered a temporary escape.

Working Vacation

Ezra had quickly realized that the purchases Asouad made from Aleppo were never going to make him a rich man. The only reason he had been able to survive previously was that his employer supported him in the early stages of their partnership. In order to make more money, Ezra needed to do more business and look for bigger international markets. He enlisted the help of Alfred Shouah from Lebanon.

Alfred had a good relationship with Ezra, could write well in both French and English, and needed some financial support. In exchange for Alfred's help in writing letters to foreign customers, Ezra would take him to lunch and dinner every day. The relationship worked very well for both parties until the day Alfred decided that he was tired of being single. He had his sister arrange a match for him in Lebanon and left immediately to get married. This was problematic since Ezra had little formal education, and while he picked up foreign languages with ease, he had only a limited ability to write official business letters. That left only one person who fit the limiting criteria of being fluent in the necessary languages, staunchly loyal, possessing plenty of free time, and costing next to nothing to employ.

While the invitation to practice my written French, English, and Arabic every morning was interesting, the prospect of finally escaping from my mother-in-law was more exciting. Ezra's one-story, cream colored office building was smaller than I had expected it to be, but was very centrally located at only a five-minute walk from Sannomiya Train Station. Ezra rented barely enough space for a big desk and a small work table, separated by a maze of rusty pipes, from his landlord Maruni-San—a good natured, traditionally dressed older man with an impressively long pinky fingernail.

The second we entered the office, Ezra's countenance changed from semi-relaxed to rigid as stone. He seemed to have forgotten that I was with him, so I set up his typewriter at the small table and got ready for instructions. My stomach was churning with nervousness, as I did not want to disappoint him. I knew that if I performed badly, I would be back with his mother in less than an hour.

After a long wait, he came over and tossed a list of thirty names and addresses from the Chamber of Commerce at me. He explained seriously, "We need to get more customers very fast, or we will go out of business here. I need you to write a letter to each person on this list, summarizing the details of the fabrics in the corner. They do not know who I am, so you need to make a nice introduction. Let me know when you are done with the first one, and I will go over it with you."

Not knowing too much about the textile business or exactly what I should be saying, I hesitantly wrote out the first draft.

Dear Sir:
My name is Ezra Choueke, and I am an exporter of textiles
from Kobe, Japan. I have many fabrics to offer you, includ-
ing cotton sheeting, cotton shirting, cotton jacquards, and cot-
ton blends. Please review the following samples and prices. I
am looking forward to hearing your positive reply.
Warm Regards,
Ezra Choueke

No sooner had I finished reading the letter to my husband in Arabic, than I wished that I hadn't.

"What do you mean, 'I am an exporter of textiles'!?" he roared like an angry lion. "Don't you know how to write a business letter? This customer has never heard of me before! You need to give him a good reason to place the order with me—and not someone else!"

As the blood slowly drained out of my face, I answered in my most apologetic voice. Using the wrong vocal tone would be a one-way ticket home.

"What should I have said?" I answered sheepishly.

He yelled out tidbits of information, and all the while, I patiently took notes. "Tell him I get the best prices, I buy directly from the maker, I am the best negotiator, I guarantee the quality... Tell him, once he gives me the order, I can often get him a lower price after a final negotiation with the factory."

I had been screamed at during my job with the French military and when misbehaving at home, so this was not a new feeling. The difference here was that home and work were now one. I couldn't make Ezra angry at work and have a peaceful home life. Also, I knew that I didn't want to be poor, like we were in Aleppo. I wanted to help him do well in the business so we would have enough to eat. I also knew that to have both my mother-in-law and my husband against me would mean much bigger problems for me personally. I would not be receiving any invitations to return to Syria anytime soon, so I kept quiet and started typing.

When we discussed the new letter, he carried on a little more but recommended only two or three more changes. I considered it a moral victory, and before the end of the next hour, we had finished our first letter.

A Lesson in Negotiation

That afternoon we received an exciting letter from Siyahou Zayat, one of Ezra's old friends in Palestine. He had purchased the fabrics we had sent to my brother Abraham. Since Abraham had chosen to pursue another business, Siyahou requested to be our distributor in Palestine and wanted to place an opening order for cotton shirting. We immediately notified our supplier.

Ishii-San's kimono flowed responsively over his stout build as he strode confidently into the office the following afternoon. His thick hair was complemented by a sparse mustache precisely groomed to accent the distinct curvature of his upper lip. He bowed to us and we returned the courtesy to show respect.

As he placed large swatches of fabric on the weathered table, I inhaled the pleasant, savory aroma of miso slowly escaping from an uneaten lunch hidden in his large bag. Joining us was an Australian who resided in Hong Kong, who everyone called Ned Kelly, after the outlaw, because he wanted to buy fabric at unimaginably low prices.

Ishii-San began in English for the benefit of our guest and I. With a patient smile, he introduced himself and explained that he had set up his factory in Osaka because the soft water there was ideal for bleaching and printing fabrics.[2]

2 Pearse, Arno S. *The Cotton Industry of Japan and China*. Manchester, England: International Federation of Master Cotton Spinners & Manufacturers' Association, 1929, p. 31.

While Ishii-San educated us in cotton, Ezra rose from his seat and examined each sample carefully. He felt each fabric between his thumb and index finger, inspected the composition with a brass thread-counting microscope, counted the strands of yarn which made up each thread, immersed a yarn strand in a candles flame to differentiate between cotton and rayon, weighed a *shaku* of cloth in *momme*, and recorded all the information meticulously in a leather-bound notebook.

Ezra then rejoined the conversation and quickly switched to Japanese. I knew he wanted to conduct the negotiation agreeably without any comments from Ned. Ishii-San gestured with an open hand to each fabric, and quickly stated the composition, width and price.

Ezra nodded and immediately had me write up a few orders. He then relayed the information to Ned.

Ned brushed his hands over a fabric of intermediate quality. He smoothly removed his brimmed hat and brandished an ugly scowl aimed at Ezra and Ishii-San. "I came all the way over from Hong Kong for these prices?" he spat. "I can't pay 25 sen per yard, you know very well that the British are trying to force Australia to ban Japanese textile imports! We have to be creative just to get this merchandise through customs."

Ezra nodded at Ned and said, "You're right!" His calm demeanor erupted into rage like a volcano, and he immediately started shouting at Ishii-San in Japanese.

Ishii-San remained motionless, listened and looked to the floor. When Ezra stopped, Ishii-San looked calmly at both of them and answered in English. "I will lower the price to 20 sen per yard for the first order."

Ezra erupted again, first yelling in Japanese, then in Arabic, and finally in English: "*Chalas! Chalas!* For this quality of merchandise we can only pay 17!"

Ned was silent but glared at Ishii-San with the edges of his lips starting to edge up towards a smile. I flushed with embarrassment in disbelief at my husband, the madman, in front of me. I suddenly leapt to my feet and ran out of the office door in a panic.

I spent a few minutes outside, composed myself, and skulked back into the room. Ishii-San, still confident, was in the middle of a description of his production process and why it warranted the extra money. Ezra spoke quickly to me in Arabic: "Lucie, wait a few minutes and then ask in English if we can both compromise on the price by meeting in the middle."

After a suitable time had passed, I shuffled reluctantly over to the desk and did as instructed.

"What do you mean!?" Ezra shouted at me in English, using all the force in his lungs. "I told you the price is too high!" His hot breath blew back some strands of hair at the edges of my face.

Ishii-San suddenly jumped out of his seat. "Alright! Alright!" he exclaimed. "We have a deal, but only to honor your wife!"

Both Ned and Ezra immediately placed huge orders.

Ishii-San gave me a covert smile as I finished writing out the details, he exchanged bows with Ezra, and hurried out the door.

Ezra's stern façade crumbled into a big smile once we were alone. "You did a good job," he chuckled, savoring my reaction. "Siyahou will be happy."

I was shocked and embarrassed. "Why did you yell at Ishi-San like that?" I asked Ezra carefully, still unsure if I was speaking to a sane person.

"Maybe you should ask me what I yelled at Ishii-San." His eyes twinkled. "I shouted, 'Don't worry about this *wakaran-mon* (ignorant person), just give us a volume discount on 30,000 yards³ and I will make up the difference in quantity.' It was all a show."

"Why did you yell at *me*?" My eyes teared.

"Most deals are straight forward, but for some people we

---

3 They measured fabric in both yards and meters. The unit of measurement depended on the customer and the factory. I have used "yards" as the unit of measurement here for simplicity.

need to create some drama. Ned wouldn't have ordered if he didn't think he was getting a good price. You played your part perfectly. And look at the result, Ned and Siyahou received a great price and Ishii-San a great order."

A Strategic Partner

That afternoon, Ezra explained the difficulties of our business. We had saved Siyahou a lot of money, but we actually made less commission by negotiating honestly. Ironically, the better we did for the customer, the less money we would get paid. There was only one conclusion: we needed bigger customers, and fast, if we wanted to eat on a regular basis.

Joe Dahab from Brooklyn was a key partner we needed in order to make our business viable. Most of his products had been coming from Shanghai and Hong Kong, China, but he needed an agent in Japan. Joe was only the third American I had ever met. He reminded me of a gentleman cowboy from one of those western movies with a full, strong face, a big bushy mustache, matching eyebrows, long thick sideburns, and bright-red cheeks. The thick cigar projecting from the right corner of his mouth accented his brash speech and stout body, but his warm personality often softened his features. The next few days were filled with lively meals at the house, multiple factory visits, and countless negotiations.

Whenever a negotiation was close to the end, Joe would stare at the supplier, like a cowboy on the cusp of a gunfight, squint his right eye for maximum effect, and hold up ten fingers.

Ezra would then turn to the supplier, "Look, he wants another ten percent discount. If you want this new customer to buy something from us in Japan, we better lower the price."

Despite appearances, Ezra wasn't only working for Joe. His goal was to find a group of regular items that made sense for both Mr. Dahab and the Japanese suppliers, so they could all make profits together for decades. When they had finally reached an acceptable price, Mr. Dahab would not smile. He would slowly take out a cigar from his shirt pocket, light it, and start puffing away, staring contemplatively at the ceiling.

Taking care of a customer was a full-time affair. Aside from lunch and dinner at our house, we spent Saturdays at the synagogue and Sundays playing cards. Many of our friends were invited as well, since a crowd of people was necessary for the synagogue *minyan* (the required ten men for a Jewish group prayer).

Sigmund, a weasel-faced, sickly pale, balding man of thirty-seven, stayed as close to Ezra as the handkerchief adorning the breast pocket of his suit. Partly, this was because they were friends, but it was mostly to keep his shifty green eyes on the business my husband was involved in. Sigmund started stalking Joe like a hungry hyena: Laughing at all of his jokes; sitting next to him when the cards were dealt; and drooling nearby, armed with the latest financial news, right when the food was placed steaming hot upon the table. He was carefully biding his time until the opportune moment to strike. One Sunday night, when Ezra was tired, Sigmund predatorily rushed in to accompany Mr. Dahab on the walk to his hotel.

"What commission is Ezra charging you?" he spouted, getting directly to the point once they were alone.

"Five percent is what he is proposing," Joe answered, unbothered by the question. He was used to people fighting over his business.

"If you give me the business, I will work on four percent," Sigmund proposed with a smirk, showing Joe a generous mouth full of crooked yellow teeth all jostling for position at the front of his mouth. "I know where the factories are as well and can do a better job for you than he can."

"I'll think about it," Joe replied ambiguously. "I won't make the decision until later in my buying trip."

Ezra kept working with Mr. Dahab for another week.

They visited new suppliers every day before finally looking to put a deal in place.

"Ezra," Joe began cautiously. "I want to make an agreement between us so we can start doing some long-term business."

"Excellent!" Ezra answered happily. "I will do my best for you."

"Yes," Joe answered more seriously, squinting his right eye. "You see... I have received many offers from men who will represent me at four or even at three percent commission."

"Joe..." he answered, smiling and confident, while whipping out a comb and running it thoughtfully through his straight hair. "You know as well as I do that if you are working with a dishonest person, it does not matter what commission rate he charges. He will just make side deals with the suppliers to increase his profits. I can't charge less because I need to pay for transportation to the factories, samples, inspections, postage, rent, and food."

Joe thought about it carefully, picked a cigar out of his shirt pocket, lit it, and took a long drag. He did not speak for about five minutes but simply blew ring after ring of cigar smoke thoughtfully into the air. He then made direct eye contact and extended his right hand, and with a vigorous shake, our partnership began.

Growing the Line

We began by shipping Mr. Dahab material, but the real opportunity for us lay in the development of new product lines such as tablecloths, shoes, slippers, baseball caps, beach hats, towels, and children's clothing. We knew he was currently buying these items from someone in another country. Getting more business for Japan was contingent upon finding the best merchandise at the best possible price. Ezra spent his time between the office and the factories developing new sources. I hired a car and traveled from factory to factory looking for new products.

Joe sent us various tablecloth styles from Belgium and I went to see Nakamura-San. Nakamura-San was the trendiest factory owner we knew. Although he was tall, muscular, and handsome, he always looked for the latest in Western fashion to complete his appearance. At first, his kimono and crew cut were complemented only by a gold European pocket watch, kept in the folds of his belt. Later, though, he abandoned his kimono altogether in favor of a navy-blue pin-striped suit, a white long-sleeved shirt, and a matching blue tie. His beautiful wife and three daughters, obviously very proud of him, hung on his every word. As was the custom in many Japanese factories, the entire family worked together, side by side.

The main reason Nakamura-San's prices were so good was that fabric was not his main business. He was a rice farmer, employing one hundred people to cultivate his fields. During the planting and harvesting seasons, all of his workers were ankle-deep in the rice fields with inverted-cone-shaped straw hats on their heads. Although his land was sizeable, one hundred people completed the required work relatively quickly. In order to occupy them for the rest of the year, he bought machines to make thread, winding machines, and weaving machines. The factory's dress code was very different from the farm's. His many female employees were carefully dressed in spotless kimonos, socks, and slippers. Their long hair was tied back in complicated buns, using only small wooden sticks to efficiently hold it in place.

Since we were concentrating on beginning the tablecloth business, Nakamura-San showed me how he prepared the cotton fibers through the drawing, roving, and spinning processes. Afterwards, he briefly explained how the automatic loom worked, and I marveled at the many cotton threads being fed into the machine's rapidly moving parts. I was quietly overjoyed when, at the end of the tour, he showed me a huge warehouse full of cancelled orders.

We were looking for situations such as these because most factories had little room for stock merchandise. They all wanted to turn their excess goods into cash in order to free up more workspace. By paying cash right away, Ezra often received unimaginably low prices on goods the factory could not sell. After having an *udon* noodle lunch with Nakamura-San and his wife, I continued on to a shoe factory. Nakamura-San promised to meet Ezra in Kobe.

For weeks, I went different places in search of stock goods and soon compiled a long list of merchandise sitting in factory warehouses around Kobe. We knew that the only way to prevent our competition from offering the same goods was to buy this merchandise ourselves. In order to rent a warehouse, buy the merchandise, and give people credit, we needed money. But money we didn't have. Intelligently, Ezra had already been working on this problem for some time.

Takai

Vegard Larson was the stodgy Dutch manager of Netherlands Industry Bank and, conveniently, a very good friend of Ezra's. Like the bachelors, he would come over for lunch and dinner a few days a week. Unlike the bachelors, he was unhappily married.

Due to the fact that he was a prominent figure in town, many wanted to be friendly with him, but the surrounding circumstances made it difficult. His Dutch wife would visit the good-looking businessmen in town, especially those who owed her husband money, and insist on a few cups of coffee. She would then wait until they were alone and seduce these younger men. Soon everyone, including Mr. Larson, knew of her adventures. Their marital issues became especially difficult to ignore when, after a long vacation to the U.S. by herself, she returned pregnant.

When our banker found a good-looking Japanese girl-friend—which everyone agreed could morally be afforded to him due to his wife's behavior—he brought her over to the house for every social event. Since Ezra and I worked together, my husband was beyond suspicion with regards to having had an inappropriate relationship with Vegard's wife, and there-fore, our house became a safe haven for him. One of the side benefits to our great friendship was that loans to grow our business were approved without any bureaucratic delay.

Ezra began negotiations around the clock to make sure that we secured as much top quality, discounted merchandise as possible.

When Nakamura-San began laying out samples of his extra inventory on Ezra's desk one morning, he could sense some lingering tension in the room from the previous sup-plier. And while happy to see an old friend, Ezra immediately picked up an exquisite two-toned, cream colored tablecloth with a floral jacquard pattern and examined it under a loop.

Nakamura-San spoke first, "Before you say *'Takai'* ('too expensive') and start negotiating with me concerning these beautiful items, let me say that there are many other very good words in the Japanese language."

"Please teach me some!" Ezra looked up from the cloth and laughed heartily.

"There is the word *yasui*, which means, 'cheap,' and you can use the phrase *eii hinshitsu no mono de su*, which means, 'good quality.'"

Ezra replied quickly, "Thank you very much for the quick lesson, Nakamura-San, but I'll never have any use for those words. They will only cause the price to increase."

They both laughed and were able to come to an agree-ment in time to go to the Oriental Hotel for lunch. They both understood that one had outdated merchandise clogging up his factory floor, and that the other could only pay a certain amount to gain possession of it.

Crowing Around

Our business grew quickly with the help of our local suppliers. As we shipped more products, hired more people, and relocated our offices, more large factories considered us as a viable outlet for their excess goods. These factories took orders from large corporate customers and there was always a "waste factor" built into their cost calculations, since there were always mistakes made on the factory floor. A standard calculation for defective products, or "seconds," was in the neighborhood of 5%. However, customers were not fully aware of the meticulousness of the Japanese worker and the defective output was far less than that. As a result, the factory would have extra goods to sell in a non-competing international market. The cost for this merchandise would be nil to the factory and anything they got for it would be pure profit. Naturally, a large producer knew the price that he was selling his products for and would ask this price when coming to us. This would be the opening price and beginning of any negotiation.

We had a client visiting from Panama and a major supplier came to meet with him.[4] I joined them at the table with paper and pen.

"Sato-San, what can you offer our dear friend from Panama today?" Ezra began.

"We have 1780 dozen of these beautiful dress shirts, some white, some blue and some striped, made exclusively for a top department store in New York." After slurping his tea (which was quite common and acceptable) and wiping his brow with a handkerchief that he brought for the express purpose of

---

4 This negotiation represents a true event, but has been moved chronologically to before 1940 for the purposes of the book.

wiping away the imagined sweat from his brow, he sighed and whispered in a crestfallen voice: "33 Yen per dozen, and my boss will have my head for quoting such a low price."

I knew that this gentleman would have no trouble finding a dramatic role in the movies or even on the Kabuki stage.

"Come to your senses man!" Ezra countered. "This poor fellow," he gestured casually in the direction of the customer who did not speak a word of Japanese and who sat on the sofa in the office, "can in no way compete with the many adversaries he has in his market. He can pay no more than 12 Yen per dozen!"

Sato-San reddened immediately, and to this day I don't know how he did it. He must have had a secret store of whisky to nip on so as to enhance the effect. "You cannot be serious Ezra-San, you know as well as I do that that's way below the cost of making. Are you trying to get me fired from my job? Maybe then I can come to work for you?"

"You know I cannot afford a highly skilled and capable businessman such as yourself," Ezra replied. "What's the best price Sato-San? That's what I ask."

"All right, because we go back a long way, I will persuade my boss to agree to 26 Yen per dozen, with payment in ready cash."

"Have you ever been to Panama?" Ezra asked. (This was a rhetorical question, the answer to which was an obvious "No.") "What do you expect them to do with dress shirts there? It's so hot and humid there it makes a sweltering August in Osaka feel like a holiday in Hokkaido."

"What are you saying? Have they suddenly abandoned their smuggling business? Don't they just buy the goods and transship them over to South America? Business as usual, wouldn't you say? It's a good deal and if you don't want them, then I will offer them to Hana-San. Did I tell you about the stripes? I think I mentioned them. It's the absolute latest in trend, the next time I come in I'll get you one for yourself. Allow me to measure your neck and your sleeves..."

"Because you are my friend," replied Ezra, "and because you know so much about the Panama business, I will offer you an exorbitant 18 Yen per dozen and that's my last offer."

"It's almost lunch time," Sato-San replied. "Let's meet in the middle and '*Chalas*.' And by the way, don't even think of diverting these goods to anywhere—*anywhere*—in the US."

"We have a deal. Lucie, please write an order for our distinguished guests."

Later that night before going to bed, I asked Ezra how it was that Sato-San spoke Arabic.

Ezra answered: "Arabic? What Arabic?"

"Well I heard him say '*chalas*' to you. And '*chalas*' is certainly an Arabic word." (An indication of finality, the end to a negotiation or other event.)

"He actually said '*karasu*,'" Ezra replied. "'*Karasu*' is the word in Japanese for crow. Also there is no letter 'L' in the Japanese language so '*chalas*' would be pronounced as '*karasu*.' It's a kind of double entendre. It means no more crowing around and let's just conclude this portion of business. They're very smart you know. They pretend not to know your language but sometimes they just can't resist letting you know they understand. I heard that Sato-San has taken to using it as his famous last word when he closes down the bar at night. He takes his last swig, declares '*chalas*' or '*karasu*' and then happily heads home to bed. Don't let his innocent look fool you. He is very much the equal of any trader in the Middle East."

From a personal standpoint, I was very happy to be employed again, and my reward was the knowledge that I was helping my new family. At first, I jumped at the chance to work for the simple pleasure of getting away from my mother-in-law. I began to love it for many other reasons as well. Working was like playing a sport, with Ezra as my teammate. The simple rule of the game was this: we needed to make more money than we spent. Focus or motivation was not a problem because if we failed, we would starve. Mutual trust was not a problem either. I knew Ezra had confidence in me, and I had confidence in him. The lack of internal problems allowed us to focus on growing our sales and decreasing our costs. However, the most valuable product of our business was not the money: it was the change it brought to our relationship.

Two Blessings

Today people commonly wait to fall in love. Love is something I never fell in. Falling, where love is concerned, describes an effortless process that could only be facilitated by the most polished movie star—complete with a tuxedo, a handsome face, and a European accent. The common saying never applied to me or to anyone I knew. A better phrase to describe my path was "*I worked into love.*"

I ran into my first few months of marriage sure that Mama had made the wrong decision, and I just attempted to squeeze any joy that I could out of the day. Learning to cook, reading books, and later going to the office were all ways to swim through the complexities of my captors' personalities, ultimately to make a better life for myself.

The transformation from thinking only of myself to thinking of us as a couple took place in Ezra's office. Our business was the vehicle by which we were either going to go hungry or succeed beyond our dreams. As our teamwork at the office grew stronger, so did our feelings for each other. The first time I noticed this happening was when I found 10,000 five-piece cosmetic bag sets in a factory outside of Osaka. The set was very cute and featured pastel-colored tulips printed on a light-pink cotton fabric. When the maker asked my opinion of the merchandise, I hid my excitement and pretended to be ambivalent.

I invited the supplier to the office, the negotiation with Ezra went smoothly, and as it was concluding, Ezra announced in

Arabic, "Lucie, you really found something great! We will surely sell this immediately! *Mafe mitlek* ['You are one of a kind']."

I smiled quickly and left the room. I didn't want the manager to know we were happy with the deal and possibly cause an unexpected price increase. The truth was that I was absolutely filled with joy. It had been too long since someone had used my name in a sentence without criticism, since someone had appreciated me, and since I had felt as though I was part of a family. We sold the goods one week after we bought them to a visiting customer from South America. With part of the profit, Ezra bought me a gold chain, which became my most prized possession. It was a token of love we had earned together, working side by side.

My mother-in-law was not as fulfilled, because once I went to the office, she returned to the kitchen. This meant she had to spend more time in the house and had no one to speak to. Ezra made sure to bring home as many Arabic speakers as possible so she would have company. Ironically, the more guests we would bring to entertain her, the more cooking she would need to do. By the time the lunch was ready, she was so angry that Ezra never dared to return home alone. For as long as the bachelors were over, Farida would either be involved in a good conversation or too polite to complain excessively in front of them. I respected my husband for all his efforts to keep his mother happy, but these efforts did not save me from her wrath. I was still her main project.

Farida's life was complicated by my going to the office, as she had much less time to bother me throughout the day.

So she complained obsessively, "What am I supposed to do here all day by myself? I have no one to talk to! I am like a slave in this house!"

Ezra had no easy way to solve this problem, as he needed me in the office. The only logical solution was to bring Farida to the office as well.

This experiment lasted a miserable seventy-two hours.

She sat on a chair in the corner of the office and bitterly did nothing all day. In addition, Ezra had to pay handsomely to take everyone to lunch at a hotel.

Farida did not like to create problems for her son, so after the third day she announced loudly on the way home, "Tomorrow, I am no longer coming to the office. There is nothing for me to do there!"

"Incredible!" I thought. Finally, I had won! I would get to work as before without trouble or problem.

"Alright, Yamo!" Ezra said morosely, concluding a few moments of silence. "Lucie will stay with you in the morning, and she will come to the office with me every afternoon."

Alas, a razor sharp samurai sword sliced through the celebratory balloons floating around in my head. Heavy iron shackles of negativity restrained my spirit. Not only would I have to return to the kitchen in the morning, but I also would have double the work in the afternoon.

I crawled slowly through the next few months, as if time had become as viscous as honey. Going to the market in the morning, cooking until the early afternoon, and taking my turn in the office weakened my entire body.

My mother-in-law, emboldened by her victory, constantly hurled insults at me, which stuck like shrapnel into my soul: "This food is inedible!" "I have no company!" "Why are you eating so much!?" "If you do not have children soon, my son is permitted a second wife!"

The only justified criticism was that about my eating. Although work had injected excitement and purpose into my life, I still faced the same issues at home. Lunch and dinner were the only activities I enjoyed there. I ate everything I could as an emotional escape from my monitor. The food was the only thing not telling me what to do. Then, one day, my escape was taken from me as well.

When preparing the daily lunch one morning, I was frying minced garlic and inhaling the fragrant aroma. Suddenly, the smell became sour, vile, and absolutely unbearable, like burnt hot peppers. I was barely able to cross the threshold from the kitchen to the garden before vomiting uncontrollably on the steps that bridged them. Farida, who was in the kitchen, watched the performance in silence.

"I must be sick," I stammered delicately. "I need to go lie down."

Farida for once did not criticize me but kept quiet. I did not ask again but hurried up to my room and lay down.

That night, I rushed to the bathroom and threw up again. The next day, while preparing lunch, I gave an encore performance on the kitchen's stone floor.

"I must be very, very sick," I told Farida with worry staining my voice. "I don't feel well and cannot eat anything. I need to go to a doctor."

My mother-in-law's stern countenance cracked as a knowing smile crept slowly onto her face. She looked up at the sky and, trying in vain to stay unemotional, she said, "You do not need a doctor for this. I know what this is, and you are not sick. Eat what you can, go upstairs, and I will finish the cooking."

Too tired to argue or question, I stumbled upstairs and collapsed in bed.

Weaving Our Lives Together

Alright, Alright, Alright... so I may have omitted some information. In those French movies I watched in Aleppo, there is usually that split second when the fiery, gorgeous woman being pursued realizes that the handsome rogue she has been resisting is actually everything that had been missing in her life. Abandoning her resistance, she dissolves into his chiseled arms, mirrors his wanting gaze, passionately kisses his sensuous lips, and declares tearfully, "You have always been the only one for me!" As the credits begin to appear on the screen, the curtains close, and the audience is assured they will live happily ever after.

This has absolutely, positively no relation to what actually took place in my life. First and foremost, in my cinematic moment of clarity, it became abundantly clear that my life, for better or worse, was with Ezra and Farida in Japan. Mama was not going to take me back, and Ezra was not going to send me back. All the fight and energy I could muster would not change that. The only objective prolonged resistance would accomplish was alienation from the only two people within seven thousand kilometers who cared whether I lived or died.

Next, I understood that Farida's threats were very real. Over the long term, if I didn't produce results for the family in the baby department, the only department they really cared about, my position would be housekeeper to Ezra's new wife. I already had a mother-in-law and a husband telling me what to do all day. I couldn't imagine having another boss and, worse yet, one that was my age—or even younger. It did not escape me that having a child would also give me an easier time with my current bosses. Having a baby would bring me a higher status in the house. I would no longer be thought of as the girl that arrived without a dowry. I would be the mother of Ezra's son and Farida's grandson.

I also have to admit that, like all the women in these French romances, I, too, had a change of heart regarding my costar. What changed? In the beginning, he was a man over twice my age wanting me for his bride and, at thirteen years old, I could only imagine what else. But by now we had traveled together, worked together, eaten together, lived together, and I realized that he was an intelligent, kind man. As my respect for him grew, the fact that he did not look like Rudolf Valentino became irrelevant. My perception of him became much richer and more elaborate than any understanding of a man that I could get from staring at a two-dimensional movie screen. He was my coworker, my husband, my provider, someone who ate my cooking even when it was burnt or barely edible, someone who had never rushed me to consummate our relationship, and someone who had to carefully take my side when his mother insisted otherwise.

While the new understanding of my husband slowly materialized, my preconceptions of him evaporated into the night. Instead, new thread, composed of the sum of our experiences together, was rewoven into a new, complex, and beautiful pattern, reminiscent of the intricately detailed, thick carpets that blanketed our floors in Aleppo. And as those carpets had magically infused an atmosphere of warmth, beauty, comfort, excitement, and structure into our home, these same characteristics radiated throughout our relationship. The complex fabric formed in the heat of weaving our lives together was something that I could love, something that could allow me to make our relationship whole.

If you expect a lurid description of what took place that night and the nights that followed, leading up to my pregnancy, you have not been paying attention. A conservative, serious girl from Aleppo would never do that!

Expanding Waistlines and Borders

No one offered the slightest help or guidance in the early stages of my pregnancy. All I knew was a strange being was growing inside my body demanding food, making me sick, hampering my blissful eating with bouts of vomiting, deforming my body, and causing me to outgrow my few clothes. My only purchase was an extra-large kimono with enough fabric to cover my ever-expanding midsection.

Japan, unlike me, did not have the luxury of buying new clothes or procuring enough extra food to adapt to the changes taking place within her borders. Those changes, however, were just as significant and demanded resources for the population growing in her belly. Although I was ignorant of the situation at the time, Japan's population was increasing rapidly, but the country's economic might was not keeping pace. Many of Japan's exports had dropped precipitously in price due to the effects of the American depression. Many farmers were also struggling as the increasing overpopulation limited the land available for agriculture. This contributed to low crop yields and created many poor people. The economic discontent manifested itself in an intense nationalism and calls for expansion. Like me buying a bigger kimono to adequately clothe my growing body, Japan looked for extra land and material resources to supply its multiplying population. Some Japanese looked to China as the source for new raw materials, farmed goods, and business outlets for their finished products.[5]

Ezra, Farida, the bachelors, and I were foreigners in Japan and did our best to stay out of politics. The daily interactions with our neighbors, business suppliers, butchers, maids, and others were of a superficial nature to achieve success and survival through cooperation. We did not offer our political opinions, and they did not ask for them. Most locals privately felt that foreigners were not very intelligent and had no real lasting interest in the success of the country. In reality, though, our politics were quite simple. Our only goal was to avoid war since war inevitably resulted in death. We were only interested in surviving peacefully and doing some business if we were lucky enough. The celebration carried out at our neighbor's house one afternoon, though, whispered warnings of tougher days ahead.

Business for us was getting better. We no longer considered ourselves poor since we had more than enough money to buy food and necessities. Ezra rented a large, English-style, two-story house up the street from the German Club. The

5 Toland, John. *The Rising Sun The Decline and Fall of the Japanese Empire, 1936-1945*. New York: Random House, 1970, p. 6.

two floors and multiple rooms could accommodate many children and customers. However, my favorite feature of the house was the big garden.

A deaf-mute, ancient man with wisps of white hair and a hunched back was the garden caretaker. We called him *Oji-San* ("Uncle"), and he lived in a small hut on the corner of the property. He had lived in the hut for an indeterminable number of years, and it was obvious that he would never leave. *Oji-San* was a curious individual who raised chickens and goats, not to eat, but as pets. The remarkably tame chickens would eat from his hands while he stroked their feathers. We would give him some food, but he stayed mostly self-sufficient by eating the chicken eggs and milking the goats. He never wondered for a moment if anything would change when we moved into the house. *Oji-San* kept taking care of the garden as he always had; he couldn't hear, so we couldn't suggest any changes, and he couldn't speak, so there were no complaints. We began eating dinner in the well-manicured garden every night and became friendly with our neighbors, the Tanakas, who often ate in their garden next door.

Tanaka-San had five children and an important position at the Port of Kobe. Most days, he would come home from work around 7 p.m., have dinner with the family, change from a business suit into a kimono, and head off towards the police station where he perfected his mastery of *kendo* (the modern Japanese art of sword fighting). His wife and mother managed the household. They prepared delicious daily meals of *okonomiyaki*, tofu, fish, octopus, *miso*, *udon*, various kelps and savory broths whose delicate aromas danced around the neighborhood. They washed clothes and hung them precisely on the line, heated water for the bath, and meticulously cared for their beautiful garden and home. Their boys, aged twenty-five, twenty, and sixteen, were very handsome, tall, muscular, short-haired, and unmarried. Their two girls were beautiful, well-proportioned, tall, and modest. We often exchanged pleasantries and discussed the simple subjects that friendly neighbors discuss without delving into anything controversial.

One evening, Ezra, Farida, a few guests, and I were having a small dinner in the garden. It was the special hour before the summer sunset, when the air would cool enough to allow us to relax and calmly discuss the day's events over cold drinks. Suddenly, a small forest-green military truck screeched to a stop in front of the Tanakas' house. Two officers jumped out of the front and one out of the back, quickly looked around, and marched with perfect coordination into our neighbors' garden. Official solemnity and seriousness radiated from their neatly pressed uniforms: green canvas brimmed hats, long-sleeved green cotton shirts buttoned down the middle, and pants that started wide at the hips, tightened over their calves, and disappeared into their ample black leather boots. We were immediately intimidated by their deliberate movements, close cropped hair, rigid faces, long sheathed swords, and holstered pistols.

The three officers approached the family, who were all seated around a dinner table set up in the garden. Everyone at the table instantly stood up and respectfully bowed low to the officers. The military men stopped and bowed respectfully back. The tallest of the three took one step forward and unrolled a piece of thick yellow paper.

"Tanaka-San," he proclaimed with vigor and politeness.

"At your service!" the father answered obediently. He swiftly walked around the table, approached the officers, and bowed low in deference.

The officers bowed back and straightened ceremoniously. The tallest member of the trio again projected loudly: "I am pleased to announce that the Emperor has requested the presence of your eldest son in the armed forces, to fulfill his duty to the nation. Do you accept?"

"Yes, of course! We are honored to be of service!" Tanaka-San punctuated his enthusiasm with another bow.

The soldier who had jumped out of the back of the truck received some instructions from his superior, saluted, departed, and returned almost instantly. He opened a bottle of sake, unwrapped a box of cookies, and began slicing a large red fish. Together the officers, the father, and Daitaro, the eldest son, ate sashimi and drank sake. They became redder and redder as the rice wine took effect. Repeatedly clinking glasses before each new sip, they yelled, "*Tenno Heika, banzai!*" toasting to the Emperor's good health. After what must have been over two hours, the officers stood up with Daitaro, and all four of them drove away into the night. A few days later, the Tanakas received a framed picture of their eldest son in full uniform, which they proudly displayed above their fireplace. Daitaro wrote to inform them that he would soon be stationed in China.

The Tanakas were very proud of their son. It was a great honor for the family to have a son serving the nation at the Emperor's request. Like every Japanese person we knew, they considered the Emperor to be a God. However, it is difficult to compare our views to theirs. As Jews, we believe in the one God who created the universe and whom we pray to daily in thanks for the blessings we have received. Our Japanese friends and neighbors prayed to many gods, including their ancestors. The Emperor was considered to be one of these numerous deities but held a special position among them. He was thought to be infallible, a beacon of morality, and like a father to all of his subjects. An order from the Emperor to go to China therefore was not treated as anything negative. Rather, it was the highest honor to be chosen to help their leader, father, and God turn his vision for a better world order into action.

In order to supply the armies in China and the Pacific with the soldiers needed, men in their twenties and thirties were chosen. During that time, men who were married, had many small children to support, or were employed in doing a job critical to the good of the country were not taken. Instead, they were encouraged to have more children. The government was interested in keeping families as self-sufficient as possible. In the case of our friends the Tanakas, only the eldest son was taken that day to further the nation's cause. The other sons and daughters were left behind to provide for the family.

My Angel

The baby in my womb was supposed to dissolve all the disagreements we had as a family. Now that I had part of Farida and Ezra growing inside my body, I was no longer an outsider but an equal who was cultivating the future of the Choueke name. I would be treated with respect, my opinion would be valued, and I would not be pestered needlessly anymore. Oh, how young and ignorant I was regarding the ways of the world! The only thing that changed was the size of my waist!

The first weeks of the pregnancy, my mother-in-law made an effort to help with the cooking and shopping every morning. Perhaps I made the mistake of being too capable, because soon I was doing the shopping all by myself again. She still helped with the cooking, but I suspected it was more to enhance the flavor of the food than to decrease my workload.

I made sure that Ezra didn't see me in any weak moments during my pregnancy. I still valued my afternoons in the office away from Farida and did not want to jeopardize my freedom. Business for me was not just something that needed to be done; it was my hobby and one of the only activities that brought me happiness. Therefore, I was careful to display my struggles only during the morning hours—after Ezra had left to the office.

Whatever my mother-in-law did to help in the kitchen she offset in other ways to make sure I didn't get too proud.

She regularly picked new characteristics, behaviors, and actions to criticize, as if she were being financially rewarded for her efforts.

Some days, with all the changes in my body, I could not cope with the abuse as before. I wavered between wanting to stab her with a sharpened knife and wanting to run away— once and for all. I probably would have done one or the other had not an angel by the name of Lily Braha come into my life.

Lily Braha was not an angel in the sense that she was divinely beautiful, with big white wings, a halo, and a mouth that always spouted words of virtue. It was actually quite the opposite. Due to an overzealous midwife at her birth who had tried to pull her out early, one of Lily's shoulders was several centimeters higher than the other and she walked with an uneven gait. Her long, curly brown hair, blue eyes, tall frame, and plain, full face made her average to look at. But the intelligent, quick-witted phrases that danced off of her lips somehow changed my thinking and gave my mind a vacation from its ever-present persecutor.

Lily and I did not have a choice but to become close. Haim Braha, Lily's husband, was a very good friend of Ezra's. They ate and played cards together daily. With one simple conversation, while cleaning up the kitchen, I finally found the ally and friend I had been lacking.

Lily—speaking in French so no one nearby could understand—spat out her questions like venom from a cobra. "Why does your mother-in-law make a face, like she has bit into a lemon, whenever she looks at you?"

I was caught off guard but was always more than willing to discuss Ezra's mother. "I don't know!" I vented energetically. "Every day she picks a new detail to criticize! Yesterday, I overcooked the rice! Today, while I was serving Mois Shayo, I leaned too close to him!"

"What? Does she think you are in love with Mois!?" she responded incredulously.

"I don't know! Last week, she thought I talked to Isaac for too long! So, maybe she thinks I am in love with him too!" I answered, laughing and turning red in the face.

"So, every day you are accused of behaving indecently with your husband's friends, even though you are pregnant?" she answered with a delightful smile.

"I suppose it is one of her favorite subjects," I responded, giggling.

"Well, from my point of view, that is very depressing." She concentrated on scrubbing the grime off of a dish, as she continued, "If she is criticizing you for flirting, and there is no flirting going on, you are getting the punishment but not enjoying the reward. If you are going to be scowled at either way, you should at least have the decency to give her something real to complain about. Ezra's friends, you, and I will at least get a good laugh out of it. It is not right to let Farida have all the fun. Follow my lead after lunch, and let's see if we can really make her nervous!" she responded, smiling mischievously.

After lunch, everyone left the house and walked together toward their respective offices. Ezra and his mother walked with a group of bachelors. Lily and I followed about ten steps behind.

"Watch this!" Lily grinned, her eyes sparkling with excitement.

She shouted enthusiastically so everyone could hear: "Dahoodeh! Dahoodeh Sassoon, come here! I want to tell you a funny story!" Dahoodeh smiled and hurried over to us. This quickly aroused the suspicions of my husband, her husband, and my mother-in-law all at the same time. It also made the other bachelors' ears perk up with jealousy, as the men wondered why they weren't chosen to hear the anecdote. It was as if she were teaching a course in manipulation.

Lily whispered to me, "Now, let him walk between us, and we'll both talk to him at once. Make sure to laugh loudly at whatever he says, whether it is funny or not."

She began weaving a ridiculous tale of an ugly farm girl who fell in love with a prince. Lily acted out everything the woman did to attract the prince's attention, while he rode through the city on his way to the palace. Lily waved at the prince like the farm girl waved, winked at the prince like the farm girl winked, whistled at the prince like the farm girl whistled, shouted at the prince like the farm girl shouted, and did whatever needed to be done to tell the story effectively. Finally, this unfortunate farm girl was put to death by order of the king due to her outrageous behavior. It really wasn't the story that was important, though—it was the reactions we received. Whenever Dahoodeh asked a question about the love-struck girl, we both carried on loudly so that, up ahead, they could all hear us having a good time. Dahoodeh thought he was being charming, and everyone else was wishing that they had been chosen to hear the scintillating tale. Lily's plan worked to perfection, and it was the most fun I had had since my arrival in Japan.

When we all separated to start work, Ezra started peppering me with questions about Dahoodeh. "What did he say?" "What did he do?" "What was he laughing at?" "What was this Lily Braha talking about?" "Why did she invite Dahoodeh and no one else?"

My new friend's charade naturally didn't help reduce the number of accusations flung at me. However, it made me realize that I could have fun with them. In addition to being tortured, I had the power to torture in return.

The following week, after lunch, my mother-in-law scowled at me again. This time, I was speaking too much to our Panamanian customer. Lily Braha saw her facial expressions almost before I did and started speaking rapidly in French. Luckily, out of all the people within earshot, only we understood the French language.

"Oh... you have made her angry again!" she said facetiously but with more than a tinge of distaste. "I have a new idea—much better than before! They obviously think you are fooling around with almost all the men in Kobe. Nothing you can do will change their minds, so let's make some money out of this difficult situation. I will rent a house in town and hang a red light in front of it. I will put up a sign that says, 'Please come spend time with the prettiest foreigner in Kobe—only twenty yen per hour for anything your heart desires.' I will sell the tickets in front and give you eighty percent of the profits."

I was shocked, stunned, and just had no idea what to say. My cheeks, initially a light shade of polished ivory with disbelief, were flooded by a tsunami of scarlet embarrassment—projecting my horrific amusement to all in attendance. Luckily, I had the presence of mind to escape quickly into the kitchen before collapsing onto the floor in uncontrollable, lung-constricting laughter. After the few minutes required to compose myself, I returned to the dining room. I brought out a large plate of apples, watermelon, and coffee, not only to explain my disappearance, but also so I could hide behind them.

The guests happily devoured the dessert and acted as if my absence had not even been noticed. However, Farida's eyes appeared to burn red, like the sun, repeatedly shining their intense energy from her bridge hand to Lily and then back to me.

Lily saw that she may have put me in a difficult situation, which she had, but before leaving, she made sure the blame lay squarely on her uneven shoulders. When everyone was getting up to go to the office, she made sure Farida was listening and remarked casually in Arabic, so everyone could understand, "So, Lucy, I will look for the red light today and will tell you tomorrow if I was able to find it."

Farida and Ezra were staring right at me, so I didn't dare answer, smile, or move.

Once the guests had left the room, Ezra demanded loudly, "What is this red light she is talking about?"

I couldn't answer, but luckily, Farida readily dove into the conversation and my silence went unnoticed.

"This Lily Braha is a bad influence on your wife," Farida erupted angrily.

"Yes, I agree!" Ezra roared. "You are not to talk to her anymore!"

I answered somberly with the only word that wouldn't get me thrown out into the street: "Alright."

However, Ezra and Farida, while masters of my world, were not the masters of Lily Braha's. It soon became clear that, even though they disapproved, my friend Lily would keep visiting. The simple reason was that Ezra liked the company of Haim Braha, and Haim liked the company of his wife. Ezra was not going to risk Haim's friendship by telling him that his wife could not come to the house. The Jewish and foreign communities in Kobe were very small, and therefore, it was not easy to replace a good friend. The people who lived there were your friends and family, whether you liked all of them or not! This was a blessing for me because I was able to keep my friend, my ally, and my sanity.

Salty Situations

Lily and I saturated our leisure time discussing a myriad of interesting subjects, but one of our favorites was reviewing the bachelors' love lives. There were many single foreign men in Kobe and no single foreign girls. The vacuum of marriage possibilities, and the abundance of beautiful Japanese women, created a recipe for adventure, deception, and plenty of trouble. This left no shortage of captivating conversation topics.

Daniel, a member of the foreign Kobe community, went through a difficult situation which served as a warning to others tiptoeing around the same life possibility. Like most young men who moved to Japan from the Middle East,

Daniel had very little money and had to work excessively to reach his financial goals. His plan was to return to Lebanon once he had a profitable business that could support a family. His parents would then arrange a good match, and he would bring his bride to Japan. The problem was that this process often took over ten years. Daniel, like many others, had to work well into his thirties before he had built up enough wealth to support a wife and children. As his business slowly improved, he had less free time to do the housework and hired a pretty young Japanese girl named Hiroko to help.

Hiroko really liked Daniel and took her job very seriously. She always bought and carefully prepared the choicest foods so he could enjoy a hot, nutritious meal when arriving home. She kept the house spotless and the garden well manicured. She thoroughly washed and carefully ironed his clothing, making sure he always looked handsome. She even put hot water bottles in his bed during the cold Kobe winters. The motivated woman always looked for new ways to please her employer and friend. One particularly cold night, she not only arranged the hot water bottles in his bed but also got under the covers herself.

Daniel came home late, walked into the room, and nearly fainted with surprise when he saw Hiroko lying there. She acted quickly, getting out from under the covers fully clothed, and assured him that she was only trying to warm the bed more thoroughly. He thanked her cordially, and she retired to her room.

The next night was colder than the last. Again, she went beyond the call of duty by using her body to warm the freezing bed. The night after she did the same, and meeting no resistance, she incorporated the activity into her daily work schedule.

Now Daniel was not a cruel taskmaster without a conscience. It troubled him that this thoughtful, beautiful woman had to warm his bed and then travel in the frigid temperatures to her room. So one night, when he was ready to retire for the evening, he soothed his troubled mind by telling her to stay. Once he slid into bed beside her, they both had the advantage of added warmth and slept comfortably.

The winter became colder, and for the sake of warmth, the space between them decreased nightly. It became so cold, in fact, that by the time spring rolled around, Hiroko found herself pregnant.

They did not want to abort the baby and, before fall, Hiroko gave Daniel a son. Daniel was not an unreasonable or uncaring man. He knew it was his responsibility to care for them both. The problem was that there was no conceivable way he could marry Hiroko. His family back in Lebanon would disown him. Marrying outside of the faith was something that was just not done. Hiroko was not pleased with this, and their relationship deteriorated rapidly. She was actually in an even bigger predicament. If Daniel wouldn't marry her, she certainly wouldn't be able to marry a Japanese man. Having a son out of wedlock was a permanent black stain on her family's reputation, and having the son of a foreigner was many times worse.

They reached the only conceivable solution. Both of them continued living together, raised their son, and never married. Over time, this created a problem for Daniel. He needed to reside in Japan to run his business. However, he was technically not in compliance with the law. A foreign man and a Japanese woman could not live together unless they were married. The crime would shackle the foreigner with a very stiff prison sentence. Hiroko would subtly bring this to Daniel's attention whenever she wanted something he refused to give.

On most fronts, their disagreements were settled peacefully, following a policy of appeasement. However, when questions arose regarding the religion of their son, both sides fought bitterly. She made certain her son had a Japanese upbringing, pushing him to attend local schools and Shinto festivals and surrounding him with local children. Daniel pushed his son to experience as much of the Jewish life as he could provide. He often brought him to the synagogue and to dinners at our house during the high holidays. He also put aside some money every month so his son could eventually open a business of his own. Daniel wanted to give him a fast start in life, so he would have a fighting chance to lure a wife away from the Middle East. When his son was of marrying age, Daniel tried to take him out of Japan to meet a Jewish woman, but Hiroko objected adamantly. Daniel then wrote his relatives, asking them to send a potential match to Kobe. A mother and her daughter were interested, so Daniel provided them the funds for the boat tickets. Knowing she would resist, Daniel didn't tell Hiroko.

When the boat arrived, Daniel brought the girl and her mother to the house for lunch. Hiroko was not deceived—she knew exactly what was taking place. She graciously served them course after course in silence until they were all full and content. When everyone was relaxed, talking, and drinking tea in the living room, she joined them. Then she suddenly broke her silence for the first time since their arrival. "What boat did you come on?" she pleasantly asked their guests in a practiced English.

"The boat from Shanghai," the mother answered politely.

"Good," Hiroko answered calmly with a slight open hand indicating the direction of the port. "That boat will leave the harbor in three days. I want you and your daughter to be on it. Until then, my generous husband will hire you a room at the Oriental Hotel. Please understand that I have nothing against you. I have only one son, and he will marry someone like me—someone Japanese."

After that incident, Daniel gave up trying to find a wife for his son. Since Hiroko was not Jewish, it had already been exceedingly difficult to find him a potential Jewish bride.

With Hiroko's wishes further complicating a marriage to a Jewish girl, it was evident that his son needed to marry a Japanese. This was positive in many respects, but virtually guaranteed that Daniel's religion would be forgotten. Most of this drama had taken place before either Lily or I arrived in Japan. For our community, understanding the difficulties of their situation helped keep others from entering into difficult relationships. The manner in which these situations were "corrected" often was unconventional at best.

Many single foreign men arrived in Kobe around the time that Lily and I were enjoying the beginning of our friendship. After Ezra or Haim invited them to lunch, we often were responsible for entertaining and cooking for them. At the midday meal, all of our new guests behaved appropriately. However, some of our guests' nighttime activities were more clandestine in nature. News of their secret pursuits often filtered down to Lily and me from our friends and neighbors.

These foreign bachelors from many different religious and geographic backgrounds spent a disproportionately large number of their evening hours at the hostess bars around Kobe. They would go to meet the pretty taxi dancers and stay for the whisky.

In these smoky, softly lit clubs, there were often over twenty girls waiting for company. The men would buy a book of ten or twenty tickets from the *Mama-San*, each ticket entitling a man to a dance with the woman of his choice. The first few times they frequented a certain bar, the men would tend to dance with as many of the girls as possible, sampling the merchandise. Over time, though, each bachelor would inevitably become loyal to one woman. The usual night would begin with them both dancing to badly played international music. When both were tired from the physical exertion, or the woman had her feet injured by the clumsy steps of her dance partner, the man invited her to have a drink at his table. Whisky or sake was ordered by everyone. The men would receive the drink they ordered on ice, and the women would receive a watered down iced tea. Of course, the tea looked enough like whisky to warrant the same price being charged for each. The girls were required by their employer to act as if they were getting drunk, so the client didn't question the potency of the faux whisky he was being charged for. These bars were not meant to be brothels, but sometimes there were extracurricular activities after closing hours.

In the beginning, the connections with these women were purely physical, but as time progressed, these connections became mental and emotional as well. The men developed relatively exclusive relationships with these girls, and consequently spent more time at the club. These bachelors, although in love, were relatively good businessmen. Too good at business to have to pay a club every time they wanted a drink with their girlfriends! When the club was no longer needed as an intermediary, they would often have a sound business conversation with their partners.

"How much is the club paying you?" the man would ask.

"One hundred fifty yen a month plus an apartment to live in," the bar girl would answer.

"I have an idea," the man would say innocently. "I don't like you dancing with other men, and I don't like having to pay every time I want to see you. I will get you an apartment and give you more money than you are making now."

Most of the time the women agreed to this, either because they didn't like working nights in a club or they had real feelings for their suitors. In this way, the relationship was transformed into something resembling a "normal" situation. Some women also hoped to eventually marry their lovers/employers. If the situation was left unchecked, there was nothing to prevent this from happening.

Ezra, Haim, and their friends developed an unwritten rule to deal with these delicate situations. Without the knowledge of the ensnared individual, they would write his parents in the Middle East, Europe, or Asia. The letter would explain the predicament their son was in and plead for them to act. The mother would write an emotional letter to their son that usually went something like this:

> *My Dear Beloved Son,*
> *I am sorry to tell you that I have fallen ill and will likely die very soon. Please come home right away so that I may see you before I pass. My only desire left in life is to see you once more.*
> *All my love,*
> *Mama*

The grief-stricken man would rush home on the next boat, only to find his mother quite well.

"Thank God! I had a miraculous recovery!" she would say. "I am sorry you had to come all this way and worry for nothing. However, God has strange ways of making his plans come to fruition. Your father and I have decided to take advantage of your being here and have planned a wedding. We have already made the match. The wedding will be on Sunday."

The wedding would take place, and the bachelor would go home a husband. Before he arrived in Kobe with his foreign wife, his friends would explain the situation to the bar girl. They would give her a nice amount of money, which she could use to start her own bar business, retire, or get married herself.

Not all of the salty stories Lily and I discussed were between our unmarried friends. One of our favorite companions at the lunch table was Omar Hussein from Baghdad. Omar was short, bald, and dark-skinned and always brought light into any room he entered. His soft brown eyes were always full of humor, and his big lips hid a mouthful of large white teeth that he brandished generously with every smile. He had been sent over to India and subsequently to Japan, due to the needs of his employer. To supplement his income, he was involved in many different businesses, including exporting green tea and brokering real estate transactions. He had arrived in Japan with very little besides his wife and longtime companion. The latter was about half a meter tall with long ruby-red plumage; a six-centimeter, razor-sharp beak; and a penchant for nuts. Omar's African parrot was both enormously entertaining and intelligent. He would repeat words and phrases heard through-out the day from his perch, such as "I'm hungry," "Give me a pistachio," and "Hello." Unfortunately for some, the charming parrot did not necessarily repeat only the phrases everyone wanted remembered.

One day, when Omar came home from work, the par-rot greeted him at the door with a new line. "Thank you for the box of chocolates! Thank you for the box of chocolates! Thank you for the box of chocolates!" the parrot shrieked over and over again.

At dinner, Omar asked his wife where his parrot had learned to say such a phrase. As far as he remembered, no box of chocolates had been given to him or his wife in some time. She claimed to have no idea where he had picked it up.

The following Friday, the unusually animated parrot greeted Omar again with some new vocabulary. "Thank you for the flowers! Thank you for the flowers! Thank you for the flowers!" he cawed.

This time Omar was troubled. He knew that he had not given his wife flowers or chocolates for a while. In fact, they were not getting along at all. He thought to himself that either the bird was hearing these comments from the street, or there was another way he was picking them up. The next Friday morning, he pretended to leave for work, doubled back, and waited behind a bamboo thicket near his front door. To Omar's surprise, a uniformed white man knocked on the door. His wife opened up and let him in straightaway. After collecting his thoughts for a few minutes, Omar ran furiously into the house. The strange man was in the living room embracing his wife.

"What is going on here!?" Omar demanded. "Who is this man?"

Omar's wife slowly shrugged off the embrace, took two steps forward, and answered with determination: "He is an airplane pilot, and we are in love!"

"Then go!" Omar shouted in a gust of rage. "Get out! Both of you! NOW!"

They both ran out of the house. She knew better than to dare stop and pack her suitcase for fear of getting hurt. The pilot, flying one of the first commercial airliners with service to and from Japan, took Omar's wife on his next flight. The plane crashed, killing everyone on board, and neither one of them was ever heard from again.

Omar was shocked at his wife's duplicity but was able to move on relatively quickly because of it. He even joked about it on many occasions, saying, had it not been for his most trusted companion and friend, the parrot, he might never have discovered the infidelity taking place under his own roof.

There was a similar situation concerning another frequent house guest of ours, who proved to love his wife despite her trespasses. Everyone in town, but him, knew his wife was having an affair with a single European man. They would meet every Thursday, while our friend was working for her benefit. When the woman's actions were too blatant to ignore, a comrade took him aside and detailed the wife's indiscretions. Like Omar, he waited outside the apartment for confirmation. Seeing that the accusations were true, he walked away intensely depressed. Instead of confronting his wife or the bachelor, he acquired a pistol and bid his time until the following week. When their meeting took place as usual, our friend waited twenty minutes and then charged into the house, firmly in control of his emotions. The cheaters were caught lying in bed naked, with no possible excuse or means of escape. From the foot of the bed, the husband leveled his pistol at the European man's chest, clicking the safety catch into the off position.

"Do you love my wife?" he demanded in between their frantic pleas for mercy.

"Y—Y—Yes," the man stuttered in abject terror, unsure what answer the crazed husband would prefer.

"Then here and now, promise to marry her!" he replied with cold, rumbling passion. "If you refuse, I will empty this gun into your face!"

"I promise! I promise! I promise!" the European agreed immediately, nodding his head vigorously.

"Get out of my house!" he shouted angrily at them. "If I see that you are not married by noon tomorrow, I will kill you both!"

We were all impressed by how our friend handled his wife's infidelity. He demonstrated his undying affection by transferring his husbandly duties over to her lover.

Another situation was simply the result of a collision between a cultural misunderstanding and the best of intentions. The bathhouse in Kobe was quite different from the bathhouse in Aleppo. Here, the bathhouse did not separate the sexes by alternating the days of the week they could bathe; a thin wall and curtain were all that kept them apart. The barrier diminished further if one decided to take a swim in the pool, where only a thick rope separated the men from the women.

The men who arrived in Kobe from Arab countries, such as Syria, Iran, and Iraq, could not believe that naked women could be sighted regularly on the other side of the barrier. Bathing soon became a very popular foreign pastime. On many visits to the bathhouse, these foreigners also noticed another scintillating detail. Occasionally, they would witness a scantily clad woman bathing a naked man.

A friend of ours decided that it wasn't fair to only allow the women to indulge the men. So, to remedy the situation, he offered his bathing services to the most beautiful females. He and his associates were promptly removed from the bathhouse and prohibited from returning. It was only later that they understood why their advances weren't as readily accepted. A Japanese neighbor of ours informed them that the women were only performing the invaluable service for their husbands or children.

Labor Pains

"Aaaaaagh!" I gasped as a sharp pain started rolling over my body late one afternoon. "This must be it," I thought. "My baby is coming." As calmly as possible, I waddled around the house like an overfed duck, gathering everything I had prepared to take to the hospital. First in the small suitcase were the diapers I had sewn out of old sample fabrics. Next, I packed the left-over food from lunch in the dishes sitting out on the counter. Last, I organized a few pairs of underwear to go under my extra large kimono, the only piece of clothing that still fit.

My heart was pumping nervous energy and excitement through my elephant-like body. For the last few weeks it had been difficult just to move, so I was ready to give birth and resume my normal life. In my super-pregnant state, I couldn't go to work in the afternoons, and staying in the house was making me crazy. My one respite from home life had been the day I visited Dr. Sakamoto.

Dr. Sakamoto had a general practice twenty minutes from the house. His office was a two-story building that was furnished with *futon* downstairs for the Japanese and a few beds upstairs for the *gaijin* (foreigners). The sixty-year-old doctor's experience showed in the deep wrinkles under his eyes, his traditional outlook from the blue kimono he wore, paired with short, silvery black hair. He had a quiet strength and kindness and acted more like my friend than my doctor, always looking out for my best interest but never losing his tone of professionalism. I wouldn't dare question the words that formed easily through his tea stained teeth or the symptoms observed through the rounded silver glasses perched on his perfect nose. After he had pressed the cold stethoscope on various parts of my lower torso, he had happily proclaimed that the baby had a healthy heartbeat. Quickly, though, I had pushed him for the information that everyone wanted to hear.

"Is it a boy or a girl?" I asked eagerly with a worried smile.

"Choueke-San, there is no way for me to tell," he answered scientifically.

"But with your experience, what do you think the sex is?" I pleaded, honestly afraid of the answer.

Seeing he wasn't going to get out of the room without giving me an opinion, he replied wisely, "What are you hoping for?"

"A boy, of course!" I exclaimed, exhaling loudly for emphasis.

"Then it shall be a boy," he said confidently. "From the size of your stomach, that is what I expect. Just take care of yourself until the day comes. That is the main thing."

My entire odd-shaped body had floated through the next weeks, knowing that I was going to have a boy. Ezra was even more excited and embarked on preparations of his own. He opened a bank account in New York City through a customer of his in the United States. He deposited money into it monthly so his son could start a business when he was old enough. He hadn't opened the account in a Japanese bank because he thought it unwise to have all his wealth in one currency or in one country.

When the day we had been waiting for finally arrived, I was ready. Taking my suitcase downstairs, I found my mother-in-law asleep and woke her so we could go to the hospital. Ezra was still at work, so he would have to meet us there.

"I'm ready to go," I announced proudly and nervously at the same time.

"Go where?" she answered back with the menacing glare of a person interrupted from a good dream.

"To the hospital, to Dr. Sakamoto's," I said defensively.

"Why? You are not ready to have the baby! It is much, much too early," she answered, annoyed, like a professor being pestered by a student.

"Dr. Sakamoto told me to come see him when I feel pain every few minutes," I pleaded.

"You have no experience in this!" she replied condescendingly and sat up. "You are not ready, and you are not going to the doctor!" she insisted.

I waddled away and sat down in the living room, waiting to see if the pains would subside or continue. I drew the curtains, sat in near darkness, and closed my eyes to truly analyze my sensations, making sure they were real. Every few minutes, a spasmodic fist clenched tightly on my lower abdomen, sending chills outwardly to every one of my extremities. After I had sat there for over an hour, it became clear that the pain was not subsiding but was intensifying alarmingly in severity and frequency. When I broke out into a cold sweat, I had waited enough. I got up noisily, took my suitcase, and walked slowly to the door. Farida came up stealthily behind me.

"Where are you going?" she demanded angrily.

"I am going to the doctor whether you like it or not! You do not have to come!" I answered, looking in the other direction.

Luckily before the most pitiful fight in history broke out between a pregnant woman and her old mother-in-law, Ezra opened the door. He saw me holding the suitcase and purse and asked in surprise, "Where are you going?"

"To the doctor!" I countered aggressively, thoroughly wound up.

"It is too early! She is not ready to go! It's a false alarm!" Farida chimed in, trying to match my aggression.

Another pain quaked through my abdomen. I screamed involuntarily and had to brace myself against the wall to keep from falling. "I am going to the doctor now!" I tried to speak forcefully, but the words slithered out of my clenched teeth at barely above a whisper.

"Good!" Ezra replied, taking my side, my suitcase, and my purse. "I will go with you!"

Farida acquiesced but didn't concede defeat. "Well... if you are going, Ezra, I will not stay in the house alone. I am going too!"

Once we entered the taxi, Farida and Ezra wisely kept quiet, as I was not in the mood to be diplomatic. Every time the waves of pain crashed over me, a shriek like that of a delicate crystal chandelier shattering on a marble floor abruptly interrupted the silence. We didn't have to say anything to the driver, who sped as if possessed by the devil, trying to avoid blood and afterbirth in his new car.

The spasms had become a rising tide of torture by the time we reached the hospital. I needed to balance on, and clutch, Ezra's shoulder on our way through the door to prevent from drowning in it. Glacial disinterest trickled from the receptionist as she reported over and over that the doctor couldn't be disturbed during his dinner. Ezra gently left me in a wooden chair as he argued raucously, unable to pierce her icy exterior. As the tide rose higher and higher, I used the last of my remaining energy to slump to the floor. A nurse appeared from within in response to the commotion. She quickly disappeared and then returned with a *futon* to slide under me.

I was lying on a thin mattress in the cold reception area of the doctor's office for an indeterminable amount of time. My constant moans were replaced periodically by screams when a spasm shook me. A sticky, warm fluid coated the inside of my legs as I waited for my baby's birth or my death. Not really partial to one outcome or the other, I only wanted the blunt pain to stop. Fortunately, before Ezra struck the receptionist, everyone in the waiting room joined him at her desk, demanding she get the doctor from his home. In fear of physical harm, she disappeared.

She returned with Dr. Sakamoto after some passage of time. I could not say if it was five minutes or two hours. I remember only the blood draining from his face as he gave me a cursory examination. He sternly barked orders to his staff, and I was immediately carried upstairs to a bed. The Japanese, at that time, did not give any drugs to women in childbirth because they believed it affected the health of the child. Consequently, for the next ten minutes, the pounding agony of every move of the baby, every involuntary action of my body, and the stretching of my flesh struck like a splintering mallet on each of my nerve endings.

Dr. Sakamoto kept repeating loudly, "Don't push! Don't push!" but I needed to bring an end to the pain. Ezra was so distressed, he ran out of the room and collapsed in a chair just outside. Farida, who had a ringside seat to the event, gave a blow-by-blow account to her son. I was not focused on any of the three, until I heard words that stung more than anything else.

"Don't get excited, Ezra—it's only a girl!" my mother-in-law shouted in disappointment over the bedlam.

The baby had not even separated from my body when I received the jury's verdict.

Dr. Sakamoto, oblivious to the Arabic background commentary, skillfully maneuvered the baby out, quickly cut the umbilical cord, and cleared the baby's airways. In seconds, the child was breathing, and the doctor was smiling triumphantly, wiping the nervous sweat from his brow.

"Congratulations!" he beamed. "It's a healthy girl!"

He handed the baby off to a nurse, who quickly exited the room with her. Dr. Sakamoto instructed a second nurse, stationed on the other side of the bed, to help me change clothes. The doctor congratulated all of us in turn and quickly departed. Ezra, happy to be useful, went downstairs to get the suitcase, which had remained in the waiting room.

When the nurse opened it, the tension in the room erupted.

"Look!" Farida shouted to her son. "Lucie brought all of our good dishes to the hospital!"

I just closed my eyes, too exhausted to answer.

After witnessing the carnage of his first childbirth, Ezra did not have the patience for another argument. "What does it matter what dishes she brings to the hospital!?" he roared.

Farida lowered her voice but persisted. "They will be stolen by the help here. We don't know the people who are coming in and out of these rooms."

Ezra did not calm down. "Let her bring all the dishes with her to the hospital! I don't care! Let them steal them all! What's the difference?"

They both paused, peering despondently at one another, until Farida carefully massaged the silence. "We have all had a long day. It is past eleven o'clock. Let's go home, and we will come back tomorrow."

I kept my eyes closed in a daze of disappointment, pain, and anger. I was angry at my mother-in-law, angry at Ezra, and disappointed in myself for having a girl. Shutting my eyelids, I let my aching body and tormented soul float freely, unrestrained, in the empty darkness. The only interruption was a warm kiss on the head and a soft caress of my hand before Ezra led his mother home. His touches were a motor that propelled me deeper into a sleepy abyss, as the nurse manipulated my unresponsive body while changing the last of my clothes.

Three Masters

Tradition, beautiful tradition... Tradition gives us the comfort of knowing where we come from, brings us together in times of celebration, determines the subjects we devote our time to learning, and most conveniently, automatically makes many of our life decisions for us. One of these time-tested, time-honored Sephardic Jewish traditions is to name your first son after your husband's father. An interpretation of that tradition is often extended to the first-born girl, who is named after your husband's mother. I guess one can say that tradition isn't always kind.

I cringed at the idea of naming my daughter *Farida*! Besides our long-running feud, she had caused me a lot of unnecessary pain by delaying my trip to the doctor and rarely came to visit while I was recovering in the hospital—an oversight I wasn't too disappointed with.

Following the pregnancy, Dr. Sakamoto would not release me for three days, until assured I had recovered completely. When he saw the diapers I had sewn for the baby, he immediately threw them in the garbage. He claimed they would give the baby a bad skin rash. There were a few stillbirths in Dr. Sakamoto's office every month, so he gave me some extra supplies, like Japanese cloth diapers, left by the parents that had abandoned them in their grief. The nurses saw that I had absolutely no idea what I was doing and taught me how to care for the baby. Due to the kindness of Dr. Sakamoto and his staff, I emerged from the hospital knowing more or less how to take care of her. It was a good thing too, because initially no one was too eager to help look after a girl.

Luckily, my daughter was beautiful. Her glowing creamy skin, raven-black hair, chubby cheeks, and strong constitution ensured that she would not be ignored by the family. Farida, Ezra, and Sakura, after their initial disappointment, quickly warmed to her. Farida cooked; Ezra bought me a typewriter, enabling me to work from home; and Sakura watched the baby in the afternoons, allowing me to get some extra sleep. While everyone seemed happy, it escaped no one's attention that the baby was three weeks old and had not yet been named.

My anger at Ezra's and Farida's hospital behavior had not gone unnoticed, so no one broached the subject at first. But after three weeks, the wait became too much. Farida pushed me to make a decision as only she could.

"Have you named the baby yet?" she asked nonchalantly when we were in the kitchen preparing lunch.

"Not yet," I replied curtly, focusing on some onions I was chopping.

Her mood spontaneously turned, going from calm to livid in less than one point two seconds. "What!?" she shouted angrily. "My name is not good enough for you??? The queen of Egypt's name is Frieda!!! It's good enough for her, and good enough for me!!! Why is it not good enough for you???"

A vermillion hue invaded my cheeks, and my mind wandered for a moment. Even though I felt like answering back, I knew that would only aggravate the problem, so I remained silent. The truth was that I wanted to give my daughter a French name like Cecile, Nancy, or Fifi. When I had introduced the subject one week before, my mother-in-law had replied condescendingly, "Fifi is a great name for a cat but not my granddaughter."

Farida pushed again, bringing my concentration back to the current argument. "You are making a big fuss over this girl, who you think is too good for my name!!! You didn't even have a boy, and you are acting like it's the most important event of the century!!!"

Again I stayed silent but shifted my concentration to the cucumbers.

"It has been three weeks already!" she continued yelling. "You must decide on a name for the child, and that name should be mine!" When she finally realized that I wasn't going to argue, she stormed out of the room.

That night I cried alone in the bathroom so neither Ezra nor his mother could hear me. Ezra did not give an opinion on the subject, but by saying nothing, he actually said everything. I did not have a choice.

The next morning, I announced that I wanted to name the baby Frieda. It was the same name as my mother-in-law's, I explained, but with a more modern spelling. Farida was thrilled, and Ezra was relieved that a disaster had been averted.

What I thought would make things easier only made them more difficult. From that day on, nothing I did for my daughter was good enough. My mother-in-law always had plenty to say: "Be careful with her! She is my name!" "You are not feeding her enough! She is my name!" "Don't let her cry! She is my name!"

My daughter initially was considered an inconvenience. When I named her Frieda, it was as if I were the inconvenience. Before the birth, I served two masters; now I served three.

Rationing

Before I could adjust to the many responsibilities related to raising a child, going to the office, and taking care of our home, help unexpectedly arrived from abroad. My brother David, in search of new opportunities in business, decided to join us in Kobe. He first helped Ezra with his correspondence and then started a business of his own.

I was thrilled to have an ally but knew it couldn't last. My mother-in-law was very aware that David's business involved exporting cotton. She correctly understood that there was the potential for competition between my husband and my brother. However, she was very gracious to let David live with us until he could support himself.

After David was earning enough to send Mama some money every month, he moved out. I missed living with him but knew my mother-in-law's opinion on the subject: "One Esses in the house is more than enough!"

After David's departure from the house, constructing my schedule so that all the needs of the family and office were met was difficult. Fortunately, with Farida's help cooking and Sakura's help with the baby, I was able to manage. Unfortunately, just when I had figured everything out, one part of my day became much more difficult.

When I had arrived in Japan, the most difficult part of shopping had been making the money to buy the food. The subsequent trip to four or five small markets was not an ordeal for an Aleppo girl. If you had the money, the shopkeepers were happy to take it. I made many working friendships with the food vendors and was able to buy everything at a good price. If I ever had time late in the afternoon, I returned to the market and bought the food for the next day at a substantial discount because the vendors' had limited refrigeration.

Like little Frieda depended on me for sustenance, we depended on the prosperity of Japan to provide us with our daily necessities. However, on the political front, the country was in a precarious situation. Japan's incursions into China resulted in European and American outrage over the military expansion. The West's hypocrisy created anger in Japan. The one-sided criticism denouncing Japan's efforts to expand into China seemed to ignore the fact that the West already maintained interests in Hong Kong, Singapore, India, the Philippines, Guam, the East Indies, Wake Island, and other territories. Internationally, the country was also ailing from deteriorating world diplomacy. Japan faced the possibility of the Soviet Union, the Netherlands, Great Britain, China, and the United States all joining up against her.[6] The threat was only magnified further when Russia signed a treaty with Germany on August 23, 1939, and World War Two began with the invasion of Poland on September first. Japan had been losing many soldiers in battles with the Soviet Union over territory along the Manchurian/Russian border.[7] The Soviet surprise alliance with Germany, which had long been sought as Japan's own ally,[8] created additional concerns over the strengths of their adversaries.

---

6 Toland, p. 59.

7 Toland, p. 59.

8 Toland, p. 59.

A few results of this political situation for Japan were more resources being diverted to the armed forces, more men being shipped out to fight the wars in China, and less of everything for the people at home. The main result of this political situation for us was that procuring what we needed to live became more difficult. The government began a rationing program and we had to queue to collect our ration books outside the French consulate. We were very lucky that a friend of ours in the French consulate made sure we were registered to receive them. Being Jews that had left Syria, we were not Syrian citizens, Japanese citizens, nor French citizens. If no one had taken responsibility for us, we would not have received any ration coupons at all, and possibly starved. We received a book for meat, a book for rice, and a book for bread. They also gave us three meters of fabric every year that we would use to make clothing. We participated, whenever possible, in the consulate's bake sales and fundraising events. The proceeds were sent overseas to aid in France's military defense.

I waited in line at the French consulate for hours to get the staples of our meals. I had to show them the pictures of my family members to prove that we required food for four people (Sakura collected her rations together with the Japanese citizens). The ration coupon did not entitle you to free food—it only gave you the right to buy it. Although the price was double that of the market, we were happy to pay because of the short supply.

The Funeral

The ration lowered our food supply but did not subtract from the responsibilities at hand. The fact remained that I was still a wife with only one girl to her credit. Therefore, the threat of competition in the house was still present. I got pregnant again quickly, so I could have the boy everyone wanted. While I had a baby of undetermined sex in my womb, it was harder to criticize me for having only girls. It would be bad luck to imply that my expected baby was anything but a strong male. In that way, I bought myself nine months of relative peace on that front.

On the China warfront, Japan was by all accounts gaining territory with very few casualties. The radio, as well as the populace, praised the gallant soldiers fighting to provide for Japan. The media explained that the spoils of war and a steady stream of resources were being sent back to better our lives.

I could soon see that the war was not as rosy as the picture that had been painted. One Thursday evening, a military van pulled up to our neighbor's house and presented them with a medium-sized wooden box, tied neatly with a ribbon. Mrs. Tanaka ran inside from the garden, trying to choke back her tears, as Mr. Tanaka solemnly accepted the remains of his eldest son. He did not show any emotion as he bowed somberly to the officers who had arrived with the bad news. The following day, he led his family slowly through Motomachi, Kobe's shopping district, with a cream-colored canvas bag draped around his neck containing his son's ashes. Mrs. Tanaka, her two remaining sons, her two daughters, and a few family friends followed closely behind, regularly ringing bells to scare away the evil spirits. Most of the procession wore black cotton funeral kimonos bordered with grey trim. Everyone they passed looked at the ground or bowed in deference to the deceased. Upon reaching the shore, they climbed into a row boat, traveled one kilometer off the coast, and spread his ashes onto the waves of the sea.

After the ceremony, Mr. Tanaka put Daitaro's box on their mantelpiece. On one side, they placed a photo of Daitaro as a little boy, and on the other side, they placed a picture of him in full Army uniform. On top of the box, they placed a sake cup with elegant calligraphy—a gift from the Emperor to the family for providing their eldest son to the nation. The Tanakas did not mourn their son like we would have. They were rather fiercely proud to have given a child of theirs for the good of the country. Every day Daitaro's siblings placed small tokens of food in front of his picture and prayed for him to watch over them. He was a role model to everyone in the family.

Two weeks after Daitaro's death, the now-familiar military van rolled up again to the neighbor's house. This time it was Hideo, Tanaka-San's twenty-one-year-old son, who was to join his countrymen in battle. Like his brother, Hideo honorably and enthusiastically accepted his obligation to the nation. As before, they all drank sake late into the night. When it was time to report for duty, he gave a military salute to his parents, who bowed in return.

Rei, the Tanakas' eighteen-year-old daughter, came to the nation's aid only a few days afterwards. She joined the war preparation effort at a factory near the port, sewing canvas shirts for soldiers' uniforms. Rei worked over twelve hours a day, every day of the week. Instead of becoming downcast from the exhausting schedule, she seemed very happy to be contributing to the country's well-being.

The Camera

The foreign community was not asked to serve in the battles or help prepare for them. In fact, it was quite the opposite. The government did not trust us to be involved at all. A team of policeman, headed by Osakabe-San, was assigned to make sure we weren't involved in anything subversive. Osakabe-San was a muscular, compact man who easily filled out a newly pressed green uniform adorned with various stripes and medals denoting his high rank. He had precisely cut short black hair, light skin, thin lips, a strong chin, and large, solemn eyes that seemed to peer knowingly into all people and all things. He took his job very seriously, knocking on the front door at all hours of the day to check on what we were doing. Sometimes, he would even enter the house without knocking, hoping to catch us by surprise. Invariably, he would walk in on me doing correspondence and taking care of Frieda or interrupt my mother-in-law in the middle of preparing one of her famous delectable dishes. I believe it was soon evident that we were not spies, but he kept coming over anyway. We soon found out that in addition to coming and checking on the foreign community, he was enlisting our housekeepers to spy for him. When the *gaijin* (foreigners) left the room, the housekeepers in foreign houses would relate the goings on of the residences in detail to him. The only way our community had to alter our behavior in response to this was to stop wagering on card games. Betting on cards was against the law and could land us a prison sentence. The help in our houses could not speak Arabic, so we could say whatever we wanted.

I made only one small mistake concerning Osakabe-San. Since he was always friendly and polite, I naturally trusted him, despite the risks. Half a year before, I had received a beautiful camera from my brother Moise, who was still residing in Palestine. The camera, my prized possession, had all the modern options, including a tripod and flash. The film was expensive, but I still used it often to take photos of our family and friends. Osakabe-San made one of his unannounced visits while I was taking a picture of my daughter. Greeting him with a smile, I showed him the camera, and his face lit up. Thinking he was also interested in photography, I proceeded to show him how the lens worked, took a picture of myself using the timer, and demonstrated how to use the flash. He departed quickly after my demonstration, and I took Frieda for a walk around town in her baby stroller. As usual, the camera was hidden in my clothing drawer upstairs, and the bulky tripod was left in the closet. When I returned home from the walk, I saw my room had been ransacked and my camera was gone. I was shocked and upset. I went directly to see Osakabe-San at the police station and told him that my camera had been stolen.

He came over with a deputy and took a full report. "Do you have anything we can use to identify the camera once we find it?" Osakabe-San questioned, while his deputy wrote furiously.

"They didn't take the tripod or flash," I answered naively. "Maybe you can use those to check against any stolen cameras you find?"

"That is a very good idea," Osakabe-San readily agreed. "Give them to me at once. It will be much easier to identify your camera if we have them."

After I gave them the remaining accessories, they thanked me for my time and left. I never saw the camera again.

When I discussed the matter over with Ezra, we reached the conclusion that the police took the camera. But we realized it wasn't for their own personal benefit. We later found out that there was a policy in effect to confiscate anything that spies could use to communicate knowledge of Japan to the outside world. Cameras were prime targets of this policy, and soon most foreigners we knew had theirs "disappear" as well.

A Step Closer to War

As my body swelled, promising the arrival of my second child, so did the hearts of military men throughout Japan. Constant military propaganda regarding the China conflict, among other factors, cultivated an already intense nationalism within our borders. The unyielding political stance of the West created a situation like putting on a tight school dress over my pregnant body: either the compressing fabric would rip, or the country's future ambitions would be aborted. As I read years later, Army and Navy leaders, supported by their troops and a large segment of the population, fiercely resented the interference of Western powers with Japan's occupation of Asian lands. Not only would the Westerners refuse to recognize any territorial acquisitions, but also the United States continuously supplied China's Chang Kai-Shek with weapons and monetary aid.[9]

From 1940 to 1941, the war in Europe, the circumstances in Asia, and a deteriorating relationship with the U.S.A. prompted Japan to embark upon certain military strategies. Germany impressed the Japanese armed forces with its efficient victories over the Dutch and French and with its continuing success against the British in May and June of 1940.[10] On September 27, 1940, Germany, Italy, and Japan signed the Tripartite Pact.[11] The agreement gave Japan powerful allies to help discourage the U.S. from declaring war against her[12] and quickly set the stage for a Japan-Soviet neutrality pact. The Japanese military also understood that it had a window of opportunity to extricate the European colonies in Southeast Asia from Western control[13] while Germany and Italy devastated Europe. Controlling these resource-rich colonies would give Japan the ability to reduce its economic dependence on the Western powers[14] and obtain what it needed to continue operations in China.[15] This step would also be necessary to establish "The Greater East Asia Co-Prosperity Sphere"—a

9 Feis, Herbert. *The Road to Pearl Harbor*. Princeton, NJ: Princeton University Press, 1971, p. 140.

10 Toland, p. 60.

11 Feis, p. 110.

12 Toland, p. 63.

13 Toland, p. 60.

14 Ike, Nobutaka. *Japan's Decision for War: Records of the 1941 Policy Conferences*. Stanford, California: Stanford University Press, 1967, p. xix.

15 Ienaga, Saburo. The Pacific War, 1931 - 1945: A Critical Perspective on Japan's Role in World War 2. New York, NY: Pantheon Books, 1978, p. 131.

desired empire "extending from Manchuria in the North to the Dutch East Indies in the South."[16]

Japan began expanding its influence to the south by completing the occupation of French Indochina (later, North Vietnam) on July 24, 1941, using diplomatic pressure instead of military means. Territory in French-ruled Indochina would supply Japan with badly needed resources, provide strategic areas to station military forces, and cut off the supply route used to shuttle western arms into China.[17]

Approximately two days following the occupation, the United States, England, and Holland retaliated by freezing all Japanese assets in their respective countries.[18] This was the latest in a series of embargoes that left Japan in a very difficult situation. The majority of the country's oil was imported from regions controlled by these governments, and now trade with them ceased. Much less important to these nations, but important to us, was the inability to trade tablecloths, beach sandals, towels, and textiles.

Working Against the International Clock

While I was dealing with my pregnancy, Ezra was struggling with the business. The problems that had plagued us during the beginning stages of our endeavors had been replaced by more serious issues. Finding customers was no longer the priority—now we had to find ways to ship the goods. We were well aware that Japan's international friendships were growing weak and, with them, the hopes of maintaining our livelihood. In response, Ezra spent much more time in the

---

16 Ike, p. xix.

17 Ienaga, p. 130.

18 Ienaga, p. 132.

factories. He pushed them to finish our customers' goods, while our accountant spent the majority of his time securing the ships needed for their transport. We had just finished a large shipment for Hanan, in New York, when Mr. Dahab began pushing for his merchandise.

Joe Dahab had given us one of our largest orders to date, consisting of Christmas merchandise for the United States market. After reading about what was transpiring between the U.S. and Japan in the newspaper, he sent Ezra a telegram:

Ezra Urgent U ship goods immediately or order cancelled. Dahab

We were in a difficult situation. The cash deposit had been sent to our suppliers over one month ago, and if we didn't ship the order, we would forfeit large amounts of money. Ezra left right away.

When the security guard opened the massive wooden gate and the taxi drove up the long unpaved road leading to Ishii-San's factory, it was obvious there was a problem. On Ezra's previous visits, the workers had spilled out of the workshops, darting one way or the other, in the organized chaos of the workday. Today there was hardly anyone outside, except for two men pushing large carts overflowing with grey cotton fabric. A receptionist met him at the door and led him through the half-empty building. Many of the machines that had clicked and clacked noisily throughout the day remained silent. Ishii-San was sitting at his old wooden desk, accompanied only by an ashtray littered with smoldering cigarette butts. He saw Ezra at the door, jumped up in surprise, and went to greet him with a preoccupied grin on his face. The good humor painted on his shaky façade quickly evaporated when he was told the shipment would have to be advanced.

"I can't do it, *taisho!*" he exclaimed, almost losing his temper in frustration. "You can see how many people I've lost. Many have left to the fabric companies producing for the

Army. In fact, I am going to have to delay your order. There is no way to advance it!"

"Ishii-San," Ezra replied thoughtfully, "you have always been a man of honor with me. When you made a promise to finish the order in three weeks time, I trusted you. Because of my confidence in you, I made a promise to my customer that the order would be completed. Now we both have our reputations on the line. No delay will be accepted. My customer advised that he will cancel the order if we do not ship in one week and a half."

"One week and a half? That is impossible! Look in the factory! I have very few people! Most of the people I do have are working on other orders."

"Well, then put them on my order!" Ezra argued, his face reddening.

"I can't put my entire factory on your orders," Ishii-San reasoned, maintaining composure. "You negotiate so much, I make very little money from you. If I only do your orders, I will go out of business. The only reason I accept them at such low prices is to fill up my production. But now I have hardly any workers and too many orders."

Ezra smiled and calmed down. "Let's have some tea," he proposed. An office girl brought green tea in ceramic cups, and they drank in nervous silence for a few minutes.

Ezra spoke in a warm conceding tone, verbally dispelling the tension in the room. "Alright, Ishii-San, it is obvious you are having a difficult time. If I can get my customer to increase the price fifteen percent, can you advance the shipment? I am trying to help you with some increase, but please don't make it impossible for both of us to take an honorable path."

"Twenty-five percent is the best I can do, or you can wait one month like everyone else!" Ishii-San replied, simultaneously annoyed and unbendingly confident.

"Agreed," Ezra replied without a pause. "I will bring the payment personally in ten days and will inspect at the same time. However, when I arrive, we will need to cancel all unfinished production." They both got up, bowed to each other, and Ezra made a quick exit before Ishii-San could change his mind.

Ezra continued on his route, having the same difficult discussion with each supplier. Half of the businesses were still operating at full force, but half were handicapped by the loss of employees to the war effort. The following week he returned to check their progress, pushing the factories that needed to be pushed and motivating those that needed to be motivated. If luck held, the shipment to Dahab would be sent early as requested.

Relations between the United States, England, France, and Japan were deteriorating rapidly. Our customers realized this and, fearing the worst, were pushing us to advance the remainder of their shipments. We were not too optimistic with respect to the political situation, but we could do nothing besides try to comply with their requests. If we stopped shipping and no war came, we would lose the loyalty from our business partners. Everyone understood that if war commenced, all would have to endure hardships—irrespective of our country of residence.

These financial hardships officially began for us on July 26, 1941. We had packed and paid for Dahab's goods, and booked the shipping vessel for their transport, when trade between Japan and the Western world screeched to a halt. In response to the Japanese occupation of French Indochina, the United States, Britain, and the Netherlands froze all Japanese assets in their respective countries. There was nothing we could do. We had just paid out a large amount of our savings for Dahab's merchandise, but trade between our countries had ceased. To make matters worse, the goods had already entered the port area and passed customs inspection. This meant we could not take the merchandise back and resell it somewhere else. The goods had to stay in port until the next shipping vessel to the United States arrived. The wait could be one week, one year, or the rest of our lives.

Ezra and I were crushed but didn't have time to pout. We went straight to the factories and cancelled every follow-up order we had placed. Nakamura-San, Ishii-San, and the rest of our suppliers were furious. They had just completed a nearly impossible job for us and were rewarded by the suspension of business. It was no comfort to them that our livelihood was ruined as well. Two days later, once all the orders were cancelled, we told our employees to go home until further notice. It was impossible to pay salaries with no money coming in. The first wave of anger from the factories was followed by a second wave of anger from our employees. It was obvious that we didn't have a choice. However, that was little consolation for people who had to feed their families while the prices of necessities were increasing drastically.

Every foreigner had to make the crucial decision to leave the country or remain, hoping to improve his life with respect to the international situation. Many who had been in Japan for only one or two years departed. However, there were not many places where one could travel at that time. I was depressed when my brother David left for Shanghai but understood that he could no longer make a living in Kobe. Other acquaintances of ours went to the Philippines. Ezra and I couldn't leave. We liked working with the Japanese, we enjoyed living in Kobe, and we had invested a large amount of time and effort to establish ourselves in the country.

Nonetheless, consciously making that decision did not make our lives easier. Ezra, like many others, had lost the ability to run his business. In addition, he knew that the large amount of money sitting in our United States savings account was inaccessible and possibly lost. Instead of going to work, he stayed home, depressed. Working on long-term projects was pointless if there was no certainty of selling what one produced. Even if Ezra were lucky enough to make money, there were few secure places to put it. He morosely went through the passing weeks with no direction, no focus, and no hope. Only fear of an inevitable black future pervaded every air particle in the house. The darkness was closing in.

Cutting Back, Adding On

The loss of the business made my job all the more crucial. Ezra had cash hidden in our bedroom for uncertain times. Now that uncertain times had arrived, the money had to go much farther. It was no longer permissible to spend five yen buying necessities when four would be sufficient. We didn't know how long we would be without income, and the cash we had hidden upstairs had to last. In addition, we had funds in Japanese banks but were permitted to withdraw only a small, fixed amount per week. Everything I bought for the house needed to be at the best price possible. Every morning, I left the house early in order to spend more time at the markets in our search for food. We replaced some expensive vegetables by buying more rice and eggplant. We bought less. We ate less. Despite the economic difficulties, we didn't stop inviting people to the house. The bachelors had lost their businesses as well, and as a result, the card games got longer. However, the laughter that had formerly accompanied the games was replaced by haunting fears of worse to come. In the afternoons especially, many arguments erupted from the stress and anger accompanying the fortunes lost.

I retired to my room early one day, partly to avoid the emotional outbursts and partly to be near the toilet my body forced me to frequent every five minutes. While I lay on the bed in between visits, familiar cramps began their spasmodic dance triumphantly over my pelvis. I kept still as the tightness slowly radiated to my mid-stomach and lower back, like a storm slowly forming at sea. The waves of tension ebbed and flowed over my abdomen for a few hours before I arose to go to the hospital. I didn't mind going a little early this time. If waiting in the doctor's office for a few hours would spare me the unabated torture of my first try, it was alright with me. When I announced to Farida and Ezra that it was time to go to the hospital, there was no argument, no complaint, and not even a backwards glance. They abandoned their card games immediately, and we all filed out of the house into a taxi.

I was worried about maintaining a cool and confident exterior, but inside I was shaking like a tree in a typhoon. After nine months of speculation, all would be revealed within a few hours. Would I be redeemed with a boy, or would I burden the family with another girl? The birth of a boy would be a tremendous source of hope to the family among the great uncertainty that permeated our lives. A girl would mean another mouth to feed, another dowry to pay, and the possibility of another wife in the house. Dr. Sakamoto's assurances that my desire for a boy would be fulfilled were important, but he had said the same before Frieda's birth which left me with some lingering doubts.

My previous traumatic experience finally benefited me in one way. The long period I had stayed in the hospital had given me the opportunity to make friendships with many of the nurses. This time, I didn't have to wait for a bed, and they made me as comfortable as possible. Dr. Sakamoto was very kind, as usual, and the birth proceeded with relative ease. It was only in the last few moments that I was no longer in command of my faculties. My muscles convulsed every few seconds as if I were repeatedly being shoved from a spot in front of our toasty warm fireplace into the chilly cold waters of Shioya beach. I didn't get nervous though since Dr. Sakamoto and Farida, who waited at the side of the bed, both looked very calm. It was only at the end, as I pushed through a burning, numbing cloud of pain, that everyone panicked.

My eyes were closed, every fiber of my being fighting to

expel the life from my womb at any cost, when I heard those frightening words.

"Don't worry!" Farida yelled before the baby had fully left me. "It's only another girl!"

Even though the pain still burned within, I managed to force open my eyelids. My mother-in-law's red face demonstrated that her words had been the truth and not a cruel joke.

Dr. Sakamoto quickly and successfully cleared the baby's airways. He glanced at me for a quarter of a second, a pink hue of embarrassment invading his cheeks, and dejectedly pronounced with scientific precision: "It's a healthy girl."

He immediately vacated the room after delegating instructions to the nurses, above the chaos of Farida's complaining, my crying, and the soft, delicate first breaths of my newborn child.

Visiting Hours

The raw physical act of giving birth the second time was much easier than the first. We arrived on time at the hospital, the doctor was ready, and there were no complications endangering my life or the baby's. It was the emotional aspect of having my second girl that was much more difficult.

My husband and mother-in-law left right at the conclusion of the main event, as I drifted off into a troubled sleep. The next morning, I waited for them to bring some food, but when they didn't appear, my hunger succumbed to a breakfast of *mochi*, *nori*, and pickles. The afternoon was similar, except that the lunch was steamed rice with boiled fish. For dinner, when no one came to visit, I couldn't eat. Nothing could fill the void in my spirit. Solitary, depressing thoughts fluttered around in my mind's expanse, like fireflies on a moonless night: Was it really such a bad thing I had done? Did I deserve to be ignored and left at the hospital? What would we do with another girl? I was born a girl but was able to contribute to my family. Why couldn't my new daughter contribute as well? Did any of these questions have rational, logical answers?

The bitterness at my family and my luck grew like a snowball hurtling down Kobe's steep mountains. It was only after a visit from Dr. Sakamoto and a long conversation with one of the nurses that I was calm enough to fall asleep. The following morning, when no one appeared, I knew I had been left there.

I felt abandoned, forgotten, and taken for granted. But the fact remained that the hospital charged by the day for the occupancy of my room. I knew we needed to save the money we had, so I dressed, got the baby, and prepared to leave. Luckily, I had brought some cash for the bill, which I turned over to Dr. Sakamoto. It was obviously not enough. The doctor only smiled and said softly, "Pay me the rest when you can. There is no rush."

He then returned several sen so I could take a taxi back home. I think he felt sorry for me. While I didn't want his pity, I appreciated his warmth and understanding. It partially melted the icy bitterness that had been packed around my soul.

Home life was rough for the next few days. Ezra and Farida didn't go out of their way to make amends, and I didn't offer any apologies for producing the wrong sex. We focused on the jobs at hand and spoke as little as possible. I brazenly named my daughter Simone after my father, Simantov, and my mother, Stella, without consulting anyone. I became only more livid when they didn't offer any objection. They didn't seem to care one way or the other. Ironically, with my first child I resented their intervention in the baby naming, and now I resented their disinterest.

Farida and I eventually fostered a tenuous truce. We owned only one crib, which was purchased with gifts from the bachelors after the birth of Frieda. When I brought Simone home, my mother-in-law took my elder daughter to her bed, and left the crib for the newborn. It was probably more to begin educating her namesake than to help me, but either way I appreciated her sensitivity.

She even took a step closer to reconciliation one week after Simone's arrival, when she finally took a good look at her. She held the baby, inspected her like a watermelon, and with tempered excitement, the corners of her mouth moved slightly upwards to form a small grin. She said, "Well... she *is* a girl... but never mind that... she is a beautiful girl!"

"Yes, she is," I agreed happily and left them alone to get to know each other.

My reconciliation with Ezra did not come as easily. I couldn't believe he had abandoned me at the hospital. He couldn't believe I had produced another girl. It was a full two weeks later when I finally gathered the courage to break the silence between us. The tension had reached an unbearable crescendo. We were lying in bed with our backs to each other, as had become the custom, when I decided to slice through the dreadful silence, like a sharp knife through fresh goat cheese.

"Wh—Why—didn't you come to visit me at the hospital?" I stammered.

Only silence greeted me from the other side of the bed.

"Why did you leave me in the hospital?" I whispered, crying softly.

"I was embarrassed..." Ezra replied softly, after a pause as big as the ocean. "I was embarrassed to tell my friends that I had another girl. I was afraid they would start talking badly about me, saying that girls are the only thing I am capable of."

Silence followed as we both independently pondered our current situations.

The conversation for the evening concluded, but we had softened the barrier between us. The next few days we increased our cooperation, little by little, to conquer the new obstacles set out before us. However, the argument did not end without leaving deep emotional scars. I promised myself that I would have no more children. I also realized that I was expendable. If they didn't even show up after the second girl, I doubted whether I would be invited back into the house if there were a third.

A Little Background

Unfortunately, diplomacy between the United States, the Netherlands, Great Britain, and Japan continued to go as well as the relationship between Farida, Ezra, and me. The decision to freeze all Japanese assets in the U.S. as well as trade between the two countries put Japan in a precarious situation. The country had imported the majority of its oil from the United States,[19] and the suspension of trade required the continued use of its precious reserves just to meet demand.[20]

The government understood that it had sufficient oil reserves for a two-year period of peace and much less if a war were to develop.[21] Therefore, the military recommended an attack on the United States while Japan was strong.[22] To most, it appeared that there were only a few possible courses of action. One extreme was to bow to the wishes of the U.S. The other was to initiate a war with a devastating attack—making future victory achievable.[23] The former course of action was not popular since placating the U.S. meant abandoning the Tripartite Pact;[24] abandoning the occupation of French Indochina;[25] and

---

19 Ike, p. 188.

20 Ike, p. 154.

21 Ike, p. 154.

22 Ike, p. 138.

23 Toland, pp. 150-151.

24 Ike, p. 97.

25 Ike, p. 179.

most importantly, abandoning all hard-fought gains in China[26] by completely pulling out of the country. Most were fervently against bowing to U.S. demands, which undoubtedly would constrict Japan's economic and military influence, as well as ultimately signal an end to their aspirations of becoming a leader in Asia.[27] Their acquiescence would also imply that Great Britain, the Netherlands, France, and the U.S. rightly controlled Southeast Asia.

Comprehending America's power, some initially tried to steer their government towards a peaceful solution with the U.S. through diplomacy. Nonetheless, at the same time, it was deemed a necessity to prepare for war as an alternate solution. The oil stocks that were dwindling day by day required the country to put a deadline on diplomatic efforts.[28] If the government negotiated too long with the U.S., Japan's oil reserves would be too low to fight an effective war.[29]

The diplomatic process was cumbersome and slow because of vast language and cultural differences.[30] In addition, there were divisions of opinion within the governments, slowing down the process even more. A third issue causing confusion concerned the ability of the United States to intercept Japanese government messages, codes, and information on troop movements.[31] They were fully aware that while discussing peace, Japan was preparing for war.[32] The stark contrast between what the Japanese government was saying and what it was doing cultivated distrust on the other side of the negotiating table.

---

26 Ike, p. 179.

27 Ike, p. 196.

28 Feis, p. 265.

29 Ike, pp. 138-139.

30 Toland, pp. 134, 147.

31 Feis, p. 219.

32 Toland, p. 142.

The American's price for peace in response became uncompromising and rigid, insisting on the complete withdrawal of all troops from China.[33] It was an insult to everyone in the Japanese government who had attempted to forge a peace agreement.[34] It was a confirmation of the true American intentions for those people in the Japanese government who, from the beginning, wanted to fight for control of Southeast Asia. The last diplomatic hopes of avoiding war faded into obscurity.

A White Horse in the White House

We were not privy to the diplomatic struggle waging between the leaders of the U.S. and Japan. We were aware only of a nationalistic fervor gripping the nation. Many of our neighbors and associates, who had sons and daughters involved in the wars, were eager to expand and strengthen the glory of the nation.

Morale was high, but life was not getting any easier. Our morning shopping trips steadily became longer since many of our vendors ran out of food early and prices rose dramatically. As a partial solution, the government gave us vegetable seeds, and we were responsible for planting them in our garden. They issued us rice, potato, tomato, and beans, ordering us to organize them in rows. The police, who were always close by, explained the specific care required for each plant. Planting what the government needed was not an option but a requirement. The police would cut our ration if too much of the garden was allocated to an unnecessary vegetable. They explained to us on a few occasions, "If you are not producing enough of what we need, you must have enough to eat.

33 Toland, p. 143.

34 Toland, p. 144.

Therefore, you don't need as much of the ration allocated to your family." When the vegetables were mature, the government would bring a truck to our house and take a percentage of the harvest. Most food went to the troops, and the remainder we used for ourselves. After the harvest, the police would show us how to dry some of the vegetables, extract the seeds, and replant them. The vegetables supplemented our food supply, but we still needed to go shopping every morning to make up the difference.

One cold morning, I visited my favorite vegetable seller who always saved me some eggplant and cucumber. I was picking out our day's requirement, when suddenly the radio crackled. After a brief announcement, the customers in the store started grinning, celebrating, and chatting feverishly with one another. I didn't understand what was taking place, but the shopkeeper was obviously elated.

"What is happening?" I asked with captivated interest.

"Shhhhhhh! Be quiet!" he whispered forcefully, his left ear pressed up against the radio. Deep parallel furrows of concentration spontaneously appeared, running the length of his forehead, like a planted field.

I waited a few seconds and pushed again, "What is it?"

His smile became so unnaturally wide, it looked as though it would get stuck in that position. The brown in his almond-shaped eyes shone fiercely with pride, and his short, grey, thinning hair bristled on top of his head in excitement. "We are at war with the West!" he exclaimed proudly. "We invaded America! They say in a few months' time, the Emperor will ride his white horse into the White House."

I was shocked. For a few seconds, my body stood frozen until my mind was able to thaw my nerves. I knew the United States was a much larger country than Japan and any war with them would be a long one. All of a sudden, it was evident that our business could no longer be at the top of our list of priorities. We would likely be out of work for a very long time.

Our immediate problem was to find a way to survive a long, drawn-out struggle. I noticed cases of canned lentils, beans, sardines, and tuna to the right of the counter.

"How many cases of fish and vegetables do you have?" I asked the shopkeeper, trying to keep my voice nonchalant and returning the generous smile he had displayed earlier.

He checked quickly and replied, "Two cases of lentils, three cases of sardines, one case of beans, and two cases of tuna."

"You seem to have a lot of extra stock," I declared. "How much do you want for all of it?" I asked the question as calmly as I could manage. I knew if I acted too eager, the price could triple, or he could decide to save the canned goods for later. If food became scarce, the price would quickly jump.

Luckily, he only checked the price per can, multiplied the amount by the quantity of cans in the case, and then added the case costs together. He announced joyfully, "The eight cases of food will cost eighty-one yen."

I didn't want to negotiate and give him a chance to change his mind. "Very well," I quickly agreed. "I will buy it all. Just do me one favor. I will pay you a little now and will return this afternoon—after getting the rest of the money from my husband."

"No problem," he answered, now even happier than before. Not only had Japan invaded America, but he had also made some money that morning.

I hired a car, brought the food directly to the house, and with Ezra's help, hid it in the basement. The canned goods would be our reserve supply—to be used only in case of an extreme emergency.

War Time Eating

Japan had unleashed a devastating attack on the U.S. and Southeast Asia. The offensive began on December 7, 1941, with a surprise attack on Pearl Harbor, Hawaii, damaging most of the American Pacific fleet. Over the next five months, they occupied Guam, Wake Island, Hong Kong, Singapore, Dutch Java, and the Philippines. The nation appeared invincible.

At home, while Japan won victory after victory, we still felt vulnerable. The stateless people were now required to go to the German Club in order to redeem their ration coupons. This presented a problem for us. Some German employees did not like to see Jews collecting the scarce, valuable food. One older lady scrunched up her face like she was going to sneeze whenever we reached the front of the line. Her steel grey eyes, fading blonde hair, bony extremities, mostly toothless mouth, and skin partially wrinkled like an overripe fruit presented an impenetrable obstacle between us and our rations. After waiting in the line for hours, we conceded defeat if she lurked behind the counter, which was always overflowing with rice, bread, and meat. She would simply say, "Sorry, we are all out of food," take our coupons, and place our rations under the counter. The Jewish food allowance was given to her relatives, who sold it on the black market. Luckily, this woman was not there every week, and therefore, we were generally able to buy the government-issued rations. We were also lucky that the German Club's Japanese employees never withheld anything from us.

Not all German-led organizations were unfair to the Jews. At the onset of World War Two, there was a Jewish president of Japan's KRAC (Kobe Regatta and Athletic Club). The club members decided, for the purpose of avoiding political pressure, to replace him with a German. The new president immediately declared that every member would be able to enjoy the club without restrictions, regardless of their religious affiliation. But I digress.

The ration was reduced every so often. To make up for the food shortage and for the weeks when our rations were withheld, we needed to buy food at outrageous prices on the black market. We bought our necessities from three older

Japanese men, an Iraqi Jew named Victor, and an Egyptian man. Daily these men would visit independent farms scattered throughout the countryside and buy any available eggs, chickens, sugar, flour, and meat directly from the farmers. The black marketers would transport the goods into the city in large baskets. Blankets, old rags, or clothing were placed over the food, to hide it in case of police inspection. For added security, a few policemen were given food or yen incentives to look the other way. Although it was illegal to buy or sell black market food, everyone, including the police, was hungry. As a result, smuggling food was permitted as long as the correct "tariffs" and "respects" were paid where they were due. We would request items that we needed, but invariably would only receive what was available that day. As in any business, it was worth the extra money to buy from a trusted friend. We bought more and more from Victor as the food became harder to find. He was always fair with us—which was more than we could say for some.

One morning, the Egyptian man brought us almost one kilo of what appeared to be a good-looking meat. We were excited to see that it was very lean and already chopped up into medium-sized chunks. The price was paid after a lengthy negotiation, and we boiled the meat to make it soft. I looked into the pot after a few minutes of cooking and was surprised to see that the meat had turned black. A strange odor emanated from the broth that didn't smell like anything we had prepared before. Farida was cooking the vegetables, and while I was trying to decide what to do, she walked over to the pot.

"Is the beef tender yet?" she asked, presuming the answer was yes.

"No," I answered slowly and nervously. "Actually, it looks strange and smells bad."

"Did you ruin it?" Farida asked in suspense. She walked over to the stove and peered into the pot to answer her own question.

"It definitely looks very strange," she agreed, becoming

nervous herself. Fortunately, she had been there the entire time we were cooking and knew the foul smell was not my fault. "Try it!" she ordered.

We were hungry and couldn't throw away food just because it was the wrong color. I fished out a piece of meat from the broth, balancing it precariously on the wooden serving spoon, and waited a few seconds for it to cool. Farida had both eyes fixed on me, lending added motivation to proceed with haste. In one motion, I picked up the morsel between my thumb and forefinger and dropped it tentatively into my mouth. The texture was disgustingly slick and slimy. Small, brittle bones jutted painfully into my tongue and my taste buds prickled with a stinging sensation. I tried to swallow as I was hungry, but my body had other plans—an intense gag reflex propelled the meat out of my mouth, through the air, and onto the kitchen floor. Farida took one look at what had transpired and dumped the pot out in the garden. Throughout the course of the day, our hungry guests went to inspect the missing ingredient from their unsatisfying meal of rice and vegetables. The general consensus was that the mystery animal was probably a feral cat.

It was a waste of time to ask the Egyptian man for our money back, and we didn't even try. When we saw him two days later, we explained what had happened, and he claimed it must have been the farmer who had sold him the bad meat. The man was not dishonest. Times were difficult, and, like us, he had to find a way to make a living. Needless to say, we didn't buy any more cut meat from him, but we continued to purchase other necessities.

After the cat incident, we started to buy our meat differently. We insisted that the animal be whole and alive if possible. Our strategy would not have worked if everyone else hadn't demanded similar terms due to their own experiences with unidentified foods. The main problem with bringing live animals into the city was the noise. It is not easy to sneak a crowing rooster or a mewing sheep past police officers. Most officers were reasonable and could turn a blind eye to one or two activities. But a noisy animal would attract too much attention. A deception that these traders had practiced actually helped them develop a profitable business.

These vendors were under pressure to find food a few times a week. Sometimes the farmers didn't have the food to sell, wanted too high a price, or wanted to keep their animals for breeding. The traders found a way around this problem. If one crushed an aspirin-like pill, mixed it in with chicken feed, and fed the chickens before the farmers woke up, the chickens would experience a narcotic effect. The chickens would move very slowly, like they were drunk, and some would even fall asleep. The trader would approach the farmer in the morning and exclaim that his chickens looked as if they were dying. The farmer would see how strangely his chickens were acting and want to get rid of them as soon as possible. The trader would then deceitfully offer to buy them at a reduced price. While this deception had worked early in the war, the farmers soon understood how they were being manipulated. They discovered that after half a day, the effects of the drug wore off, and their chickens returned to normal.

The traders ingeniously changed their technique. Instead of using it to get a lower price from the seller, they used it to get a higher price from the buyer. After buying the chickens in the country at a fair price, they would drug them and smuggle the sleeping, noiseless chickens into the city. The first time one of the Japanese vendors brought this new product to our house, I was very surprised.

"Lucie, we have a special treat for you! Live chicken today," he said amiably.

"Live chicken?" I answered in surprise. "Let me see!"

They took out three dead-looking chickens and lay them on the floor.

"These chickens are not alive," I retorted suspiciously. "Are you trying to trick me?"

"Give me a bowl of water." He smiled. "They are not dead, only sleeping."

He tossed the water onto the birds, which jumped up in surprise and started walking slowly around the kitchen.

"You see, Lucie, they are only drugged. If you keep them for a few hours longer, they will run around like normal."

I was very impressed but probed warily. "How much do you want for these live birds?"

"*Yasui! Yasui!* Only fifty sen more than the regular price."

"Alright," I replied happily. "I'll take all three!"

Once demand picked up for these live chickens, Victor embarked on the more ambitious project of bringing a lamb into the city. Like the chickens, he fed the lamb a pill to make it sleepy. He then bought a basket big enough to hold the animal. The problem he encountered was the tired lamb would still make plenty of noise. He finally solved it by surrounding the drugged animal with grass and other foods. When the lamb awoke, it ate and kept quiet. To find a lamb or goat was not so easy, and therefore, we only enjoyed such a luxury on special occasions.

The biggest benefit of buying live animals, besides the freshness, was the ability to eat kosher meat. Jewish law requires cows, sheep, goats, and chicken to be slaughtered in a specific manner to promote the health of the person as well as to end the animal's life humanely. Before the war, we didn't have a *shochet* (a butcher versed in the Jewish dietary laws), so instead, the most knowledgeable person performed the function. In the absence of a person who knew how to correctly kill the animal, many of us merely ate non-kosher meat. This religious omission was brought about by a well-known story.

Most Jews in our community were originally from kosher households, but we knew of only a few people who put the dietary laws before their own health. A friend of ours left Aleppo to work in China, insisted on keeping kosher, and had a difficult time finding foods to eat. Despite his rapidly

declining weight, he didn't change his eating habits and eventually died of malnutrition. Learning from his experience,
we ate everything, except pork and milk with meat. Once in
Japan, we tried to adhere to our religious requirements without compromising our health.

Hitler's final solution for European Jews resulted in many
individuals fleeing Europe to find temporary homes in China
and Japan. A few German *shochets* joined this migration and
found their way to Kobe. The community was eager to give
them work, and everyone started eating kosher meat when
the animals were available.

Victor and the other vendors would smuggle the live animals to our house from the countryside. The *shochet* would
come over, tie up the animal, slit its throat, and let the blood
drain into a bucket, which was later dumped into the gutter.
We would give some meat to the *shochet* as payment for his
services and split the rest with our friends in the neighborhood. Everyone would pay for his portion. There was poor
refrigeration, so dividing up the meat was the only way to
keep a steady supply of fresh food in the house. If our small
family tried to consume an entire animal, most of it would
rot. A noisy goat or an early-rising rooster was also the most
efficient way to announce to all your neighbors, as well as the
local policemen, that you had a source of illegal food. So it
was necessary to kill the animals immediately and have ten
or twenty people share the fresh meat.

Kobe–a Strategic
Transit Center for Jewish Refugees

Sharing food, playing cards, and going to the synagogue
were only some of the activities that cemented our eclectic
Jewish community together. Beginning in the years leading
up to World War Two and continuing into the early part

of the conflict, Kobe's small collection of Jewish families worked together with many local Japanese to save thousands of refugees.

Despite the geographic distance of Japan from other Jewish communities, there had been Jews living in the country for centuries. The first reported Jews in Japan were among the Dutch traders in the early 1600s at the Port of Nagasaki. Many more arrived when Japan opened up its ports to Western trade in 1858 due to the United States-Japan Treaty of Amity and Commerce. The Jews were amongst the Dutch, American, British, Russian, French, and other foreign traders who conducted business within the country. Jewish communities were eventually established in Yokohama, Nagasaki, and Kobe during the late 1800s. The Yokohama or Kanto earthquake of 1923 caused many Jews to move their homes from Yokohama to Kobe, which enlarged Kobe's Jewish population and made it possible to support a synagogue.

When I arrived in the city, the Jewish community was renting a two-room apartment in a boarding house run by the Ono family, which served as a gathering place for daily prayers. They rented a room for the Ashkenazi Jews (Jews of German, Russian, and Polish origin) and a room for the Sephardic Jews (Jews of Spanish and Middle Eastern origin), but more often than not, they needed to pray together in order to have a *minyan*. It was a financial struggle to maintain the synagogue since everyone was poor. In fact, most of the community shared bedrooms to save on rent. But eventually many of us made money by exporting the high-quality Japanese goods to customers all over the world.

Many Japanese welcomed the Jewish presence in the country because it promoted trade. We served as middlemen and agents to lubricate the business processes. Factories were changing every day, whereas communication or travel took months. Therefore, the importers needed overseas contacts they had confidence in. The Jewish, Christian, and Muslim businessmen required the services of people who spoke their language, maintained relationships with the factory, inspected the merchandise, and made cash payments for them when necessary. Even if a Japanese factory owner spoke English or Arabic, they were not trusted one hundred percent. This is simply because there was a conflict of interest. A factory owner of any nationality would always want to ship their goods and receive payment, whether the quality was acceptable or not. In the low season, a good factory could control its quality relatively easily, but in the high season, there were often fights to occupy good production lines. This is when the quality suffered, the delivery suffered, and the Jewish agent earned his commissions by fighting for his foreign counterpart.

By Jewish law, ten percent of the agent's profits were required to be used for charitable purposes, or *tzedakah*. The increase in the prosperity of the Jews of Japan resulted in more money being pumped into the synagogue. Eventually, this allowed us to relocate and create a respectable meeting place for the community. My responsibility was to have a big Sabbath lunch ready after services. Our good friends were always invited. Also welcome was anyone who needed a place to have lunch or a place to sleep for a few nights.

Our guest list expanded rapidly due to the upwelling of antisemitism in Europe. The Jews who left Europe in the early stages of Hitler's attempted genocide were generally wealthy and immigrated to North and South America, among other areas, by ship. From autumn of 1938 to the middle of 1940,[35] they escaped on the Lloyd Triestino line, which sailed to Shanghai and other ports in Asia. After a brief stay, they would continue on to their final destinations. They used a similar route to the one I had taken on the *Conte Verde*, until Italy's June 1940 entrance into the war closed the escape route via the Mediterranean Sea.

---

35 Sakamoto, Pamela Rotner. *Japanese Diplomats and Jewish Refugees: A World War 2 Dilemma.* Westport, CT: Praeger Publishers, 1998, p. 43.

In September of 1939, Germany and Russia attacked Poland and divided the country between them. Lithuania was designated as a geographic buffer by the Russo-German Pact. Many Jewish Poles escaped to Lithuania to avoid being at the mercy of the German and Russian governments. Soon, the only escape route to the promising destinations of the United States, Latin America, or Australia was East through the Soviet Union. However, the refugees first needed a destination visa and then a transit visa to ride the Trans-Siberian railway on their way to Japan or occupied China. Dutch Ambassador L.P.J. de Decker coordinated with the Dutch Consul in Kaunas, Jan Zwartendijk, to stamp many travel papers with destination visas to Curacao.[36] Chiune Sugihara, the Japanese diplomat in Kaunas, altruistically issued thousands of transit visas to Polish and Lithuanian Jews.

Anotole Ponevejsky, who I called Ponve, was a leader of Kobe's Ashkenazi community. He received a cable in June 1940 from Lithuania. It asked Ponve to write a letter to the Japanese government, on behalf of the Jewish community, in which they would guarantee support for seven refugees on their way to America.[37] After Ponve submitted the first letter, he was immediately flooded with further requests. The community quickly accepted every request received.

The refugees en route to Japan rode the train through Siberia and Manchuria and disembarked in Vladivostok. The *Harbin Maru,* a small ship that rocked violently when crossing the Sea of Japan,[38] transported passengers once a week from

36 Kranzler, David. *Japanese, Nazis and Jews: The Jewish Refugee Community of Shanghai, 1938-1945*. Hoboken, NJ: KTAV Publishing House, Inc., 1988, p. 312.

37 Tokayer, Marvin and Mary Swartz. *The Fugu Plan: The Untold Story of the Japanese and the Jews During World War 2*. New York & London: Paddington Press, 1979, p. 124.

38 Sugihara, Yukiko. *Visas for Life*. Trans. Hiroki Sugihara. San Francisco: Edu-Comm., 1995, p. 139.

Vladivostok to Tsuruga.[39] Once the refugees arrived in Japan, the Jewish community of Kobe took responsibility for them. Alex Treguboff, a tall, handsome friend of ours, would board the boat to help with the immigration process. Although refugees were always advised to state Curacao as their destination, some mentioned the United States. The local officials would call Mr. Treguboff over, and he would quietly correct the refugees.[40] The immigration officials knew that half the visas were fake[41] and did their best to ignore the unprofessional forgeries made in underground stamp-making shops.[42] Similarly, when an individual came without a visa, Mr. Treguboff would quickly issue one while the Japanese officials watched and waited.[43] Once they were admitted into the country, members of the Jewish community accompanied them on the train to Kobe.

During the refugees' temporary residence in Japan, the synagogue supplied many earthly as well as spiritual necessities. Our community set up beds and *futon* in the building for the refugees to sleep in, and the extra people were accommodated in everyone's homes. We personally set aside two rooms for displaced Jews, one for women and the other for men. Many of the individuals that arrived were very religious and, as a result, wouldn't eat in our home. To remedy this common situation, everyone initially donated into a fund that supplied kosher meals through the synagogue for whoever required them. Fortunately, very large donations from American charities provided the financial resources to assure the continuation of these services. Community representatives would purchase the food with the donated funds, and the refugees would prepare the meals. The Jews

39 Sugihara, p. 139.

40 Sakamoto, p. 142.

41 Sakamoto, p. 142.

42 Sakamoto, p. 142.

43 Sakamoto, p. 142.

with more liberal eating habits were welcome to eat where they were staying.

There was also other help available. The Japanese government helped supply the refugees with food through the synagogue. The synagogue reported the number of people living on the premises to the police, who in turn issued extra rations. They were even sensitive enough to issue us a ration for flour instead of bread on Passover. In this way, we could make our own *matzah* (unleavened bread) for the holiday. The community paid for the rations with strong support from abroad, but we were happy to do so since food was in such high demand. The Red Cross also distributed supplies periodically to the refugees in the city. Every long-term member of the community additionally contributed clothing, shoes, and extra material to those in need. Money was in short supply, but each person gave as much as possible. For security, all donations were anonymous to prevent German retribution. Despite the generosity of American charities and the Jewish community, there were still periodic food shortages. Friendleib, a German bakery run by a German man and his Japanese wife, would give their extra bread to the Jewish refugees. However, it had to be done quickly and secretly. Many Jews lining up in front of a German bakery for free leftovers would definitely arouse suspicion and risk getting the bakery's flour ration cut. Another local German bakery would not give or even sell bread to Jews.

Some members of the community provided valuable services to the refugees. The Stolovi family and Sam Evans[44] specialized in obtaining money for the refugees. Many people would arrive in the country with diamonds or precious metals hidden in the heels of their shoes. Sam had many Japanese contacts from being a ship's chandler (a food procurer for

---

44 Sopher, Lisa, "Introduction and Summary of Lisa Sopher's Notes from Interviews Conducted together with S. David Moche About the History of Jewish Life in Kobe, Japan 1936 – 2000." History of Jewish Kobe, Japan, 2009, http://historyofjewishkobejapan.blogspot.com, 2009, p. 1

passenger vessels), and would sell these valuables to them at the best price he could. He would give the cash to the refugees and help them buy food on the black market.

Some individuals were only able to afford the trip to Kobe and did not have any funds to continue on. American charities subsidized most activities, but there were often shortages of money. In these cases, when money was available, the community would pay the boat fare to their destinations. In late 1940 and early 1941, our community was able to give a lot to help finance these passages. At the conclusion of 1941, it became more difficult, as money was harder to come by.

From 1940 to 1941, many Jews were stranded in Japan without proper destination visas. Many of these refugees lived in Kobe for over six months and were the recipients of generous support and tolerance from the local Japanese population. In the middle of 1941, the government began to move the refugees to Shanghai, which was under Japanese control. Around this time (August 1941), our friend Maurice Wahba was traveling to Shanghai with approximately two thousand Jewish refugees. When the ship neared the destination port, the Japanese immigration official called out, "All Jews on this side!"[45] Maurice joined the refugees until he realized they weren't referring to him. Maurice possessed an Egyptian passport. He understood that the Japanese immigration officials were referring to everyone without adequate travel documents as Jews.[46]

By September of 1941, the eleven hundred remaining Kobe refugees unable to obtain destination visas were relocated to occupied Shanghai.[47] A few refugees who remained in Kobe during the war were relieved to be able to use the synagogue as a home—but many were far from happy to be

45 Sopher, p. 13.

46 Sopher, p. 13.

47 Tokayer and Swartz, p. 200.

alive. They related unspeakable tragedies of their entire families' being snatched out of their hands by the Nazis. While they lived in the synagogue to meet their physical needs, a few gave up praying to meet their spiritual ones. Some would say, "If there were a God, he would have shown his face when we were in Germany!" However, we could not judge them. Even to fathom the depths of agony enveloped around their fragile souls was impossible. With care and understanding, we hoped to assuage their wounds, knowing full well the source of their pain could never be forgotten.

It was not enough to only focus on Jewish issues in the synagogue. Everyone understood that we were in a foreign land and needed to live in harmony with the local population. A Japanese flag was placed in the synagogue, and we prayed daily for the health of the Emperor, his family, his advisors, the cabinet, and the stability of the government. In the prayer, we asked God to help the Emperor guide Japan out of the war.

The Curious
Questions of Osakabe-San

All the stories recounted to us by the refugees flooding into Kobe, in addition to the German officers and propaganda appearing in our neighborhood, made us fear for our lives, although it gradually became apparent that Japan's relationship with Germany had everything to do with politics and nothing to do with religion. At the onset of war with the West, some American and British citizens, whether Jewish or not, were put into internment camps. Some of these camps were uncomfortable but some were relatively humane. Certain guards would even allow prisoners to go to a local bar as long as they returned before a preset time. The prisoners knew not to escape because they could be recaptured in a different prefecture that would not care for them as generously. The Japanese treated foreigners from non-combatant countries relatively well, regardless of their religion. We lived side by side with Catholics, Muslims, Hindus, and Protestants who were all treated humanely. Being foreigners, we were under constant scrutiny, but we were not subject to cruelty.

One situation illustrated the sentiment of the local people quite well. Rahmo Sassoon, a member of the Sephardic community, painted the name *"Ohel Shelomoh"* (the tent of Solomon, Solomon being the first name of his father) in big gold Hebrew letters on the door of the Sephardic synagogue. As the political relationship between Germany and Japan grew closer, Mr. Ocheimer and other Jews in the community, fearing violence or vandalism, told Rahmo to remove the letters. Less than one week after Rahmo complied with their wishes, a Japanese policeman inquired about the old sign's disappearance. When he heard of the Jewish community's reservations, the policeman told Rahmo to repaint the letters. "This isn't Nazi Germany," he said.[48]

The Nazis' specific goal was to destroy Jewish lives. Thank God the Japanese did not bow to their request. Dear friend, please understand that I did not influence any of the political decisions in Tokyo, and therefore, the true reasons we weren't all murdered immediately are beyond the comprehension of a poor girl from Aleppo. I believe what kept us alive in the early parts of the war was a combination of three things: we were from a non-combatant country, we had been in Japan from before the war, and we were the recipients of abundant kindness from the Japanese people. From my point of view, we were not treated any worse or any better than the foreigners in Kobe belonging to other religions. That being said, the police were monitoring us daily to watch for any suspicious activity subversive to the local population or to the country.

---

48 Sopher, p. 5.

The Japanese caretaker of the synagogue grounds was a police informant. She would watch our movements every day, especially on the Sabbath, and review the activities later with Osakabe-San. A member of the congregation overheard a conversation between them on a spontaneous visit to the synagogue to retrieve a forgotten book.

"What happened today?" Osakabe-San asked her.

She answered carefully, reviewing the religious service, "Today they opened up the wooden cabinets, took out the big red case and the big blue case. They brought them to the table in the middle of the room and read from them. Then, they put them back in the cabinet."

Osakabe-San went to the *bimah* (cabinet for the Torah), opened it, gingerly picked up the Torah with the red velvet covering, and carried it to the table. He carefully, respectfully removed the red fabric and unrolled part of the scroll he found inside. After looking at the peculiar Hebrew words for approximately fifteen minutes, he rolled up the scrolls, replaced the covering, and returned the Torah to the *bimah*. Osakabe-San and the caretaker exchanged some parting words before he quickly left.

The following week, he began a cursory investigation and showed up unannounced at our house. Simone was in my arms and Sakura was feeding Frieda at the kitchen table when we heard his familiar forceful knock. Opening the front door, I bowed respectfully, led him into the kitchen, and excused myself to put Simone back in her crib. I then made him a strong coffee, accompanied it with some cookies, gave him a spoon, and placed our sugar bowl in front of him.

Sugar was rationed and expensive, so this was not a small gesture. The farmers who prepared the sugar mixed it with as much water as possible. They sold it by weight, and the water increased the price they could get for their product. The result was that the sugar often was unusable after a few days because the moisture caused mold to grow in it. Even so, we kept buying the luxury chiefly for situations like these. By giving him the spoon and the entire bowl, I was giving him the ability to take as much as he wanted of a sparse commodity. It was merely a small way of showing respect. Furthermore, it was common knowledge that many people, including us, were buying food from the black market. We always offered him the best of what we had, as a sign of thanks for his discretion.

He asked about the children, as this was our favorite safe topic of conversation, and then he promptly got down to business. "What do you do in the synagogue?" he asked with feigned nonchalance.

"I pray," I answered slowly, a bit confused. He had never shown interest in my religious habits before.

"What do you pray for?" he probed patiently.

I paused for a second, saw this was important, gathered my thoughts, and tried to impress him. "I pray to God for many things: good health and many sons for the Emperor, health and good judgment for the government, health for you and your family, and health for me and my family."

Osakabe-San smiled, nodding in approval. "What words are written in the scrolls you keep in the cabinet?" he asked amiably, but steeped in concentration.

I continued after a few seconds, careful not to pause too long. I didn't want him to think I was making anything up. "This is called the Torah. The scroll tells us about the lives of our ancestors, Abraham, Isaac, and Jacob. It tells us about the prophet Moses and how he led the Jews out of Egypt. It tells us how we received God's instructions on Mount Sinai. It also tells us how we used to worship God in Israel, thousands of years ago, in a temple now destroyed. Most importantly, though, it tells us how we should act in order to conform to God's will. This includes treating our neighbors with respect, improving the world we live in, and helping the people around us in any way that we can."

He thought for a while, nodded, bid me goodbye, and left.

Ezra came back an hour later from buying the rations for the week. I told him of the curious questions Osakabe-San was asking. We warned all of our friends to prepare themselves for inquiries into the synagogue. All of our answers had to be as similar as possible to avoid suspicion. To our surprise, he had already been to a few houses. After researching the matter, Osakabe-San appeared convinced at our benign intentions. Not only did he leave the synagogue open, but he also appointed a security guard to protect us while we prayed.

Taking Sides

They say hindsight is twenty/twenty. Had I known of the emotional abuse I would receive upon having a second girl, I would have relished the relatively little they bothered me after the first. But alas, I suppose life doesn't work that way. After taking care of Simone for a few months, I realized how giving my mother-in-law her wish gave baby Frieda her complete protection. Whenever she cried or wanted for anything, I heard the familiar call: "Lucie, hurry quickly! She is my name!"

I soon found out that my father's name was not as valued in the house. When Simone cried, the reaction was quite different: "Concentrate on what you are doing, and Simone can come later! Girls are strong! She won't die!"

Little Frieda would eat, sleep, and cry with her *Tetta* (Arabic for grandmother). Simone would eat, sleep, and cry with me. Between our two camps, a gigantic chasm developed that seemed to continually widen with new daily conflicts.

One afternoon Frieda, who was now walking and talking, managed to sneak up on Simone in the living room and yanked her hair as furiously as her young, developing muscles allowed. Simone, who had been sleeping on the couch, started howling in agony. I was reviewing our warehouse inventory list but saw the scene develop in slow motion from the corner of my eye.

"Frieda!" I yelled angrily. "Bad girl! Get over here now, and I will give you a big spanking with my *zori*!" I jumped up, yanked off my *zori*, and charged towards her menacingly. I created as much drama as I could, hoping to scare her with my actions instead of having to hurt her.

I don't know how Frieda, at barely three years old, perceived the solution to her problem. Instead of listening to me, she turned and ran. I rushed after her like a crazed maniac with my slipper above my head. Frieda sped down the hallway like a young Arabian thoroughbred. Once she reached the kitchen, she slid behind the formidable figure of her *Tetta*. I entered the room with my slipper held high and a snarl on my lips. Seeing the obstacle in my path, I put on the brakes and skidded to a halt just a few centimeters in front of my mother-in-law.

"What is this?" asked Farida, pointing at me accusingly.

I explained the situation melodramatically, trying to punish my daughter psychologically. "Frieda pulled Simone's hair, and now I'm here to give her a big spanking!" Instead of meeting the pointed gaze of Ezra's mother, I glowered at Frieda, who promptly hid her face behind her *Tetta's* thigh.

The words out of my mother-in-law's mouth ambushed me with surprise. "You don't touch a hair on her head!" she exploded menacingly. "Frieda has my name, and she will not be spanked!"

I was shocked into silence. I slowly turned around, slunk back to my desk, and continued my work, fuming in anger. The die was cast, the precedent established.

A few weeks later, Ezra bought Frieda a pair of beautiful black patent leather boots. She loved them so much, she even refused to take them off before bedtime. It did not take her long to figure out that they could be used as weapons. One afternoon, as Simone crawled by, Frieda stomped one down with a quick, shiny flash on her sister's fragile pink fingers. My mother-in-law and I, slicing eggplant at the table, turned our heads suddenly as we heard the sturdy boot smack the cold kitchen floor. Simone erupted simultaneously into a fit of agony. Her face scrunched up and contorted, flushing crimson red. No sound, only short, sporadic pained gasps of breath left her quivering mouth.

Farida and I both sprang into action. Luckily, both of us had a different target in mind or there would have been a nasty collision. I ran to Simone, grabbed her arm, and forced her swelling hand into a bowl of cold water. She scooped up Frieda and continued out the kitchen door, heading straight to her room. On her way out, she shot me a backward glance, and strongly enunciated, "Don't lay one finger on her! That is my name!"

The fear of eventually having another girl enveloped my soul. The misery of fighting for control of my eldest daughter's upbringing stung my heart. I didn't want to fight anymore with my mother-in-law, and I didn't want to have any more children. I was resigned to the idea that Ezra would take another Syrian wife as soon as the war was over. He did not treat me badly or seek out other women. But he was obviously depressed that I couldn't give him the boy he wanted.

When I found myself pregnant, yet again, I knew what to do. I went straight to Dr. Sakamoto and got an abortion. The doctor did not want to do the procedure because it was now against the law but conceded after seeing I was not going to leave without one. I wept leaving his office but knew that having three girls was just not an option.

Danger Mounts

The United States military was beaten repeatedly in the five months following Pearl Harbor. President Roosevelt, hungry for a victory, approved a plan to surprise the Japanese mainland—even though the capability to maintain a consistent air attack was years away. In a risky maneuver on April 12, 1942, B-25 bombers uncharacteristically took off from the deck of an aircraft carrier. Their targets were Tokyo, Yokohama, Nagoya, Osaka, and Kobe.[49]

Ezra, Farida, and I began putting all the cash we had left towards food. Luckily, our office warehouse was partially stocked with tablecloths and other goods, which we used for various necessities. In the early afternoon, I was working on some dresses for the girls. I took a small tablecloth and began to cut the patterns for the garments. I planned to decorate the hemlines with small embroidered flowers once the sewing was finished.

Downstairs, where the usual card game was being played, I could hear a large commotion. I hurried downstairs to see what it was, and everyone was on the veranda looking towards the ocean. From the Kobe foothills, we could see a heavy column of black smoke near the coast, billowing into the air no more than a few miles away. We didn't know what had happened. Some thought it was an explosion in a factory, and others thought it could have been a bomb.

The next day there was confirmation of a bombing over the radio. None of the foreigners we knew still possessed such a valuable piece of equipment, due to government efforts to keep radios out of the hands of possible spies, but the news filtered down to us through our Japanese neighbors and friends. They reported that there had been an enemy bombing, the Japanese Air Force had repulsed the attack, and all the enemy

---

49 Chun, Clayton K. S. *The Doolittle Raid 1942: America's first strike back at Japan.* New York: Osprey Publishing Limited, 2006, p. 51.

aircraft had been destroyed. They also mentioned that they had captured some of the enemy airmen who had parachuted out of their planes. We didn't know how much truth lay in the reports we received from our friends. But for the next day or so we watched the tower of black smoke wind its way into the sky. When we asked a policeman why the blaze wasn't put out, he answered that water had no effect on such a fire.

About one month later in Motomachi, Kobe's shopping district, a bloody uniform with bullet holes in it, a ripped parachute, and the wing of an enemy airplane were displayed to the public as all that was left of the American aggressors.

The attack did not significantly damage Kobe, but it did significantly change the mindset within our city. It provided irrefutable evidence that the enemy could bomb the mainland. In the months that followed, we prepared for a more intense future siege. We organized into neighborhood groups. And in the garden, we constructed a shallow concrete pool that we filled with water for the purpose of fighting fires after a bombing run. The neighborhood security, especially on the foreign section, increased greatly. We needed permission in the form of a pass from the police station to travel even one or two miles. This greatly limited our movement.

Whenever the air raid siren blared, we quickly gathered together in our fortified garage. Since our garage was the predetermined meeting place for the immediate neighborhood, Ezra had to run down to let everyone inside. If the air raid siren rang at night, all lights had to be extinguished before we gathered together. The local police supervised our reaction to the siren and criticized us vehemently if our performance was less than perfect. Here a problem developed.

Oji-San, the garden caretaker, who could neither hear nor speak, was not about to change any aspect of his life for me, the government, or anyone else. When the air raid siren rang, he was oblivious to the entire drill, and left his fire and candles lit. At first, I would run into his rickety hut, blow out the candles, and throw a bucket of water on the fire. But that didn't work because he would just relight them. The police criticized our neighborhood's performance and blamed the bad result on our house. They explained that the enemy's bombs were very large and that only one overlooked light could lead to the destruction of the entire surrounding area. The next time, I tried to stay in his shack during the simulated air raid, making sure he kept the fires out. It didn't work. He became livid with anger, threw his body around the room in a chaotic tantrum, and I ran outside in fear. Later, others tried to reason with him but to no avail. We decided that, in the case of a real bombing, we were going to have to force him into the shelter.

Difficulties for Neighbors and Friends

To be honest, the problems with the practice air raids were not what was most worrying me. I was pregnant again and, after petitioning the local police a few times, was finally able to obtain a pass to see Dr. Sakamoto. He gave me a checkup and announced cheerfully, "Congratulations, Lucie. It seems that you have another healthy baby on the way."

Reading my downcast facial expression, he answered my request somberly before I even asked. "Last time, I did something I shouldn't have. I will not do it again. I am under more pressure than before from the police and can lose my license doing such things."

"But I cannot have another girl!" I explained sadly, looking straight into his soft brown eyes, while tears welled up in my own. "My family will barely talk to me now!"

He kept silent for a few moments, took a half breath, and answered unwaveringly. "Go home. I will make your follow-up appointment for three months from today. If there is anything wrong at that time, I will give you what you request."

I walked home depressed, but at the same time I knew that my problems were minor compared to those shared by the soldiers fighting in the war, the citizens supporting the war effort domestically and overseas, and even their family members who were left behind. The daily reminders of suffering were too prevalent to ignore.

We spoke often with a poor sixty-year-old widow in town whom I called *Oba-San* ("Auntie"). Her coffee-colored scalp was only sparsely covered with barely visible, colorless hair. She didn't need to tell anyone her story. It was evident from her crossed eyes, twisted, gaunt figure, and five remaining teeth that she had traveled a rough road. Despite time's weathering scars that had been imprinted upon her face, she always wore a crooked smile for her two pretty daughters, who usually accompanied her on odd jobs around the neighborhood. Whenever we had money available, I let her assist with the laundry or other tasks so that she could support herself. This was the only way to help, since she would not accept charity.

Oba-San finally caught some luck when a nice young man asked for her elder daughter's hand in marriage. The upcoming happy occasion lightened *Oba-San*'s spirit, and neither the past nor the war could dampen her mood. The wedding was to take place in two weeks' time, and the daughter saw no harm in consummating the marriage early. She wanted the life with her future husband to begin immediately. In a cruel twist of fate, her fiancé was suddenly taken to begin his military service. *Oba-San*'s daughter, soon after his departure, found herself pregnant. She did everything in her power to hide the pregnancy, including tightly wrapping cloth around her stomach. As the baby grew bigger, she wrapped the fabric tighter around her body, until the day her indiscretion was impossible to conceal. The shame of having a baby out of wedlock, coupled with the departure of her future husband, was too much for her. She stopped eating and bathing and became crazy with grief. The abuse to the fetus was too significant, and the baby came early. After a painful labor, *Oba-San's* daughter delivered a stillborn boy, and as a result of complications, she also died later that night. The following week, *Oba-San's* younger daughter was sent to undergo training as an overseas medic for wounded soldiers. *Oba-San* was never the same afterwards. The tragic hand that fate had dealt her blanketed her already breaking body in a shroud of depression.

Months before, the Tanakas' youngest son and younger daughter had been sent overseas without the pomp and circumstance that had accompanied their elder brothers' departures. The boy had been sent to battle in the southern islands. The girl had been sent to the warfront as a nurse. The only child our neighbors had left in the house was their daughter Rei, who continued working daily making uniforms for the soldiers. They were proud of their children but very worried as well.

The sudden return of the Tanakas' daughter should have been a happy event for them, but the circumstances of her return further depressed their spirits. She was over five months pregnant. There was definitely a degree of embarrassment from getting pregnant without a husband, but her shame was tempered by the chaos she had witnessed near the front lines. The Tanakas took care of their daughter until she had a healthy baby boy. Less than one month after giving birth, she was sent overseas again for another tour of duty. The child was left in the care of his grandparents.

I returned to Dr. Sakamoto three months later and found out that my baby seemed perfectly healthy. I didn't ask the sex of the child because I knew it was of no use to speculate. At almost seven months along, I would have to go through with it and hope for the best.

Hungry Neighbors and Spies

As losses mounted, our Japanese friends and acquaintances were constantly informed of new military victories against the West. Some of the accounts were true, and some were not. Aside from the heavy toll the war was exacting on our neighbors, which we could see evidence of, all of our foreign friends were completely cut off from news concerning the rest of the world. Therefore, everyone we knew was entirely ignorant of the true state of international affairs. It was not until years later that I was able to read historical accounts of what was taking place at that time. The Japanese Army and Navy had spread themselves out over a myriad of territories, including many island chains in Southeast Asia. Their supply lines were stretched very tightly considering that staggering amounts of resources were en route from the United States and Australia to combat their ambitions. The Allies stood up to Japan's prodigious naval might in the Battle of the Coral Sea and emerged victorious in the Battle of Midway, strengthening the West's naval presence in the South Pacific. In addition, the Allies took control of Guadalcanal and used its captured airstrips to start the offensive in the Pacific. They planned to jump from island to island and establish bases that could be used to bomb the mainland into submission.

Daily life in Kobe was already getting difficult due to a lack of food. This caused neighbors to turn on one another and the police to intensify their search for any wasteful practices.

One night, little Frieda was in a terrible mood. Everything I tried to feed her she threw on the floor, wore on her face, or left smashed on the table. Even though I was hungry, the frustration from trying to push a little food down her throat got to be too much. I picked her up, put her in my mother-in-law's bed, uncharacteristically threw her half-chewed dinner into the trash, and fell asleep.

The next morning, there was a stiff knock at the door, and two local policemen in full uniform barged into the house. Skipping the usual polite greeting, the taller one spat in official solemnity pureed with anger, "Can you come outside with us?"

"Yes," I answered meekly. I didn't know what I had done or what they wanted from me. I didn't know whether to beg for my life, run, or sit there calmly waiting for my punishment.

The taller policeman led me into our garden, pointed to my daughter's half-digested dinner sitting in the trash and accused, "Is this your rice?"

"Yes," I responded fearfully, hoping for leniency. I knew that lying to the policeman would only earn me a long-term prison sentence.

At my immediate admission of guilt, he calmed a little. He spoke condescendingly, scolding me like a five-year-old. "We are all struggling here in Japan! We are in an intense war with the West to protect our nation, and you have the audacity to throw out food! People are starving, and you have so much that you are throwing it away!"

I stared towards the ground, partly in my own personal shame, partly out of respect for the officer, and partly to avoid his fiery stare. "You are right," I replied apologetically. "I'm sorry. My young daughter was crying all night. I tried to feed her, but she was sick and couldn't eat. I won't make the same mistake again."

He paused for half a minute, moderately satisfied with my response, and handed down my punishment on the spot. "Since you have so much food, I am lowering your ration by thirty percent on everything! If I see that you throw food out again, I will cut it another thirty percent!"

"Alright," I responded, nodding three times in agreement but avoiding eye contact. I bowed to both policemen, and they left as suddenly as they had come.

I was very angry but had no one to blame but myself. The chewed rice I had thrown out was less than a thimbleful, but nonetheless I had committed a wasteful act. Earlier in the war, whenever we had a little extra rice, it was made into a paste and given to the chickens. Now we didn't have anything extra. When I explained what had happened to Ezra and my mother-in-law, they both didn't speak to me for the rest of the week. It increased their animosity towards a wife with no dowry and no boys, who now added wasting precious food to her scant resume. In the month that followed, we had to purchase much more illegal food from the black market, greatly increasing our grocery bill.

One morning, Osakabe-San stopped by the house to have a conversation with Ezra. Osakabe-San did not mention our decrease in rations, and Ezra didn't mention them either. As usual, we gave him some coffee, a cigarette, the bowl of sugar, and something to eat. He was in a good mood and very talkative. His wife was pregnant and almost ready to have the baby. We insisted on making a present for him, and he admitted that he needed a blanket for his new child. A few days afterwards, I was able to buy some cotton from the black market and chose two of the softest tablecloths we had in the warehouse. In my free time, I began sewing them together by hand and stuffing the cotton inside little by little.

One week later, we found out that the police department's sudden inspection of our trash had not been an isolated incident. Victor was able to smuggle a lamb into the city, but we couldn't locate the *shochet* until nightfall. The *shochet* agreed to come to the house early the next morning to slaughter the animal. In the meantime, the lamb was making lots of noise in the garden. The soft baaaing sounds alerted some of our hungry neighbors that we were able to find some food. The next morning, we had barely finished slaughtering the lamb and dumping the blood in the gutter when our Italian neighbor showed up. The shine in the man's eyes hinted at trouble. We kept him in the living room because we didn't want him to see the butchered animal carcass in the kitchen.

"I know you have a lamb or goat," he demanded accusingly, rubbing his hands together, a sinister grin emerging from his dark overgrown beard.

"This food is not all for us!" Ezra reasoned. "We have to share it with many people, and everyone pays for their portion."

"We are hungry too!" our neighbor shot back, quickly getting to the point.

"We can give you some meat if you pay for it," Ezra countered, trying to reach a solution without making an enemy.

The man persisted without blinking or flinching, the grin vanishing from his face. "If you don't *give* me a portion, I will report you to the police."

Ezra didn't answer right away. He looked our neighbor up and down, grimaced at him disapprovingly, and walked rapidly towards the kitchen. As an afterthought, he sullenly commanded, "Wait here!" without interrupting his stride or turning his head around to make eye contact.

He returned with half a kilo of meat wrapped in white paper and pushed it roughly into the hands of our visitor. "Here!" he shouted. "Now go!"

The man nodded almost imperceptibly, expressing an apologetic form of thanks, and disappeared out the door.

The issue with our Italian neighbor was easily solved, but we did not foresee a bigger problem that was only just developing. The following week, Osakabe-San entered our kitchen again, but this time he was fuming with rage. Ezra was downstairs reasoning with him while I was upstairs in our room. He launched an accusation angrily: "We have received reports from a police informant that you have a lot of black market food!"

"That is not true," Ezra politely explained. "We kill a lamb or goat from time to time, but we share it with over ten families. We are struggling to survive just like everyone else."

"*Ah, so desu-ka,*" he replied, listening carefully but apparently not fully convinced.

"Please come with me," Ezra invited calmly. "I will show you around the entire house. Give me an opportunity to prove our innocence." He began by giving him a tour of every downstairs room, most now empty and bare. He explained how we needed to sell the furniture to pay for our food and expenses. Ezra showed him our liquor cabinet and the one bottle of black market whisky we had left. Ezra took out two glasses and carefully poured a generous serving for Osakabe-San and himself. They savored the expensive, potent liquor and chatted about his upcoming child. When they were finished, Ezra insisted they continue the tour upstairs. He showed the Chief of the Foreign Section one empty room after the other until he opened the door of our bedroom.

I was on the floor, hand sewing the blanket for Osakabe-San. Frieda was running around the room, Simone was sleeping on the bed, and I had a big baby inside my very pregnant stomach. Ezra smiled warmly and said to him, "I wanted it to be a surprise, but this is the blanket we are making for you."

Osakabe-San looked a little embarrassed, seeing me on the floor working on his present and at the same time taking care of the children. He realized that although we once had been successful, we were obviously in the same boat as everyone else. He advised with understanding, "Watch what you are doing carefully! I can only protect you from so much. Your neighbors are watching the drains, the garbage, and listening to see who has food. If you are butchering an animal for the neighborhood, do it at night and bury the remains immediately."

He explained that Ezra would need to appear in the local courts and refute charges that he was buying from the black market. The police had been secretly compiling records of the illegal food each house was procuring. Osakabe-San, in complete seriousness, instructed him exactly how to behave. "They will say that you killed twenty animals at your house. You need to say that you are guilty of killing two. I will accompany you to the trial and help you avoid prison."

On the way to the front door, he thanked Ezra for his hospitality and promised to bring us a gift of his own the next day. The following morning, some men installed a telephone line that went directly to the police station. They explained it was so the police could call me a taxi when I was ready to give birth. It would save me the difficult process of applying for a permit to see Dr. Sakamoto. Since labor pains could start at any time, and the day I would eventually need the permit was unknown, this gift was positively priceless.

Victory

Sabbaths at the Choueke household were always very diffi-cult since Jews are not permitted to light fires or work on our weekly day of rest. The cooking and place settings could be prepared beforehand, but unfortunately, the mother-in-law could not. Farida was still smoking heavily throughout the war, and we made it a priority to find cigarettes for her. Earlier we had been able to buy them. Later, we needed to look for tobacco weeds in the mountains, dry them, and roll them ourselves in paper. Any effort expended to procure cigarettes, no matter how difficult, was generously rewarded with a docile temperament from the mother-in-law. If one wanted evidence of what a break in the supply line would bring, they only needed to be present on Saturday after-noons. By that time, Farida had gone about eighteen hours without a puff, refusing to bend any of the Sabbath rules to satisfy her craving.

It was at this approximate time on this difficult day that she had a nicotine fit that endangered my life. We were in the kitchen, cleaning the dishes, when she all of a sudden stopped. Anxiety invaded her face, and she sat down at the table a few feet from me. She repetitively laced one set of fin-gers through the other and stared at my oversized body in an all-encompassing trance. She abruptly grimaced, like I had given her a grave insult, and unloaded what was on her mind.

"What are we going to do with your next daughter when she gets here?" she remarked snidely.

I just ignored her but increased the speed I was scrubbing an iron pot.

She tried again to elicit the desired reaction. "Why are you standing there so proud when you know, as well as I do, that we will have another girl to feed in a few weeks?"

"It might be a boy," I retorted, only half paying attention, not believing my own words. In fact, I had already taken care of a few details freeing me from apprehension. I had purchased a train ticket to Shioya that I kept in my handbag. If I had another girl, I would take the train to the seaside, put stones in my pockets, and drown myself. I couldn't go back to Syria and I couldn't suffer endless abuse for my entire life. If the result was another girl, my death would free me from torment. If the result was a boy, my child would free me from torment. Either way, I would be free. The comfort in that sentiment buoyed my spirit and allowed me to peacefully ignore her.

"Look at you!" she crowed, jolting me out of my serene state. "You are so fat! You are so huge! You are so disgusting!"

I kept scrubbing the pan, but now a tinge of red, boiling rage leached into my skin.

She got up from her seat and started closing the distance between us. Every step she took was accompanied by another insulting remark. "Your body is so big! Your *tiso* is so fat!"

When I could feel her about to touch me, I couldn't stand it. I dropped the pot and cloth in the sink, turned my back on her, and started waddling around the table as fast as I could. She followed me close behind, hurling a deluge of insults, while I tried to increase the distance between us.

"You're so ugly! You're as big as an elephant!"

Suddenly, my worn black canvas shoes lost all traction with the tile floor, and my legs shot out from under me as fast as bullets. I landed with a tremendous thud in a pool of soapy dishwater on the ice-cold hard floor. Farida froze immediately in nervous silence. I groaned, crumbling onto my side and involuntarily curled up into the fetal position. A haze of disorientation and shock overcame me for ten eternal seconds, while I tried to determine the state of my body. Then the pain began moaning inside me, growing in pitch like a wailing air raid siren in the early morning until I could hear nothing else. My tailbone started throbbing in agony, and something deep in my stomach twisted unnaturally with a watery crunch.

I lay quietly in the puddle for three minutes. I slowly inched myself up to a chair and then to a hunched standing position, holding onto the table and countertop. A sharp stabbing pain was radiating from my abdomen. I struggled over to the phone, still using the counter for balance, and called for a taxi.

Farida became as still and silent as the Japanese stone lamps in our garden. After hearing the tail end of my conversation with the police station, Ezra rushed in from the living room. He needed only one look at my swelling, wincing, splotchy red face and the big watery mark on my dress before he grabbed my suitcase with his left hand and helped me outside with his right. My mother-in-law, once she composed herself, followed at a safe distance behind.

I stayed quiet. Since I had stood up I felt duller, blunter, independent movement in my body, accompanied by a sharp surge of pain. I let the tears stream down my face with wild abandon and bit my tongue until Ezra helped me into the taxi. On the way to the doctor, I couldn't help moaning and gasping in anguish, which made everyone else utterly silent.

We arrived at the hospital, and my body was no longer responding to the directions I gave it. I couldn't get out of the car, so Ezra ran into the hospital and brought out two people with a stretcher. They carried me quickly upstairs and put me on a hard bed.

They told us the doctor was with another patient and would attend to us in a few minutes. But my body was not going to wait for anybody. A nurse I recognized came into the room, examined me for about three seconds, and sprinted off to get Dr. Sakamoto.

I felt as if I were giving birth to a serpent. There was something thrashing back and forth inside me, and every movement brought my nerves to a boil. "It's a snake!" I yelled in panic. "I am giving birth to a snake! God help me!"

Dr. Sakamoto rushed in with the nurse. His face became as white as bone. "Don't push!" he yelled. "Don't push!"

I had no control of my extremities; my body was pushing, and there was nothing I could do about it.

The legs came out first, and Farida's face became flush with concern, suspense, and trepidation. She virtually stopped breathing, stayed motionless and silent.

Dr. Sakamoto worked quickly and quietly. He gave up telling me what to do, since I was not listening to a word he said.

"Aaaaaaaaaahhhhh!" I screamed and pushed hard, over and over again. My stomach muscles tightened, relaxed from fatigue for milliseconds, and tightened again until the baby's head left my body. Everyone remained completely quiet, saturating the room with suspense and terror. The baby was motionless, and the umbilical cord was wrapped around its neck. Dr. Sakamoto quickly cut the cord, untangled it, and held the baby upside down by its ankles.

For the first time, I saw why my mother-in-law was so engrossed in the process. It was a boy. I had given birth to a boy... I had given birth to a boy!!! This was the answer to all my problems!!! I produced a male heir!!! But he was not moving.

Dr. Sakamoto ignored the drama surrounding him and deftly stuck his hand down the inverted baby's throat. He made a quick movement with his hand and grimaced... He tried again, stomping his foot on the floor in frustration... The third time, a brown colored liquid gushed out of the baby's mouth and splattered on the spotless white floor. A jet of air raced into the child, causing his lungs to expand, and his whole body suddenly convulsed like an earthquake. Dr. Sakamoto spun the body one hundred eighty degrees, quickly cleared the nasal passages, and we all heard the sound we were waiting for.

"Waaaaaaa...Waaaaaa!" A soft cry emanated from the fragile being in front of me.

He was alive!!! Success!!! Victory!!! Sweet victory was won!!!

Barter, Indigestion, and Prison?

The two days' recuperation from the pregnancy was physically painful, but emotionally it was like receiving a massage and a hot bath. Farida and Ezra brought food from the house, were attentive to the baby, and even complimentary of me. Naming my first daughter had been politically difficult because tradition supplies only vague guidelines for girls. Any name can be selected, and therefore, everyone fought to be responsible for the one chosen. Naming my son was very easy. In the Sephardic tradition, it was required to name the baby Yaoub Choueke after Ezra's father. There was no room for interpretation, no one could object, and no one could even suggest an alternative. At last, there was some comfort in tradition.

Dr. Sakamoto knew everyone was having money problems. He told us just to pay what we could. This was a further testament to what a remarkable person he was.

We had a big party for the baby and placed Osakabe-San at the head of the table. No one had a lot to celebrate with, but everyone brought what they could. The guests helped finish off our last bottle of whisky and played cards late into the night. Osakabe-San must have taken note of the community's lack of food since, soon afterwards, he told Rahmo

Sassoon's pretty Japanese cook where we could all find more black market goods. Osakabe-San instructed us to say it was for his personal use so we could receive the best available.

Despite the help, procuring food was only getting more and more difficult. The ration was constantly getting cut, and the black market vendors would not accept cash. Money was becoming useless since there were fewer and fewer goods to buy with it. We could only use it to buy the scarce government rations. Instead of going to find food with cash, we now had to go find food with items we had in the house.

I needed to get creative with our shopping methods. The first time I bartered for food, I walked around our neighborhood for hours. I was not able to travel longer distances since the local police would demand to see a permit. When a man with some chickens and eggs appeared on his way to market, I tried to buy the food from him.

"What do you want for those chickens?" I asked politely.

The vendor looked me over carefully, trying to pick the most expensive item he saw. His eyes panned from my gold watch to my leather belt to the extra pair of pants hanging folded on my arm.

"Let me see your watch," he exclaimed, his interest perking up. He examined the watch, held it up to the sun, turned it over, brought it to his ear, asked questions about it, and then named a ridiculously low asking price. "I'll give you three eggs for it," he declared shrewdly.

I countered, taking the watch back, "Three eggs! No, no, no! This is a twenty-four-carat gold watch with a Swiss timing mechanism and a leather band. If you want it, I need three chickens and twelve eggs!"

"The watch may be nice, but you can't eat it," he replied facetiously. "There is no more food left in the country, and we are all going to starve to death. I'll give you one chicken and six eggs for it."

"I tell you what I'll do," I pleaded with him. "I'll give you my leather belt and my watch, but I need to have three chickens and twelve eggs."

"My final offer for the watch *and* the belt is two chickens and ten eggs!" he responded abruptly, letting me know the negotiation was over.

"Agreed," I replied quickly. "But only if I get two hens." I liked the hens because they could make eggs as well as be used for food. We exchanged goods, and the man kept walking with the rest of his merchandise into town. I was happy with almost every deal we made. Gold had no value to us. It didn't matter what we paid for something. The only thing that mattered was to get enough food to survive the week.

While almost everyone purchased from the black market, it was dangerous for the seller as well as the buyer. If the police found contraband in the house, both parties could be thrown in jail. With the scarcity of resources, everyone started searching for what remained.

Charlie Alfia, one of the bachelors, liked to drink whisky every night. When the war began, he couldn't legally buy any more liquor and thus made an arrangement with a bartender in the city to sell him some in secret. He slowly sipped a glass or two every night before sleeping. Occasionally, he would bring a bottle out for everyone to taste. However, this was dangerous due to the constant supervision by certain housekeepers, our neighbors, and the police. One such evening, feeling generous, he poured a glass for each of the men playing cards at his table. The next morning, there was a heavy knock on his door, the housekeeper opened it, and five policemen stormed into the house. Immediately, they walked directly to the main cupboard, threw aside a bag of rice on the bottom shelf, and found three dusty bottles of whisky. They interrogated him for hours, asking him over and over to reveal his supplier. He could not answer. His Japanese friend would get in enormous trouble for supplying liquor to a foreigner. They brought him to the police station and tried to pry the answer out of him again. But Charlie was honorable and kept silent. His reward was a three-by-five-meter prison cell with cellmates and little more than a bowl of rice to eat every day. With his diet drastically altered and withdrawals from the lack of alcohol, Charlie's health deteriorated rapidly. He sat day after day in a dank prison, wondering who had betrayed him. We had a clever spy in our midst, and we were all in danger of being discovered...

We suspected Ezra was turned in by the same spy. Ezra was in danger of sharing Mr. Alfia's fate when he visited the local court. We knew that the principles running Japanese courts were very different from those running Western institutions. In Japan, maintaining your innocence was a guarantee of a long, arduous prison sentence. Instead, the correct course of action was to admit guilt and obtain a mild sentence from the presiding officials. This was also dangerous. Everyone knew that being stuck in a jail cell during the ongoing war was possibly a death sentence. As resources dwindled, the prisoners would be the first to get their rations cut.

Unbeknownst to Ezra, Osakabe-San stayed in the police station late one night. After his colleagues left, he removed the handwritten list of families guilty of procuring black market goods. He found our family name and noted the indication that we had slaughtered twenty animals, including chickens and goats, during the recorded period. He quickly erased the zero, leaving only the two visible. When Ezra arrived in court, he admitted to slaughtering two animals, as Osakabe-San had suggested. The officials first berated his illegal activity and then admonished him against doing it again. Ezra expressed his heartfelt apologies for the offense, groveled, and explained that he broke the law only to satisfy his family's hunger. On a recommendation from our friend, Ezra was set free with only a slight cut in our ration as punishment.

Nevertheless, to buy only rationed food was not an option because there just wasn't enough food in the country allocated to meet peoples' needs. As a result, we needed to keep buying illegally and stay vigilant. As the fighting wore on, the quality of the food got progressively worse. The rice became infested with various beetles and flying insects and the bread became inundated with brown-colored worms. To prepare the bread for consumption, I would slice the loaf into very thin pieces, poke out the cross sections of worms I had sliced through, and then toast the bread thoroughly to kill any other insects hiding within. Preparation of the rice was slightly more complicated. Every week, Lily Braha and I took the rationed rice into the garden and ran it through a sieve onto a white bed sheet. The large bugs could not fit through the metal sieve and would either fly away or be squashed. The small bugs would prance around—easily spotted on the white background. I would grab two corners of the sheet, and Lily the other two. We would throw the rice up in the air repeatedly, and most of the smaller bugs would be carried away in the afternoon breeze. Many bugs would inevitably stay in the rice mixture and be cooked into the food.

One day, I complained to Lily about our strange-tasting rice: "Lily, I'm tired of eating all these bugs. How long do we have to keep doing this?"

"The way I look at it," she answered laughing, "is either we eat them above ground, or soon they will eat us below ground."

"Very true, and I suppose they are also a good source of vitamins," I agreed with a thin smile.

Besides rations and black market food, we had our garden to make ends meet. Initially, the vegetables we grew were plentiful and tasted good, but after a few growing cycles, they were smaller and scarcer. The problem was that many animals had died in the countryside, and there was very little fertilizer to replenish the soil nutrients. We needed to start fertilizing the plants with our own human fertilizer. Putting our excrement in the garden was a dirty job, but worse were the fat white worms we contracted from eating the produce. The children had a multitude of various parasites in their bodies, which created upset stomachs, numerous soiled diapers, and overall bad morale.

It was a difficult time. The fat people became thin, and some thin people passed away. There was hardly any food and definitely no medicine. When someone became ill, we went up to the mountains to gather white marguerite flowers. We boiled them and then spooned the liquid into the sick person's mouth. This was the only treatment available. The water quality got worse every day, and as a result, we were always on the toilet with diarrhea. Countless animals had died, so the extra human feces left over from people's personal gardens was carted out to the countryside and used to fertilize the remaining farms.

Only the very old and the very young were left at home in Kobe. Anyone with a shred of ability was either shipped out to the front or required to work in the factories producing goods for the war effort. Our neighbors, the Tanakas, felt the brunt of these programs. After working in the manufacturing plant, their elder daughter Rei was shipped overseas to work as a nurse. Soon afterwards, the ashes of her brother Hideo were displayed on the family's mantelpiece. A second sake cup from the Emperor stood proudly next to the second wooden box they had received. Sakura, my friend and companion, left for Nagasaki to be with her family. I understood that it was easier for her to suffer with them than to suffer with us. She left some clothing behind, but when months later a friend of hers came by to pick up her belongings, it was clear that she wouldn't be returning. Everyone was preparing for the worst, which was yet to come.

First Contact

While our country's military position was deteriorating, we were completely ignorant of world events. The problems in Southeast Asia, however, could not be concealed any longer. New Georgia, New Guinea, Guam, the Mariana Islands, Saipan, Iwo Jima, and many other territories were under American control. Saipan and Iwo Jima gave the Allies airbases from which they could bomb the Japanese mainland with B-29's.[50] In addition, invasions of Okinawa and the Philippines were underway that would eventually make the country even more vulnerable to air attacks. Beginning in June of 1944, foreign aircraft appeared with increasing frequency over the foreboding skies of Japan itself. In the beginning, these raids were conducted from China and India, but later, these conquered islands served as the main launching points to Tokyo—and eventually Kobe.

Warnings of the approaching enemy planes were anything but subtle. The air raid sirens would wail alarmingly as we all dashed for our neighborhood shelter. Most of us would already be hunched down in our reinforced brick and concrete garage when the antiaircraft guns would boom from the port. We watched our neighbors and friends cringe with every round the guns hurled up at the invaders as we sat sullenly, introspectively, impotently on the bare wooden benches. In frayed clothing, gaunt, skeleton-like people, who had once been rich, stared wide-eyed at each other, huddling together in their abject poverty—like beggars around a fire, except the luxury of a fire would alert enemy planes, so we were left with the cold grey floor beneath our feet and the warmth of adjacent bodies as our only solace. The fear pooled in the neighbors' eyes was mirrored in ours as we waited for the bombs everyone predicted would come.

50　Toland, p. 519.

But they didn't. No bomb was dropped. No one was hurt. We were only suspended in a living nightmare of terror, waiting for the cataclysmic event that would end our lives. Our schedules did not go by the sun or the moon. We awoke with the air raid siren, busied ourselves as the country's defenses roared on, and slept with the clanging and whooshing of guns being forged in the port factories.

It took us a few weeks to realize that these planes were not there to bomb us but instead to take photos of the area. Their chrome bellies and bird-like wings were zooming overhead at all hours of the day, scouting the perfect location from which to strike. Sometimes the planes flew so low that I could see the pilot perched in his aerial throne, skimming the horizon. Occasionally, the antiaircraft guns and defending aircraft found their marks and were able to damage the enemy planes. The foreign pilots ejected from their metal fortresses and floated precariously down to the ground with their parachutes fully extended overhead.

In the soft light of one early morning, the air raid siren moaned continuously as we made our way to the shelter. Half a block away from us, we saw two foreign soldiers parachuting towards the ground. They both wore khaki jumpsuits, leather helmets, strange sunglasses, and were trailed by tan parachutes. The police and soldiers in our neighborhood noticed the men coming a long time before we did. Six were waiting for them to land, their machine guns out, tracing the men's paths in the air. At approximately ten meters above the street, one of the foreign pilots un-holstered a small gun from his belt. Simultaneously, the six soldiers on the ground opened fire with a yell, his body jerked, the weapon fell to the road, and he glided into the ground, collapsing in an awkward heap. Three soldiers surrounded him and blocked my view. The other foreign soldier waved his arms frantically above his head as he floated down the last few meters. One Japanese soldier kept a machine gun trained on him, while the other two grabbed him from each side immediately after his rough impact with the street. In organized exuberance, they quickly walked away from us to the corner house, where they imprisoned them both. The first one died, and his bloody uniform was put on display in the shopping area. This was to demonstrate the stiff punishment being handed out to the invaders. The second one seemed unhurt and, in the next few weeks, was joined by other prisoners of war.

The POWs were walked through the streets every day to further remind the neighborhood that Japan's defenses were holding strong. Some were in good health, but others limped along using the shoulders of helpful comrades as crutches. They spoke in hushed voices, scrutinized heavily by the eight or so guards who walked with them. We had walked by them a few times when a tall, shirtless, brown-haired POW grew brave and made eye contact with us.

His voice shattered the glum, nervous silence accompanying the procession of prisoners. He yelled in Arabic, "When will the war be over?"

Caught by surprise, Ezra answered back, "Soon. Very s—" He blushed red and regretted speaking before the words had even finished leaving his mouth.

A muscular Japanese soldier quickly punched the tall POW in the stomach, instantly dropping him to the pavement. The soldier then walked slowly, confidently, resolutely towards us with a scowl on his face and a machine gun ready in his hands.

He stopped just three centimeters from Ezra's face and yelled at him in Japanese. I was too frightened to look at either one of them. "What did he ask you!!!??? What did he ask you!!!???" the man shouted.

Ezra answered truthfully in an apologetic tone, bowing low to the soldier and looking down in shame. "I'm sorry. I shouldn't have answered him. He caught me by surprise," he almost whispered.

"What did he ask you!!!???" the soldier shouted, veins in his neck pulsing dangerously under brilliant red skin.

"He asked when the war will be over," Ezra answered. He continued to stare down at his feet, his face devoid of all color like the inside of a radish.

"And what did you answer!?" he questioned angrily with spit flying everywhere, accentuating his authority and belligerence.

"I said it would be over very soon," Ezra replied obediently, still looking down, even though angry gobs of the soldier's saliva had peppered his forehead.

"And who did you say would win?" the soldier asked suddenly in an eerily calm voice. It was obvious that this question would determine whether my husband lived or died, and the man who would make the decision abruptly tightened his grip on the machine gun.

"I didn't say," Ezra paused for thought and continued in a stronger voice, laced with years of frustration. "We don't know who is going to win. We only know that we are all going to die."

The soldier thought for what seemed like an eternity but was actually only a few shudders of a watch's most slender hand. I had only enough courage to glance up once. I saw a bead of sweat escape from under his hat, run across his forehead, and catch in his left eyebrow. He commanded very slowly and carefully: "Never speak to the prisoners again." He didn't have to say anything else. We knew what disobeying him would mean.

Not everyone obeyed the demands of the armed soldiers. There were two Jewish Ashkenazi girls who had escaped Germany and lived in Kobe throughout the war. Despite all warnings, they took it upon themselves to care for the POWs. Early every morning, before the sun came up, they would sneak extra food into the house on the corner. The extra nourishment was invaluable to the soldiers since it was virtually impossible to survive on a prisoner's ration alone.

A Brush with Death

On the cold winter night in early 1945 when bombs started exploding in Kobe, no one needed to tell us that the war had arrived. Earlier that evening, before the horrible event, dinner had been difficult to prepare. I had lit a small fire in the garden since our gas was turned off, and put a few handfuls of rice in a small pot. I had then inverted a bigger pot over the small one to mask the fire from any enemy planes. The air raid siren had maintained its silence, but unidentified planes would periodically cross the darkening skies. I had fed the children quickly and put them to bed. Frieda slept with her grandmother, Simone with me, and Yaoub (whom we now called Jack for short) in his crib.

For a while, we had been aware that death and destruction were getting closer and closer to our door. The Americans would dump leaflets in surrounding cities, telling the population at what time and what date they would be pummeled. The leaflets were on cream-colored paper and written in Japanese and English. They generally said something like, "We are not against you. We are against your government. At 4:00 p.m on Friday we will bomb Osaka." The explosives always fell at the time and place indicated.

The Americans did not destroy the trains. When the leaflets carpeted Osaka, the people jumped on the train and traveled from Osaka to Kobe before the onslaught. The population of Kobe swelled until after the bombing, when the people would return, finding their houses demolished. Those who didn't heed the notices were destroyed with the buildings. This had the desired effect of demoralizing all of us. It became evident that the enemy could bomb whenever and wherever they pleased. Although many of our neighbors wanted to fight to the death and were intensely patriotic, no one could deny that the Allied forces could kill us at any time. We were like *koi* in an American's fish pond, completely vulnerable to the wishes of our captors.

In addition to leaflets, we saw food on the ground as well. Tuna fish, sausages, chocolate, and rice were just some of the items we saw fall from the planes. However, the police and soldiers would shoot anyone they found collecting the food or reading the literature. The soldiers would destroy the leaflets and bring all food back to the police station, ostensibly to check it for sabotage. Whenever I saw leaflets or food dropped from a plane, I ran in the other direction. The American intent must have been to discourage support for the government and promote the idea that the Japanese people would be better off surrendering. Regardless of the difficulties, the people in our neighborhood would support the Emperor until death. Giving up for the promise of a few cans of food was unfathomable.

The air raid siren howled mournfully at a few hours past midnight. Ezra, Farida, and I shot up quickly, put on our jackets while rushing out the door, and finished dressing the children inside the shelter. I placed black felt hats on Frieda and Simone in case cinders or fire fell on them. The heat would hopefully sear the hats instead of their heads. Leaving Jack with his grandmother, I ran out of the shelter to check on *Oji-San*. Not wanting to give him a chance to complain, I crept quickly into his room, blew out a low burning candle, and left before he detected my presence.

In a symphony of terror, the antiaircraft guns boomed like bass drums accompanying the screaming sirens. In the distance, we could hear the steady drone of a legion of airplane engines approaching. The engine noise grew louder by the second until we needed to put our fingers in our ears to partially escape from the mechanical crescendo. That's when some new instruments joined the orchestra for their first performance. Whishing sounds, like the splitting of air by giant cellos dropped from the heavens, complemented and overlapped each other. CRASH-BANG was the punctuation as each whish collided in an enormous, explosive crunch with the earth. The first explosions were joined by seemingly unlimited numbers of their brothers in mere seconds, creating so much noise that soon I could hear none.

I slipped off of the wooden bench and crumbled onto the cold, hard concrete floor. Instinctively, I cradled Jack in my arms and folded my legs below me. I tried in vain to shield Jack's ears and eyes from the surrounding chaos with my body. Simone and Frieda clung, white-knuckled, to either side of my skirt, looking at me to stop the pain. My mother-in-law joined us on the floor, shivering, shaking, and crying nervously. With every explosion, she flinched and screamed, her frigid body pressing closely against mine. Ezra, seeing everyone together on the floor, sat on the bench behind us, placing his right hand on his mother's head and his left hand on mine. While the bombing was ripping apart so many families that night, ours was cemented together. Gone were the petty fights and the conflicting interests that divided us. Now we were all one unit, in the same shelter, with bombs falling out of the sky. One small red button pushed at the correct time by an American pilot, and we would all cease to exist.

A few hours after the bombs fell, the city was shrouded in a peculiar silence—save for the woeful cry of the air raid siren. We left the shelter and looked down on the Port of Kobe, glowing with red flames. Occasionally, a new explosion would light up the ocean as another gas storage facility suddenly caught fire. Cotton-like ash littered the sky like confetti. We stayed outside until the sun came out and illuminated the countless towers of black smoke gushing from the port's industrial area. Neighbors of ours pointed out an especially thick spout coming from the main oil depot used to refuel airplanes and ships.

We slept for a few jittery hours, after which Ezra and I went to see if we could trade for some more rice. It was a surreal feeling, walking around Kobe after the first bombing run. Neighbors who had rarely shared a word before stopped to talk and congratulated us for making it through the night. The shopkeepers were happy to see us and were extra courteous. No one knew how many more days they would be alive, so it appeared they were trying to make the most of them. It was also as if everyone who had survived shared a common bond, which gave us the feeling of being brothers and sisters, even though before we wouldn't have made the effort even to say hello.

The next bombing came a few nights later. Again, we huddled together in the freezing darkness and listened to the explosions pound closer and closer to our shelter. I fed Simone little pieces of fruit and boiled egg throughout the raid to keep her calm. Little Frieda and I played a game. We competed to see who could best guess when the bomb would explode. After hearing the whooshing sound, we tapped the ground at our estimated time of impact. The first person to tap after the bomb exploded was the winner. The point of the game was to keep us alert and Frieda calm until the bombing stopped; the trick was that if we heard the explosion, it meant the bomb had fallen somewhere else. If we didn't hear it and were engulfed in a ball of fire, it wouldn't matter who won that round. My mother-in-law screamed hysterically with every loud boom. There was really nothing we could do to calm her, so Ezra and I just pushed tightly up against her for comfort. The night ended as before, with fires at the port and ash in the air. There was only one difference.

The next morning, on our return to the house, we saw a large, cylindrical metal object partially buried in the middle of our garden's tomato patch. There were no markings on the visible surface, but there may have been some on the underside. We didn't know what it was and did not dare get close enough to find out. We notified a soldier outside, who, after a cursory inspection, declared it an unexploded bomb. We left the weapon alone in the garden, and the Army later removed it.

A few weeks later, Osakabe-San came to check on us. We were overjoyed that he had survived the bombing, and we sat down in the kitchen to have some tea together.

On his way out the door, he reached into a canvas shoulder bag and gave me a rectangular bar wrapped in foil. I thanked him with a bow and unwrapped a corner of the gift in front of him. "No!" I thought. "It couldn't be!" I broke off a little piece with my back teeth and let the brown fragment sit on my tongue. Soon it melted and left me with the sweetest, richest taste I had ever experienced. It was an entire bar of milk chocolate, and it had been over three years since I had last tasted such a treasure.

"Thank you so much! Thank you so much!" I repeated, enthusiastically squealing in delight, unsuccessfully trying to contain my excitement and maintain my respectful behavior. "Where did you get this?" I exclaimed with a tremendous grin.

"This is a present for you and your children. Shut up, eat it, and don't ask any stupid questions! *Sayonara*," he replied in pretend anger and quickly disappeared down the road.

There was a degree of freedom in knowing that a certain day of your life could be the last. Never was there any talk about saving our gift for a darker day. We gathered the family together in the kitchen, and I cut the chocolate carefully with a knife. Ezra took the first piece, then Frieda, next Simone, then Ezra's mother, and last me. Frieda and Simone raced around the table, enjoying the sugar rush from their first piece of chocolate ever. We all smiled at each other as we were given a temporary respite from the horrors of war.

We didn't need to wait for confirmation that gobbling down the chocolate immediately was a good idea. An especially long and intense bombing raid took place that night. Ezra's mother screamed in agony with every impact, and the terror lasted unabated for half the night. The next morning, I had reached my limit. I honestly didn't care anymore whether I lived or died. People were dying all through our beloved city. Why were we fighting for survival? What good would it be to struggle for a few more weeks, only to be killed in a month? It looked as if death were the only way out of the war and the only way to find peace.

The air raid siren cried out again a few hours after daylight. I was finished running or hiding. I quickly brushed my hair and put on my jacket. Leaving the kids in the house, I walked out on the veranda and waited for the planes to come. I saw some silvery objects approaching fast from the ocean. I started jumping up and down, frantically waving my arms in the air like a crazy person as they roared overhead. I didn't really know what I was thinking or what had possessed me. My half-starved, sleep-deprived, frazzled brain could think of two favorable scenarios. The first was that the pilot would see I was a white woman and not bomb our house. The second was that the pilot would think I was Japanese and send me to my death. Honestly, I didn't know what option I preferred.

The air raid siren kept wailing, and three or four more airplanes hurtled towards me. I kept waving my arms to attract their attention and force a decision to grant me life or death. A Japanese soldier suddenly yelled, "Get in your shelter now!" as he appeared below the tree line at the fringe of our garden. I didn't listen. I kept waving my arms at the approaching airplanes and jumping hysterically. He raised a machine gun to his shoulder and shouted, "I will shoot if you don't get in your shelter!"

Luckily at that instant a few seconds of clarity washed over me. I thought about my children, my husband, my brothers and sisters, my mother, my friends, and even my mother-in-law. I did not want to leave them and let them struggle without me. I did not want to die a cowardly death. I suddenly flinched, turned around, ran inside, and took the kids with me to the shelter. It occurred to me later that the reason I was not burned to a crisp in an explosion was very simple. The airplanes that had flown over in my moment of insanity were not bombers. They were photographing the damage from the night before. There were likely a few American pilots who had photos of a crazy foreign woman jumping up and down on her veranda.

There was one more bombing before the City of Kobe was showered with an especially large number of leaflets. I was too afraid to read them, but Osakabe-San paid us a personal visit in order to communicate the news. He told us the air raids were only going to get worse and, if we wanted to preserve our lives, it would be best to move. He suggested that we all relocate to the mountainous rural area of Arima, where there were a few cottages built by Catholic priests who had vacated the area on account of the war.[51] Ezra left that day to Arima and found us a new place to live. He chose a small vacant house in the village of Bunkamura, a tiny clearing in the woods with thirty or forty small residences. There were thirteen other houses in the village also sheltering Jewish families, such as the Sherbanees, Fattals, Tawils, Moches, and Mizrahis.[52] Other foreigners who had more money went to Karuisawa and Mianoshta.[53] Packing for the journey was not difficult. We didn't expect to live too much longer, so we took only what we needed. The only additional items I brought were for the purpose of bartering. We also packed a few bags with extra items we owned and sent them to our various friends around Kobe. Our friends sent us some luggage in return. We each stored a few of our superfluous items in various houses in order to ensure something would outlast the conflict. If one house was bombed, at least the goods in the other houses might survive.

---

51 Sopher, p. 15.

52 Sopher, p. 16.

53 Sopher, p. 15.

Sass and the Serpent

The three-quarter-day journey, which included a train, a car, and plenty of walking, brought us from a city under siege to a countryside with dangers of its own. The trip itself was uneventful, but I was then four months pregnant and found it physically challenging. We settled into a tiny, two-room, rickety wooden house with a tin roof, rough timber floors, pine cabinets, and a window. The one bed in the house was shared by Ezra, Simone, Jack, and me. Frieda and her *Tetta* slept together on a *futon* in the other room.

Our neighbor was a handsome, muscular, dark-haired man named Sass. Sass had arrived in Kobe from Iraq three years before us at the age of thirty-two. Before the war, he had exported textiles to his brothers in Baghdad.[54] He was elected the foreign liaison who coordinated the defense of the village with the Japanese. Immediately, Frieda, Simone, and Jack were enlisted, with the other children, to protect the village. There was a network of men who watched the coast from the mountains for approaching enemy airplanes. When the enemy was sighted, a warning was shouted from one man to another until the message reached the village. The message would then be passed on to a large group of children who would run around town shouting, "*keikai keiho* ("warning alert")." We didn't have a proper shelter, and instead everyone in the village gathered under a humongous tree. Once the planes would pass, the children would relay a new message: "*keikai keiho kaijo* ("warning alert cancelled")." The children took their jobs as the air raid sirens of Bunkamura very seriously. Our village was small, insignificant to the war, and in the middle of a forest. Therefore, the Allies would never target it on purpose. Nonetheless, it was important to keep the lights off and the people out of sight to prevent extra bombs from being sent onto our heads.

---

54 Sopher, p. 2.

As before, a large portion of our day was spent searching for food and hiding from the Allies. We could not collect our rations in the countryside. Therefore, Ezra had to make a weekly trek back to our old neighborhood in order to buy the family's food allowance. When I was not taking care of the kids, we took long walks along the earthy mountainous roads and visited local farms to exchange goods. Mainly, we traded for rice and eggs, which we placed in a barrel inside one of our splintering pine cabinets.

If we were fortunate enough to find cheese or vegetables, we needed to store them in a cool place to preserve them. The neighborhood's solution was to dig an *L*-shaped cave three meters deep into the mountainside. Wooden supports were set up every half meter so the cave would not collapse in on itself. The end of the tunnel was curved and served as the main food storage area. The cave would cool at night, and the mountain would help to trap in the cold air during the day. A thick cover of branches was placed at the cave mouth to help with insulation.

The cold country nights were alive with millions of insects, wild boars, and poisonous reptiles. I lay awake for hours listening to the chirping of crickets, the ribbeting of frogs, and the occasional rustle of larger unknown animals. Sometimes, at around midnight, I would hear noises that would make the hair stand up on the back of my neck. Something large was bumping and thumping around the inside of our cabinets. I tried to muster up the courage to confront the beast but repeatedly couldn't will myself to open the door. Early in the mornings, when I would throw open the cabinets, the intruder would be gone. Amazed that there was nothing staring back at me, I would check our food inventory. I was almost sure that one or two eggs were periodically missing, but when I told Farida and Ezra, they blamed my overactive imagination.

I half believed them until one night I heard the eerie noises again as loudly as ever. Everyone was sound asleep as I tiptoed stealthily in complete darkness towards the cabinet. I slowly, carefully pried the door open, flinching at an unnaturally loud groan escaping from the rusty hinges. My first thought was to protect the food, so I reached my hand into the rice barrel, making sure everything was still there. Instead of a handful of rice, my hand closed on a frigid, scaly appendage.

"Aaaaaaaaaaaaahhhh!!!!!" I screamed, emptying my lungs completely of air, while goose pimples and shivers crawled like ants and spiders all over my skin.

Ezra shot up like a lightning bolt and ran into the dark room. "Are you hurt? What's the matter? Is there a robber?"

I couldn't answer right away. A fist of terror compressed every one of my muscles in a bony grip. A few seconds passed before it unclenched enough to allow an anxious shake of my hand in the cabinet's general direction.

Ezra ran outside, knocked on our neighbor's door, and called out loudly, "Sass! Sass! Wake up and come quickly!"

Sass stumbled out of his house, wearing white long under-wear and wielding an ax. "What is it?" he probed, wondering whether to panic or go back to sleep.

"There is a big animal in our cabinet!" Ezra explained as they arrived in our kitchen.

"Give me the sheet off the bed!" Sass ordered profession-ally. He approached the cabinet slowly, the sheet in his hands, ready to cast his net on the menacing beast. Ezra trained a flashlight beam on the cabinet and threw open the door in one terrified motion. Nothing was there.

I gestured soundlessly to the rice barrel, and Sass threw his net over it. He then carefully inverted the barrel, leaving the sheet in place so the intruder couldn't escape. He left the barrel upside down and lifted his ax into attack position.

"Remove the barrel quickly!" he commanded.

Ezra lifted the barrel and jumped back, letting the rice and eggs spill out onto the sheet. The monster was nowhere to be found.

Sass set his ax down with a sigh and complained, "What are you doing? Are you crazy? Do you think it's funny to wake me up in the middle of the night?"

Before Ezra could say anything, I interjected. "There was something there! I promise! I touched it myself! Next time, you will see!"

Sass looked at me, shrugged in doubt, and left.

Although everyone treated me like a lunatic, the next morning I emptied everything out of the cabinets. In the corner of one of the shelves was a twenty-centimeter round hole, leading to an area below the house. I found a smooth, round stone and placed it in front of the opening. To double check my sanity, I counted the number of eggs remaining. Sure enough, we were two short.

Three nights later, I heard the noises again but this time made no effort to confront them. I concentrated on the creaking cabinet doors nervously until morning. I was worried that the animal, whatever it was, might sneak out and attack the kids, but nothing happened. When I gathered the strength to open the cupboard, I noticed the stone and three more eggs were missing.

One week later, I heard the noises again, but this time something was different. I could see the earliest signs of morning peeking through the window. The approaching daylight gave me the courage I had been lacking. I slipped out of bed, crept to the cabinet door, and threw it open. In the dim light, I could see the tail end of a huge snake leaving the cabinet through the hole in the wall.

"Ezra, come quickly!" I shouted. "Quickly! Quickly!" I pointed to at least two meters of a brown, scaly, impossibly thick snake that still had not fully escaped through the wall. Ezra raced outside and pounded on Sass's door. Luckily, he was already dressed, and they left his house just in time to see a five-meter serpent slithering its way towards the woods. The snake's head was as big as a dog's, and its glimmering body was as big around as a wheel of cheese.

Sass ran behind his house and woke up a friend. They both returned brandishing long bamboo poles and rapidly took positions on either side of the animal's head. I cowered in the window as they approached the monster with their improvised weapons. When Sass was about five meters from the animal, he grabbed one end of the bamboo pole; swung the other end over his back; and in one arching motion, slammed the pole's tip, with all the force his muscular frame allowed, onto the serpent's head. The snake's head hit the ground momentarily but ricocheted up, lightning fast. It focused its round, predatory eyes on Sass and suddenly lurched toward him at a speed unimaginable for an animal of that size. But Sass's friend was ready and crashed his bamboo pole onto the beast's head from the other direction. The snake, confused and distracted, turned his wrath from one man to the other. But before it could decide to advance in the other direction, Sass knocked it on the head again. Both men took turns whacking the snake, and the bewildered animal could not decide which man to attack. With every strike of the pole, the snake lifted its head more and more slowly from the earth until it lay completely still. After waiting to make sure the serpent was dead, they wrapped the animal around a branch and gave it to some of the villagers. That same day, I received an apology of sorts. Without prompting from me, Sass and Ezra patched the hole in the cabinet.

Devastation

Unfortunately, snakes were not the only things terrorizing us. The Allies unleashed a deadly incendiary bombing campaign on the city of Kobe. One day, from our hiding place in the mountains, we witnessed a thick, black smoke that had formed over the city. The noxious blanket of black gases started at the coastline and stretched miles over our heads. The man-made fog steadily descended, and we waited to die in a cloud of poison gas. There was no escape, and we all readied ourselves for the end. It was only when the black air slowly seeped into our lungs that we discovered it wasn't poisonous. Someone suggested that the smoke was probably to blind the antiaircraft defenses from an approaching swarm of bombers.

The incendiary bombs devastated Kobe, charring buildings and bodies with reckless abandon. Families disintegrated into twisted heaps of ash. Fortunes and edifices, taking lifetimes to build, were destroyed in minutes, while the irrepressible spirits of countless individuals were consumed by hungry fires. We were too far away to witness the tragedy. But we were close enough to choke on the towers of smoke and feel the ashes of our neighbors and neighborhoods flutter past our faces.

The women in the countryside were able to stay away from the burning city. However, the men needed to make their weekly trip to collect the available rations. The city was littered with charred remains and festered with the putrid stench of decomposition. But most husbands, Japanese or foreign, were careful not to divulge the horrors they encountered to their families hiding in the surrounding mountains. The government expeditiously cleaned up the city until the visual scars of half-destroyed, deserted buildings were all that remained of the damage.

The Eggplant

There is an old Middle Eastern superstition which warns that if a woman has a food craving during pregnancy, she must satisfy it at all costs. If it so happens that she ignores this craving and by accident scratches herself, a birthmark in the shape of the food will appear upon her baby's body, gracing the exact spot where she blemished her skin. An unfortunate friend of mine had an intense craving for watermelon before the birth of her first child. Despite all warnings, she ignored her desire and dismissed the old wives' tale. Not long afterwards, she had the misfortune of drawing a drop of blood while scratching her nose. She quickly forgot about the incident but was reminded of her insolent attitude toward such wisdom of the past on the birth of her son. She stared in disbelief at a twelve-centimeter black birthmark staining the otherwise perfect features of her boy's face. The middle of the birthmark was located on his nose, and the shape was, as you have probably guessed, that of an oval watermelon.

I was not one to disregard the wisdom of my ancestors. I woke up one morning with a burning desire for an eggplant. We didn't have any eggplant that day, but Ezra was going into Kobe to buy the ration. I put in my order, but unluckily, he was unable to find any. As the days passed, my cravings for the vegetable grew and grew, until it was the only subject occupying my thoughts. I was afraid to touch my face, knowing that if I left a scratch, a big birthmark was bound to scar my child's face for life.

Finally, the pervasive desire to taste the elusive food became too much. I resolved to find one by any means necessary and encountered the purple jewel in the community's cave refrigerator. I crawled into the cave, saw the object of my desire sitting with a few others on a red cloth, and excitedly scrambled the last meter towards it. In my intense focus to arrive at my goal, I carelessly scraped my outer right thigh, causing it to bleed a little. Ignoring the sting, I grabbed the raw eggplant, wiped the dirt off, and took a tremendous bite, letting the cool juices run down my chin. The taste was absolutely amazing.

Only afterwards did I start to feel guilty about taking our neighbor's eggplant. I took the longest route possible to a house only three doors away from ours and trudged up the muddy road to confess my crime. The Baghdadi Jew who lived there with his family laughed at my confession.

"It is important for you to eat well while you are pregnant," he replied generously. "If I had known you wanted one, I would have given you three. We all have much bigger things to worry about."

That very night, our cave refrigerator collapsed. All the men from the neighborhood came together and dug out every piece of buried food. Nothing could be wasted, but kindness among friends abounded.

In fact, all of us were left with our last few tradable items. When only a few valuables remained, one needed to prioritize what to buy. A German Jewish friend of ours, Mr. Ocheimer, traded his gold wedding ring for some food and six cigarettes. He joked that after he had lost nearly everything, he possessed the best of the world's treasures: a wonderful wife, the new freedom to live life as a bachelor, and the ability to have a good smoke.

An End, A Beginning

In Bunkamura, no one had any idea that the war could end soon. Everyone was primarily focused on their day-to-day survival. We were completely oblivious to even the most profound world events: first, that Germany had surrendered unconditionally to the Allies on May eighth; second, that the atomic bomb had been dropped over Hiroshima on August sixth and Nagasaki on August ninth, killing almost three hundred thousand people; third, that the Philippines and Okinawa had fallen into American hands; fourth, that Russia had declared war on Japan; and fifth, that the Japanese government had been debating an unconditional surrender of its own. The only thing we knew for certain was that Kobe was being bombed regularly, and we assumed that other cities were sharing the same fate.

On the morning of August fifteenth, we received word from a Japanese neighbor that the Emperor was going to address the nation at noon. We still didn't have access to a radio, so in order to hear the message, Ezra and I had to be resourceful. Ezra took me to the barbershop, one of the only places where the owner let foreigners listen to the radio. We entered the crumbling wooden shack and walked across the earthen floor. I sat in an ancient wooden chair in front of the barber. The friendly man began cutting my hair, while Ezra conversed informally with a few locals. When the radio began to squawk, everyone stopped what he or she was doing and stood at attention like marble statues.

After a brief introduction, the Emperor started speaking in a high, strained voice. It was the first time I had ever heard him talk, and I was surprised that I couldn't understand what he was saying. He was speaking in the imperial style. The ultra-grammatically correct Japanese was much different from the language I had learned on the streets of Kobe. I stayed silent until the speech had finished. Two women in the corner of the room started crying, while a few men filed outside solemnly, their heads bowed in sadness.

After the speech, the barber kept listening to the radio and cutting my hair in absolute silence. His movements were slow and deliberate as he listened intently to the news. I summoned the courage to ask him what was happening only at the last possible moment, when he was evening the bangs on my forehead.

"What did the Emperor say?" I asked as politely and respectfully as possible.

"The Emperor was crying into his white gloved hands," the barber explained sullenly. "The people on the palace grounds were looking at him and offering to sacrifice themselves for his glory. He put up his hand to quiet his subjects and commanded: 'We must stop fighting.'" The barber then resumed his silence, and I knew our conversation was over.

"Thank you very much," I replied somberly. "The Emperor is a great man."

Ezra and I were ecstatic with the news, but we couldn't act that way. Every Japanese resident of Bunkamura was crying in despair or sulking in sadness, but we didn't share their point of view. The truth was that no one in our village knew what had really happened internationally during the war. Everyone had been cut off from international communication for close to five years. The only thing we knew for certain was that bombs were falling and there was no food. From all the propaganda fed to our Japanese friends, we believed that Japan was bombing the United States as well. We assumed that the Emperor's announcement, signaling the end of the military campaign, was good for everyone. Japan and the United States would be able to return to positions of prosperity. The war had brought Japan nothing but starvation, poverty, and grief. Now the Emperor was leading the country out of the fray by telling everyone to stop fighting, and that *had* to be good. It *had* to signal an eventual return to good times ahead. Therefore, we were not sad or depressed. We were happy that the war would soon finish. Who won or who lost was a question that had no relevance whatsoever. In this war, everyone I knew had already lost treasures of incalculable value.

The Emperor's statement to stop fighting did not end our troubles with the flick of a divine magic wand. We were at the beginning of a long operation to bring Japan back from the dead. Many farmers, who had produced food for the country, were now buried on mainland China and on numerous islands across Southeast Asia. Most businesses and organizations were torn apart, there was no food available, and the Allies were still bombing Japanese cities.

Ezra's daily priority remained the search for food, and my mind was clouded by another worry. I needed to prepare myself to give birth. Making the long trip into the city was too risky, so I knew I would have to give birth in the countryside, without the luxury of a hospital. Not being able to rely on the help of my friend Dr. Sakamoto worried me, but luckily, it was not difficult to find another doctor.

Dr. Weinhold, a German Jew, lived only a few houses away from us. His tall, thin frame; confident posture; and serious, intelligent face helped me worry less about the fact that he had never delivered a baby before in his life. His experience in the Holocaust had caused him to become devoutly unreligious, but his spiritual irreverence seemed to give him a tremendous confidence and dogged determination to effect change on his own terms. The only other small negative, besides his inexperience with babies, was that we could hardly communicate. Our only language in common was a poorly spoken Japanese. But the truth was, I was very lucky that anyone with a modicum of medical training was available. Ezra asked for his help, and he quickly agreed. His only instructions were to call him once the pain came.

Since the bombing and the birth of Jack, Farida and I had been on much better terms. She helped bring up the children and complete other household chores. She even said some nice things from time to time.

Her support was vital since Ezra was absent when my contractions began. He had left for Kobe the day before in order to buy the rations, but the trains had stopped running. It was too expensive to take a car all the way, so he had walked. He returned a few hours after my contractions started but was too exhausted to accompany us. He announced that he needed to sleep for a few minutes before doing anything. Ezra's journey had lasted over thirty-six hours, so Farida waited until he lay down and then nervously ran to get the doctor.

Dr. Weinhold arrived quickly, checked my progress on the bed, and asked Farida to bring some hot water. When she returned, I was having trouble. The pain was getting too intense. I began hyperventilating, and Farida tried to calm me down.

"Don't breathe too hard," she muttered uneasily. "Everything is fine. Let it come naturally."

The pain burned, stretching my body and soul to the limit. Tears wound over the topography of my face like rivers, and although I couldn't pinpoint what was wrong, I thought death was near. "Call Ezra!" I blurted out in agony. "If I die, I want him near me!"

Farida ran to get Ezra. He stumbled over beside me, still half asleep, as Farida watched the proceedings in breathless suspense.

The head came, then the neck, then the shoulders, and then the stomach. I gave one last push with a barbaric scream, and Dr. Weinhold was holding the baby. He cut the cord, applied a bandage near the baby's belly button, wiped the blood off with a cotton towel, and wrapped the child in Jack's old blanket. I didn't need to ask the sex of the child. The big smile on my mother-in-law's face told me everything I needed to know. When she gently placed him in my arms, I held him close in content exhaustion. I had just enough energy to rewrap the blanket around him. While doing so, I noticed a curious, eggplant shaped birthmark on his right outer thigh.

Friend to Foe, Foe to Friend

I collapsed into an incredibly deep, dreamless sleep for the rest of that September second morning. Ezra and Farida used the time productively to call all of our foreign friends in Bunkamura for a party. Once I woke up, I helped prepare some of our remaining rice for the guests. Ezra was so happy to have another boy, he didn't utter one complaint when I suggested we name him Simantov after my father. I would call him Tony for short.

We didn't have enough food, so I opened almost all of the remaining cans I had stored since the attack on Pearl Harbor. Some of the cans of lentils were bloated, and a foul smelling gas rushed out when I opened them. It was truly painful to throw them away, but they were inedible. I saved a few cans of sardines

for possible darker days ahead. We found a few wooden tables suitable for playing bridge on, a neighbor brought a battered guitar-like musical instrument, and we set out the tuna fish, lentils, and rice as the guests began to arrive.

Fifteen of our friends and family were enjoying themselves when two angry-looking villagers with sharp bamboo poles stopped in front of the house. They were dressed for manual labor with long-sleeved tan work shirts tied at the waist and dirty brown canvas pants. Their stance was aggressive, their jumpy movements predatory. Wide frowns monopolized their faces as they gestured towards us in furious disbelief. One of them sported a conical straw hat that served to shield us partly from his venom-filled eyes, but the other simply wore a *furoshiki* (Japanese towel) wrapped around his head, revealing the deep hate collecting in his. As the sun sank behind the hills their forms blurred, but we could still easily trace their aggressive pacing with worried faces pivoting on our stationary bodies.

I thought maybe they had an argument with one of our guests, but I couldn't imagine what could make them so angry. I also couldn't understand why they were just posturing outside our house. Why didn't they come to the door and tell us what they wanted? As the minutes went by, our celebratory mood turned sour. Instead of enjoying ourselves to celebrate the arrival of the new baby, the entire party was preoccupied with the threatening individuals out front. Suddenly, the confusion concerning their objective became horror, their intentions crystallizing to all in attendance.

Three more villagers with long machetes came to join the two. Next, two more with crude wooden clubs staggered over purposefully. Soon afterwards, a group of over ten rowdy men pushed to the front of the swelling crowd with a myriad of weapons. Their blazing torches bathed the group of uninvited guests in a sinister light.

The leader of the mob stepped forward with his torch held high above his head. His tanned skin glowed, his knife glinted, but his conical straw hat left his face in a shadow of complete darkness. "Come outside!" he shouted, silencing his compatriots.

We stayed quiet, not knowing who should answer, what to do, or what they wanted.

"Come outside one by one!" he roared again menacingly.

Sass and Ezra spoke quickly to each other in hushed tones but didn't decide on any course of action before we heard his threatening voice again.

"Come out or we will come in!" There was a rumbling of approval from the group behind him.

"Oh, my God!" I shrieked, accompanied by other colorful outbursts from our guests. Besides our immediate reflexive actions, we were frozen with indecision.

From our window, I saw two people shove through the group of men to the front. The torch light glinted off the black metal of their holstered guns and illuminated their drab uniforms and hats. They quickly marched the distance between the mob and the house, turning around to face the angry men when they reached the front steps. It was only then that I noticed they were the town policemen.

"What do you want with these foreigners?" one policeman challenged loudly.

The leader of the group took a lunge forward. "We want to punish them for celebrating our surrender! They are feasting and laughing on the day of our defeat!"

The policeman whirled around and pushed open the door to the house. "Is it true!???" he boomed incredulously. "Are you celebrating today???"

Ezra walked up slowly to meet the policeman and bowed low to him. "Please excuse us. We are not celebrating Japan's defeat. We are celebrating the birth of my son. Today, my wife gave birth to a healthy boy."

"Let me see the boy!" he retorted in disbelief.

Without being told, I arose from the floor; walked quickly into the other room; woke Tony up; and carried him, as he cried softly, to the front of the house. The policeman looked at the baby in surprise, lifted the blanket, and inspected the umbilical cord before the anger rapidly ebbed from his cheeks.

He shouted to the gathered crowd, "This is a misunderstanding! They are not celebrating the defeat of Japan. They are celebrating the birth of a baby boy!"

The leader of the mob saw the baby from a few meters away and fired back. "We do not believe this is a coincidence! These foreigners are not celebrating the birth of a son. They are celebrating our surrender in Tokyo Bay!"

Ezra, worry creasing his forehead, spoke to the policeman before he could reply. "None of us have radios or have access to the news. We had no idea that Japan surrendered today. If we had known, we definitely would not have celebrated. Please accept our deepest apologies."

The policeman yelled out to the mob, "They did not know about the surrender! Did any of you tell them it was happening?"

"They are lying!" the leader of the mob accused in a rough sandpaper voice crawling with impatience. "We need to punish them!"

Ezra leaned gently up against the wall, repeatedly bumping his head softly in exasperation, trying to come up with a plan. But the policeman stood up straight, took one step towards the mob, and unleashed a typhoon of words.

"Do you know what is happening now in the country!?" he bellowed. "I will tell you! The Americans are in Yokohama as we speak! They are making their way here! For every foreigner you kill, they will kill one hundred of you! Is that what you want? Do you want your families to be massacred in return for killing a few defenseless women and children?" The policeman's voice ran hoarse. But he stood his ground, statuesque and intimidating. More importantly, his right hand never left the pistol belted to his waist. Under his determined stare, one by one the angry men melted slowly and silently into the warm, humid night.

The two policemen stayed with us until morning. On their departure, we thanked them profusely for saving our lives. Their answer was stone-faced and rigid: "You need to leave Bunkamura. We protected you last night, but those men will return. Go back to the city and find a place to live as soon as possible. You are not safe here!"

For the record, we were not lying. None of the foreigners in our town were aware that Japan was formally surrendering to the Allied forces that day. I believe it was because the event was too depressing and embarrassing to our Japanese neighbors, who were all devoted, patriotic citizens, for them to voluntarily share the news with us. Furthermore, the news of Japan's defeat did not please us. The Japanese had treated us very well during the war, and we did not suffer any more than the citizens who lived beside us. We were not American, Australian, or European, and therefore not part of any winning team. We were stateless expatriates who had adopted Japan as our home. Our only joy lay in the promise of a better future without death and destruction.

Ezra left the next morning to find us a new place to live. He returned a few days afterwards carrying only disappointment and bad news. Most of the Kobe we knew was severely damaged. Many people had died, and numerous buildings had been destroyed. Some people whose residences were bombed lived in caves on the way to Lake Futatabi. The house we had lived in, as well as *Oji-San's* house, had been burnt beyond recognition—likely collateral damage from the bombing of the nearby German Club. Ezra had searched a large portion of the city, but there was no safe area in which to live. The only course of action was to reside longer in Bunkamura. After the celebration of Tony's birth, all of the foreigners were regarded with suspicion. We were very careful not to provoke anyone. We stopped washing our clothes and wore only our dirtiest outfits. We were very careful with our appearance because it was important for our neighbors to understand that we were not proud or better off than they were. We needed them to understand that we were all suffering to a similar degree. As a precautionary measure, much of our remaining food and many of our supplies were given to the police, thanking them for their protection.

Ezra repeated his journey to Kobe once a week in a constant search for a place to live. The government was in the process of cleaning up the city, and eventually he expected a house to become available. One morning, after Ezra departed on his weekly trip, Simone, Frieda, and I were sitting in front of the house. Suddenly, a green military jeep rumbled down the road and screeched to a stop beside us. It was a surreal moment when the four white soldiers in green uniforms disembarked with their large machine guns shining in the early sunlight. Frieda and Simone gasped in fear and ran into the house. The enemy everyone had been warning them about had arrived to destroy, maim, and pillage. I didn't really know what to do. Part of me wanted to run away and thereby demonstrate my loyalty to the Japanese we lived with. The other part wanted to see if the foreigners could help us. While my mind was racing between both opposing decisions, the soldiers closed the gap between us. Realizing I had lost my chance to act, I sat glued to the ground, numb, and in shock, staring only at the steel guns in their hands.

"Hello, do you speak English? Can we help you with anything?" a friendly voice asked.

It took a few seconds for me to decipher the strange accent, but soon my mind kicked into gear. "Yes, I speak English," I answered politely. "I only need some food, please. Do you have any extra that you can spare?" It was only then that I had enough courage to look at their smiling, unshaven, tanned faces and notice their unkempt hair partially corralled under green helmets.

One soldier rummaged around in the back of the jeep and quickly returned with a canvas sack full of rice, canned tuna, sardines, corned beef, and ham. "Here you are!" He grinned.

I quickly took the precious food and, for the first time, smiled back at them. "Thank you very much!" I almost exploded with joy, standing up out of respect. Frieda, Simone, and Jack, who were gathered at the door, sensed my change in tone and ran to join me in front of the soldiers. Another soldier grabbed three chocolate bars out of his pack, extending them towards the children. Frieda and Simone looked up at me for approval and, on my nod, gingerly accepted the present before quickly retreating back into the house. "Thank you!" I repeated enthusiastically. "I wish I could help you in some way."

"Actually, you can," one of the soldiers replied. "In Kobe, the police told us we could find some foreigners and Jews in the villages around here. Do you know where they are?"

"Yes," I answered. "There are over ten families, in addition to ours, living in this village." I then proceeded to point out the other houses they could visit.

"You're Jewish?" he asked in surprise.

"Yes, I am," I assured him.

"Can you prove it to us?" he responded, still a little unsure.

I called Frieda from inside the house, and she approached warily with brown chocolate smushed all over her face. I unclasped her silver necklace which boasted a charm with *chai*, the Hebrew symbol for life, as its centerpiece, and handed it over to the soldier.

The young man nodded and answered emotionally, a tear coming to his eye. "I am Jewish also." He made a notation in his book, went to the truck, and presented me with two bags of flour. "We have just arrived in Japan and may need your help in the future. When we return, can we bring you anything?"

I responded hesitantly, embarrassed to ask for their charity but hungry enough not to care. "All the extra food you can spare would be appreciated... We are all very hungry here."

The soldiers climbed back into their jeep and drove down the road to the next house. No sooner had they disappeared, than the two local policemen showed up. Their mood was extremely serious but courteous. "What did the soldiers ask you?" they demanded.

I did not want any trouble with the policemen who had saved our lives. The honesty and courage they showed us deserved the same in return. I recounted everything discussed with the soldiers and, before they could ask, presented them with all the food. "You can distribute this among the hungry people in town," I offered respectfully. Their entire demeanor transformed instantly, and thin smiles grew on their faces. The men took about sixty percent of the hoard and left the rest for our family. I made sure they took the non-kosher ham, which we would not eat anyway. The soldiers, who had identified themselves as Americans, came back the following week, and we repeated the process. The precious food made us useful to the town and bought us some time with the villagers, who still saw us as the enemy.

Forty painful, danger-filled days after Japan's formal surrender in Tokyo Bay, Ezra found a house. It was unoccupied, and we needed to move immediately while it stayed that way. Ezra, Farida, Frieda, Simone, Jack, Tony, and I began our journey back to Kobe in a rickety truck holding only two mattresses, one worn wooden crib, five live chickens, one bag of rice, one bag of flour, a case of sardines, and two partially empty suitcases. The war was over, but the battle to rebuild our lives had only just begun.

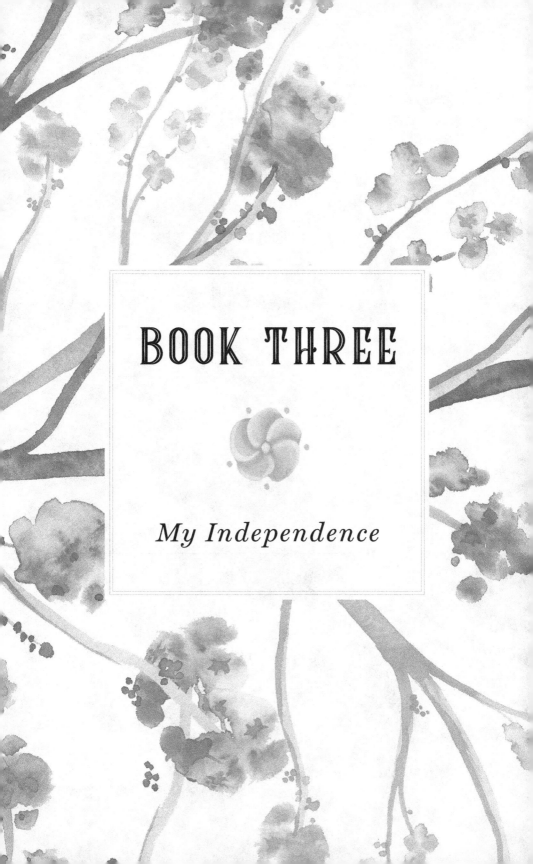

BOOK THREE

My Independence

The Dust Settles

Kobe looked like a sheep slaughtered in haste. The city was generally recognizable, but large quantities of buildings had been reduced to bulky mounds of rubble, as if quickly cut down with a few hacks of a sharp knife. Where one expected to see a head, one saw a head—but with an eye missing and an ear slashed off. The firebombing of the city had left ebony-charred wood, dirty grey ash, and cracked, seared blocks of building material strewn around the neighborhoods like animal entrails after a final, messy struggle. The buildings that had survived intact were occupied by American forces and terrified citizens.

The beginning of the war had brought people from different corners of the world together. In the end, each person who was lucky enough to survive had to decide exactly where he or she belonged. Most of our European Jewish friends who remained in Japan planned to leave the country as soon as possible. The two Ashkenazi girls who had bravely fed the POWs had stayed in Kobe throughout the war. Undeterred by the constant danger of bombs, fire, and bullets, they had continuously supplied the POWs with extra food. After Japan's surrender, two of the rescued soldiers married them and took them back to America.

Charlie Alfia, our friend who had been arrested with black market liquor, had deteriorated in a jail cell for months after his incarceration. His alcoholism, coupled with the lack of food in prison, caused his health to decline rapidly. When the bombings of Kobe were approaching, the Japanese guards recognized that he could no longer survive in jail. Because his offence was a minor one, the prison guards kindly set him free. He was able to move to the countryside and survive the bombings. Charlie, like many others who had spent time in Japan before the war, had no intention of leaving the country. He regained his health and began reconstructing his life.

After the war, the remaining community used their contacts to find the spy responsible for both our friend's incarceration and the detailed investigations into other families in the neighborhood. We all understood that the only reason Ezra and many of our friends had been fortunate enough to avoid joining Charlie in prison was Osakabe-San's help. We wanted to know who had callously endangered all of our lives. The culprit was discovered to be a half-Caucasian, half-Japanese man. His dual cultures gave him access to everyone and had allowed him to extract information about the community's food purchases for the police. Once the spy knew his identity had been uncovered, he ended his own life.

The Jews who remained in Kobe were very much involved in Japan's transition from war to peace. David (Dahoodeh) Sassoon and others spoke on behalf of many local Japanese, petitioning the U.S. government for food and supplies. They worked with the American occupying forces and were able to broker many agreements between the two sides.

Ezra and I had no intention of leaving the country, so we had to look for opportunities in the sadness and desolation of postwar Kobe. Finding solutions was difficult since our old life was virtually nonexistent. We were unable to renew contact with many old friends and neighbors. We feared that they had been victims of the bombings but hoped that they had decided to rebuild their lives elsewhere.

The Japanese Police
or the American Soldiers

Although we had survived in the countryside for forty frightening days after nearly getting butchered, we lived in continuous fear that the men would return. Our new home was therefore an improvement on the old. However, the reason it was available was not due to its exclusivity but, rather, that no one else was brave enough to live in it. We claimed the three rooms on the second floor, while some foreign friends of ours claimed the first floor. The fragile stairs in between our families creaked and groaned under the weight of even little Frieda's feather-light frame. Whenever the rains came, small holes in the roof gave birth to mini cascading waterfalls, terminating triumphantly on our heads or soaking our mattresses. The lack of gas, electricity, and a stove required us to cook outside and warm our bodies near the fireplace.

A well-groomed, middle-aged Japanese man with a dirty, tattered kimono had watched with interest as we moved into the dilapidated house. He had appeared surprised at our attempt to live there but had not broken his silence. It wasn't until three weeks later, when he returned and rapped loudly on the front door, that his motive was finally revealed. Without wasting time on pleasantries, when Ezra answered the door he bellowed: "This is my house! You and your family must leave immediately!"

Ezra was temporarily taken by surprise, and studied the man for a second before shouting: "What are you talking about!? If this is your house, why aren't you living in it?"

"This is my rental property, I need you to leave now! You are preventing me from making a living!"

"Why didn't you say anything when we first moved in!?"

The man relaxed somewhat, lowering his voice. Unlike Ezra, he was not ready to get into a fistfight. "I thought—I thought you would leave on your own. The house is barely standing up. It is very dangerous!"

My husband threw up his hands in exasperation. "We are not leaving. There is nowhere else for us to go!"

"Then, I will have no choice but to involve the Kobe police."

Five American soldiers suddenly poured out of the house next door to see what all the commotion was about. The shortest, toughest-looking of the five decided to make the disagreement his problem too. He positioned himself between Ezra and the man, waving one hand wildly and clutching his machine gun in the other. "What seems to be the problem here?" he demanded in English.

Ezra acted with deference towards the soldier and slowly described the circumstances of the dispute in English. The property owner became pale, knowing he had lost the argument. He did not understand the language enough to argue his point, and he was smart enough to know that the white soldier was not going to side with him.

Before the soldier came to his verdict, the property owner intelligently interjected, speaking to Ezra calmly in Japanese. "We are going about this the wrong way. Let us discuss this issue inside—just you and me. I am sure we can come to a fast agreement."

Ezra nodded and profusely thanked the American.

Ezra and the landlord walked upstairs and I served them tea. They quickly agreed on a fair rent for the property, smiled, and bowed. Involving the Japanese police and the American military in our day-to-day arguments would not bring about a favorable verdict for anyone. We were all tired of fighting and wanted to focus our attention on the difficult choices ahead.

The PX Business

Ezra and I knew we were lucky to be alive, but we also knew there was a pressing need to find ways to support our hungry family. Ezra immediately realized that restarting his business would require months of hard work in a very risky and uncertain international environment. More critically, it would take a minimum of half a year to receive the first payments—if he were fortunate enough to succeed. Since we simply didn't have the money to wait that long, we decided to divide our efforts. While Ezra worked to restart the export business, I would use our limited resources to find other ways to feed our children. My new responsibility electrified my spirit, as I recalled the feelings of pride that had swelled inside me from my days working at the *Parc de Réparacion*. I thought about Ani, Yesenia, the gypsy with her chicken bones, and all the other women I had known who had helped provide for their families, even though they had very little of anything to their names. And I knew if they could employ themselves effectively in Aleppo, where the opportunities for working women were few and far between, I could employ myself effectively in Japan—a country where such things were not common but not discouraged either. As I thought for a few hours about the personal attributes I could use to my advantage, I realized something of profound importance. My biggest liability before and during the war was my greatest asset after its conclusion—the color of my skin.

At first, my skin color attracted the wrong kind of attention. When my children and I took our daily walk through Kobe's rubble-strewn streets, the American soldiers would snap pictures of us in our torn clothes. I didn't understand why they were so interested in my family until the day I approached one of them. The soldier answered that they were very surprised to see white refugees in Japan. They were taking pictures to show their relatives and superiors the poverty that existed within the country. I was very embarrassed. I didn't want to be on the cover of a magazine with a sad, dirty white face to make a political statement. I was just a poor woman who wanted to take her children for a walk.

However, the entire situation got me thinking. It appeared that they were more concerned about us because of the color of our skin. Previously, they hadn't realized that people who looked somewhat like them were also suffering in Japan. I understood that I could use the attributes I shared with the occupying soldiers to better our lives as well as the lives of the people around us. As with the political situation at the *Parc de Réparacion* in Aleppo, I understood that my course of action would raise some difficult moral questions. However, I rationalized that the benefits I could provide my family and the surrounding Japanese population would outweigh any inconvenience to the occupying American forces.

The Americans quickly set up a PX and an OSS in Osaka to provide goods for the troops stationed within the country. A few U.S. dollars from every paycheck gave them access to foreign food, clothing, alcohol, books, and cigarettes. Due to the death of many Japanese farmers and the suspension of many farming activities during the war, the local food supply remained extremely limited. Therefore, everyone living in the country was still on a very tight ration. The PX was a guarded oasis, and I needed to find the key to get inside.

I took the short train ride to Osaka and quickly approached the PX. In the afternoon sun, a tall, burly soldier leaned against the wall to the right of the front door. He quickly studied everyone entering and exiting with a disinterested glance. I figured that my white skin would help me blend in with the foreign workers and nurses. My heart pounded like a *taiko* (a Japanese drum) as I walked right up to the entrance, held my breath, looked the soldier straight in the eye, nodded hello, and entered the store without saying a word. Three seconds after crossing the threshold, I exhaled the nervous energy out of my body and looked at the bounty surrounding me. I had not seen luxuries like these in over seven years: different kinds of foreign chocolate, whisky, soft drinks, coffee, bread, baking necessities, eggs, meat, shoes, clothing, magazines, and cartons of cigarettes. When I was making my final selection, my heart sank. On closer inspection of the price tag, I saw that all items were in U.S. dollars. I only had yen. It was not an option to ask the cashier to accept payment in Japanese currency, since I knew he would throw me out of the store. I would have to find a way to get U.S. dollars.

I walked sullenly through the streets of Osaka, unwilling to go home and depressed at my failure to buy food for the family. I only knew that I couldn't give up. I understood that this was a unique opportunity and that everyone in my family was depending on me. An hour had passed when I noticed a few Japanese street vendors conducting a brisk business on the street corners by selling artwork and fruit to the American soldiers. The soldiers were buying plenty and were paying in yen instead of dollars. My steps and heartbeat unconsciously quickened, as my brain churned out a beautifully simplistic solution to my problem.

I stopped two handsome soldiers walking towards me. "Pardon me," I said, interrupting their conversation with the nicest smile and tone of voice I could muster.

"Yes, ma'am, can we help you?" they answered.

"I was wondering if you were in need of some yen to buy Japanese products?" I asked hopefully.

"We do need some yen. But we usually get it from the bank," one answered politely.

Instead of begging for their help, I appealed to their intelligence. "Maybe we can help each other," I said. "I need some U.S. dollars. How much does the bank give you for a dollar?"

"About forty-eight yen," one replied.

"I will give you fifty-five yen per U.S. dollar. Can we make a trade?"

The men smiled and nodded their heads, and I changed all the yen I had in my pocket to American currency. I thanked the men many times and walked as fast as I could back to the PX. I nodded at the guard again and walked quickly into the store. I gathered all the wonderful food I could carry and waited until the store emptied out. Two men were at the cash register, a supervisor and a cashier. I waited patiently for the supervisor to go into the back room. I then nervously laid out all my purchases, while the blood started racing frenetically around my body. I made small talk with the cashier, asking him where he was from and how he liked Japan, but was too nervous to comprehend the answers. He gave me the total and asked for my identification card. I put the money for my purchases on the counter and pressed two bills into his hand. I peered into his eyes as earnestly as I could and tried to get my message across. "I seem to have forgotten my identification at home. Can you help me this time?"

He winced, turning red for a split second, but recovered quickly, flashed a smile, and stuffed the bills in his pocket. "No problem, ma'am. Please remember it next time you come."

My shoes barely touched the ground on my way home, and big smiles greeted me on my return. I had more food in my arms than our family had seen in years. Before we tore into it, I related how it had come into my possession. Ezra, Farida, and I agreed that there was a rare opportunity to do a good deed and make some money in this line of work. We kept half of the food and sold the other half to our neighbors at a small profit. We were ecstatic because we made back a good portion of the money we had spent and finally had some good food to eat. Our neighbors were happy because, even at a markup over the PX price, the food was not only less than half the price of the inferior black market goods, but also cheaper than the available rationed goods. I knew I needed to find a way to do this business on a larger scale.

It was not wise to go back to the PX the next day, since

I wanted to maintain a low profile. The following morning, I walked around Kobe exchanging yen for U.S. dollars with every soldier who agreed. Some I paid fifty-five yen to the dollar; some I paid sixty yen to the dollar. It didn't really matter. I needed the dollars to buy goods at the PX. If the dollars were more expensive, I would just have to increase the price of the food, which I would resell in yen. I gathered ten times more money than I had the first day, hired a car, and drove to Osaka. I waited until the store was empty, nodded to the soldier at the entrance, gathered my purchases, waited until my contact was alone, and took my food to the counter.

He eyed the gigantic pile of goods before him. "Why do you need so much sugar and flour?" he questioned suspiciously.

I smiled, opened my handbag, and showed the cashier pictures of our family and friends, including as many children's pictures as possible. I explained that we had all been without good food for over seven years and that the children wanted me to bake cookies, cakes, and other sweets for them. I took out four bills and pressed them, as before, into his left hand.

"This is for my identification today," I said seriously, pleading with my eyes. "Nothing will go to waste. I promise."

He smiled quickly and looked over his right shoulder nervously. He totaled the food, took the money, and helped me carry the merchandise to the car. He wanted to be polite, but especially wanted me out of the store before his supervisor returned.

Farida and Ezra were very pleasantly surprised when I returned with a carload of food. We kept one fifth of the treasure. One fifth was given free of charge to the Japanese police, who had helped us during the war, and the rest was sold immediately for a profit. Before I realized that I could not possibly satisfy our neighborhoods' immediate demand for extra food with only one PX contact, a friend walked into our lives who would help us achieve loftier goals.

Alison was one of the American WAC nurses who lived sprinkled in among the soldiers occupying the surrounding area. She often came to the house for food, company, and especially, to play with the children. Although she had long, pretty red hair, Alison did not have many suitors due to some thick glasses, false teeth, and a little extra weight partially masking her beautifully kind soul. Therefore, she didn't miss too many social occasions and liked to be around the bachelors who often came by our house. We became good friends, and I tried to set her up with a Russian friend of mine. Since Alison was usually present during our get-togethers, she saw firsthand the food shortages that were facing many of our friends and neighbors. When she asked if she could help us, I quickly agreed.

Instead of going to the PX only twice a week, we began visiting four times. We made sure to alternate our days in order to prevent the shopkeepers from growing suspicious. Our food purchases more than doubled because Alison had an identification card, giving her legal access to all the goodies. Occasionally, I would be denied by a new guard at the door or an employee I didn't know.

Many Japanese from the community would arrive at our house daily to buy the extra food we had procured. As they became more comfortable with us, our list of groceries grew. Soon, we also expanded our line into the medical field. Some Japanese doctors were unable to get the required supplies to treat their patients so they asked us to help. We solved this problem since Alison was able to buy a variety of medicines, bandages, and other items to fill their needs. After all the help I had received from them, I was happy to finally be able to help in return—free of charge.

Running the PX business was close to a full-time job. In the mornings, I found people to change the yen my customers paid me for groceries into U.S. dollars I could use at the PX. I would also need to meet with the customers, organize their orders, and make sure we found what they needed. In the afternoons, I would either go to the PX or wait for Alison to return with her goods. I paid Alison twenty percent of her purchases so that she would make money as well. But we never lost sight of the fact that we needed to provide a service to the Japanese postwar population. Our prices were kept much lower than the black marketers', the police were given free merchandise, and we sold all medicine at the price it cost us to obtain it. When the military opened another PX in Kobe, we were able to double our business and lower our prices. Alison and I could each visit the Osaka PX one day and the Kobe PX the next. The different people at each store had no communication with one another, so we increased the frequency of our visits but still maintained our relative anonymity. Our main difficulty was changing enough yen into dollars for our shopping trips.

My solution to overcoming this obstacle added an entirely new dimension to my business. The rich people in postwar Kobe were the American soldiers and not the Japanese. I needed to find something to sell the people who had the money. Luckily, the answer was already there. I noticed that the soldiers were constantly buying Japanese art, samurai swords, locally made guns, kimonos, and many other items to take home as souvenirs. I started making trips to different cities and bought many beautiful Japanese items for the American soldiers. Instead of only changing their money, which allowed them to go purchase Japanese goods, I would start selling them the Japanese goods directly. This business also succeeded very quickly. I was a pretty white woman who spoke English, and so, naturally, the young soldiers wanted to buy from me. Secondly, my prices were very good, since I needed a lot of business to obtain enough U.S. dollars for the PX. Soon, half of the yen I obtained from my Japanese customers went directly to buying souvenirs, which, when sold to the Americans, would convert my yen automatically into dollars. This helped me sustain my food business.

The proceeds from the PX business allowed us to start inviting our friends for meals once again and allowed us to resume serving big Sabbath lunches. A new temporary Synagogue replaced the old one which had been bombed and brought in many Jewish guests from the American military. On most Sabbaths, a few would join us for lunch. One Sabbath, I was stunned to see the supervisor of the Osaka PX in the synagogue. My contact in Osaka was always very careful not to arouse the suspicion of this man, as it would mean dismissal from his post. I was nervous, but the worst thing I could do was to act that way. When we were introduced, he gave me a covert smile of recognition but said nothing. I smiled back at him as nicely as I could. After the prayers, many of the servicemen were departing. I meandered over to him and invited him for lunch. I was thrilled when he accepted. I seated him at the head of the table and entertained him well into the afternoon with the rest of our regular guests. I made sure he received the choicest pieces of lamb, the most rice, the first choice of cookies after dinner, and a few glasses of whisky. After nightfall, Ezra and I accompanied him to the train station. When we said goodbye, he thanked us multiple times for the lunch, and we assured him that he had an open weekly invitation. As we were turning around to go home, he spoke up.

"Oh, yeah! One more thing!" he exclaimed, grinning widely. "If anyone ever asks you too many questions in Osaka, just tell them I sent you!"

"Thank you very much!" I laughed, smiling even more broadly than he was. "I really appreciate all of your help!"

With a tip of his hat, he jumped on the train and left.

Exporting Again

The PX more than covered our food requirement, so Ezra had the luxury of focusing on his business. He spent a few weeks renewing his contacts by traveling through the countryside, visiting the suppliers that had survived and offering his condolences to the families of those who were no longer with us. I then wrote letters to his old customers, informing them he was alive, well, and ready to do some more work for them.

One morning, out of the blue, Joe Dahab showed up at our front door. Overjoyed to see our favorite American customer, we reviewed the last few lean years for hours over a hearty meal. Ezra and Joe danced around the big question with clever conversation until all other subjects were exhausted.

Then Joe began. "Ezra tell me," he said with heightened interest, "what can we do about the big shipment from 1941 that got stuck in the port?"

"Honestly, Joe," Ezra replied gravely, breaking eye contact. "The shipment was in the port before the war, but now it is probably only ashes and dust."

"Are you sure it was destroyed?" he pressed, leaning forward in his seat.

"No, I am not," Ezra replied, shrugging his shoulders. "I have no idea one way or the other. I tried to get some information on our old shipments, but the Americans are controlling the port now. I can't even get in there."

Joe answered with excitement, "It would be excellent to get that shipment out! My customers are screaming for goods now! There is nothing in the market anymore! Can I try to locate it?"

Ezra responded with cautious optimism, "With your American passport, Joe, you might be able to succeed where I failed. I can take you there tomorrow."

The next morning, Joe was admitted into the customs area with his American passport. Although Ezra could not enter with him, he handed over the shipping documents to help in the search. Joe returned to the house later that evening in a jubilant mood. The goods were not only there, but he had also arranged to load them on the next shipping vessel bound for the United States. It was a brilliant business maneuver on his part. He was going to possess the first shipment of

Japanese textiles imported to the U.S. in over three years. He would be able to charge a premium price, and the customers would only be able to buy from him. The next few days, he worked with Ezra and placed a huge new order. Ezra would need to ship immediately, if not sooner, to capitalize on the lack of Japanese textiles in the U.S. market.

A few weeks later, Ezra was advised that his shipment for Moshe Hanan had miraculously survived Kobe's bombing as well. We completed the paperwork and were overjoyed when the shipment left the port. A few days afterwards, Hanan was given some bad news. Some of the items on their way to the United States would be subject to an additional import tax taking effect in fifteen days.[55] He would have to spend extra money to take possession of the goods. This would either increase his price to the customer or lower his profit. We thought there was no way around this, but Hanan was a very intelligent man. The next day he sent us instructions to have the goods offloaded in Hawaii, instead of San Francisco. He cleared customs in Hawaii at the old tax rate, and then the goods resumed their journey to New York. When the cheaper goods sold rapidly, we were rewarded with a large reorder.

Soon after the American occupation of Japan, General MacArthur installed his headquarters in Tokyo, and his office had to stamp the export documents for each shipment of merchandise. To receive these invaluable stamps, Ezra had to prove that he hadn't fought against American forces during the war. Even though most foreigners were beyond suspicion, it was difficult to cut through all the new bureaucratic red tape. Ezra began working seven days a week. Saturday he bought from the makers in Osaka; Sunday he conducted business in Kobe; Monday he bought from the makers in Yokohama; and the rest of the week, he navigated the bureaucracy in Tokyo.

---

55 This is a true story, but may have taken place at a later date.

Luckily, a Muslim friend of Ezra's named Yusuf met an American woman who was directly responsible for stamping General MacArthur's export documents and convinced her to help. She thought Yusuf was good-looking and tried often to close the distance between them, but Yusuf made certain he was never left alone with her. At the same time, she controlled our ability to export, so he never went so far as to reject her outright. She stayed with us whenever she traveled to Kobe, and Yusuf visited often—always accompanied by plenty of friends. We were ecstatic to be back in business and had plenty of work to do.

Renewing Contact

Although our minds were occupied with all the opportunities in postwar Japan, it was impossible to keep concerns for my Aleppo family out of my thoughts. From 1940 to 1945, every letter that I had sent had been returned with a stamp reading, "Address Unknown." During the war, I had not known if my family members were alive or dead, but we had been too worried about our own survival to spend excessive time thinking about complex situations overseas, situations that we could not have changed nor relieved. In 1946, we were finally able to locate my mother in Beirut through the Red Cross. She communicated that every one of my siblings had survived the conflicts. However, unbeknownst to us, Rafoul soon found himself in a precarious situation.

Relations between Syrian Arabs and Jews were rapidly deteriorating. A few well-known factors that contributed to these tensions included the constant flow of anti-Jewish propaganda in the Syrian press; the widespread dismissal of Jewish employees from Syrian businesses and government institutions;[56] the withholding of Jewish business licenses[57] which bankrupted importers, exporters, and others; and the restriction of Jewish travel via the denial of passports and exit permits.[58] The most significant event for my family took place in the days following the 1947 United Nations resolution, which called for the partition of Palestine into independent Arab and Jewish states and the withdrawal of British armed forces, when anti-Jewish riots severely damaged The Great Aleppo Synagogue and destroyed much of our old neighborhood. Despite the fact that Jewish families had proudly called Syria home for over 1000 years, most understood it was time to leave. Everyone understood that there was a coordinated effort to separate Jews from their assets, and some also feared a massacre.

From the early forties, Rafoul experienced some of the consequences of this tension at his record store. Local patrons would come in, pick four records, and only pay for one. If he complained, the robbers would beat him severely. He could not go to the police, since they would never take his word over the word of someone from their same background. Many of the Arabs he came in contact with suspected it would only be a short time before the Jews were kicked out of Syria and stripped of all property. As a result, there was very little demand for Jewish land or products.

During these difficult years, a Jewish man named Albert Elia started bravely smuggling Jewish residents out of the country. Rafoul and others soon joined him. Rafoul often traveled to the Port of Beirut from Damascus, which was only a short trip by car, to buy the records he needed to stock the music store. After a while, instead of merely buying records

---

56 Schechtman, Joseph B., *On Wings of Eagles: The Plight, Exodus, and Homecoming of Oriental Jewry*. New York, New York: Thomas Yoseloff, Publisher, 1961, p. 161

57 Schechtman, p. 161

58 Schechtman, p. 155

in Beirut, Rafoul used the store as a front to smuggle Jews out of Syria.

The departing individuals would be instructed to follow their normal routines on the date of travel. This prevented any suspicious neighbors from advising the local authorities of their activities. A common trick was to do the wash and leave it to dry on the clotheslines. They would then take the train to Damascus and cross the Lebanese border in a car. Border crossing was accomplished by bribing certain police, sympathetic either to the Jews' cause or to their own wallets. Some would avoid the border checkpoints and travel cross-country via smugglers' routes by a combination of car, truck, and foot. Rafoul's work was very dangerous. If he was caught by the Syrian police, he risked getting killed or spending his life in prison. All introductions were made using codes that changed often. The code phrase at one time was, "Your sister Lucie sends her regards from Japan."

It is important to note that some Arabs would help the persecuted Jews. They would deliver information crucial to the success of particular undertakings, such as which Jewish individuals were to be targeted in the future. Sometimes, the escaping Jews had to flee at a moment's notice. They abandoned all their material possessions, wore modest Muslim women's clothing (covering up virtually all their skin), and took a car directly to the border.

Eventually, the local Syrian police intensified their search for anyone helping the Jews depart. One day, Albert Elia disappeared and was never heard from again. Most assume he was murdered. When the pressure became too great, it was time for Rafoul to escape. He was notified by one of his contacts to leave the country immediately. He dressed in a modest suit, pocketed all the money he had, hid five large gold coins in the hollow heel of his shoe, and left Aleppo forever.

Meanwhile, my brother David had endured difficult conditions in Shanghai during World War II. In 1946, he moved to Hong Kong and began importing general merchandise from the United States. David was informed of the swiftly intensifying Arab-Jewish conflict in Syria and extended an invitation for Rafoul to join him in Hong Kong. However, in the years immediately following the creation of the State of Israel in 1948, it was not very safe for a Jew to travel through the Middle East. Rafoul managed to enter Lebanon and spent almost all of his savings on a Pan Am ticket traveling eastbound to Hong Kong.

Before buying the ticket, checking into the flight, and boarding the airplane in Beirut, Rafoul asked the airline representatives each time if the plane made any unscheduled stops in the Middle East. Everyone informed him with a professional smile that he was flying with an American airline and needn't worry about anything else but enjoying the trip. Rafoul scarcely had time to acclimate himself to his first flight when the plane started to descend. The Captain announced on the loudspeaker that they would be refueling the plane in Baghdad, Iraq.

No sooner had the passengers disembarked when the Iraqi police started checking everyone's papers, one by one. Rafoul did not pass inspection and was promptly led away from the group of travelers—but not without the Captain's objection. The Captain insisted, "We are not moving our plane until you return my passenger! He is my responsibility!"

However, the police answered soberly, "You will leave as soon as you finish refueling, but he is staying with us." Rafoul was put in the back of a truck and then sequestered in a hotel room.

For two and a half weeks, Rafoul was interrogated by a tall, strong man named Hakim with dark skin, darker eyes, and even darker hair. At first, his questions were harsh and pointed: "What are you doing here in Iraq?" "Who are you spying for?" "Why did your government send you?"

Later, Hakim and Rafoul spoke in Arabic daily about their

families, hobbies, and personal histories. As their friendship slowly grew, they discussed everything except politics. After a few weeks' time, Rafoul confided in his captor. "Hakim," he said emotionally, "I have really enjoyed your companionship, and I want to thank you for your kindness. I understand that my fate has been written."

"Why are you being negative?" Hakim replied.

"You know that I have spent all my life in Syria and Lebanon, and I know how interrogations in these countries work. I understand that I don't have long to live, and I want to give you a gift as a token of my gratitude." Rafoul removed the gold coins from their hiding place and presented them to his companion.

Hakim thanked him, nodded, and when he exited the room a few minutes later, lent some words of encouragement. "Have some faith my friend," he advised calmly.

The next day, Hakim did not come to visit. Nor did he come the day after. The third morning, Hakim and two other men burst into Rafoul's hotel room. One man ordered Rafoul to get dressed, while another guarded the door. Hakim, stone-faced and rigid, presented Rafoul with some papers and a sealed envelope. He announced sternly, "Here are your papers and your airplane ticket. You may go."

It wasn't until Rafoul was safely flying over Iraq that he dared open the envelope. 5 large gold coins slid out into his hand.

A Religious Obligation

We couldn't circumcise Jack and Tony the required eight days after birth, since there wasn't a *mohel*, a rabbi able to perform circumcisions, residing in Japan. An earlier situation alerted us to the risks involved with such a dangerous procedure.

One of my good friends in the community, after repeated miscarriages, had finally given birth to the baby she had wished for. But it had not been easy. Due to complications, Dr. Sakamoto had ordered her to spend the final six months of pregnancy in bed. Finally, her persistence and patience were rewarded with a son. She was overjoyed and scheduled the circumcision, taking advantage of a foreign doctor's presence in town. The doctor performed the procedure, wrapped the baby's penis, and left Japan that evening. To the mother's horror, the bandages kept becoming saturated with rich, red blood hours after the surgery. I arrived at the party that evening to congratulate our friends but was surprised to find the baby extremely pale. When I noticed the blood I called Dr. Sakamoto, who came right away.

Dr. Sakamoto was furious. He looked at all of us like we were crazy for cutting a baby's foreskin so soon after birth. With dexterity, he cleaned the wound and stitched up the botched operation. He grabbed his leather case and took four steps toward the door—but he didn't get to take a fifth. I grabbed the back of his jacket and hooked my left arm around his with all the force I could muster. I collapsed onto my knees but did not relinquish my grip on him.

"You can't leave!" I wailed bitterly, my eyes becoming moist with tears. "You told her to stay in bed for six months, and she did exactly as you asked! This is her only chance to have a child, and her son may die before the night is out!"

Dr. Sakamoto looked reflectively at the baby, and at the lunatic parked at his feet. He slowly turned around towards the patient, shook his head in disbelief—at no one in particular but everyone in general—brushed my hand away gently, and walked slowly back into the fray. He hovered over the baby the entire night, changing the bandages hourly, monitoring the bleeding, and applying medicine to the wound. By morning, we noticed a thin smile burning through the gloom, signaling the baby would survive.

After witnessing this, we waited until Jack was four and Tony was two for their circumcisions.

Artillery Shells, a Cat, and a Goat

The injection of work into our lives was like eating a chocolate bar after years of starvation. Ezra and I were happily, energetically occupied for large parts of the day. The only downside was being apart from our children, but the childrearing and cooking were managed under the discerning eye of my mother-in-law. Mornings, evenings, and Saturdays, all of our free time was spent with our customers, guests, and children. Our children were the most valued of the bunch, so even when important business associates were staying for dinner, the entire family joined them at the table.

During the last two years of the war, most of my aspirations for the future of our family had been cast aside and replaced with the need to fulfill our immediate bodily needs. The education of our children, the creation of a permanent home, the performance of our religious obligations, the building of our family's wealth, and communication with our relatives across the globe had all been aspects of life we hadn't had the luxury to pursue. With the arrival of peace, it became clear that we would have to re-create our identities. Our first priority, aside from making enough money for food and shelter, was to educate our children.

Soon after the war, we were able to enroll our daughters in St. Mary's Catholic School. Ezra and I wanted to give our children an international education and teach them English. These skills would allow them to communicate with the occupying American forces and teach them another language besides the Arabic, French, and Japanese we spoke at home. We also realized that the United States was a likely destination for them later in life, since Jews seemed to be treated well there, many of our customers lived there, and it was a prosperous country. We wanted to prepare our children for change, understanding that Muslim-Jewish relationships were beginning to sour in Aleppo and understanding that they needed the ability to adapt to a rapidly changing world.

The only problem with St. Mary's was the religious aspect. Our family was not religious by Aleppo standards, but we cherished our Jewish identity. Every morning at school, Frieda had to pray Hail Marys and Our Fathers and take Bible classes. When she came home, her grandmother would hear all about her daily lessons. Frieda did not like going to church and tried to abstain, but in the school's strict atmosphere, this was not permitted. Over and over again, she was sent to the intimidating Mother Superior. She would arrive home with her curls in a mess, her eyes tainted red from crying, and the tip of her cute nose pink from friction with a handkerchief.

My mother-in-law tried to enhance Frieda's spiritual identity and make sure she remained grounded in her faith by discussing Jewish religious concepts at home. One such discussion plunged my daughter into a boiling soup of trouble.

The Mother Superior herself was giving a lecture in class and, at the conclusion, asked if there were any questions. Frieda uncharacteristically raised her hand and the Mother Superior, pleasantly surprised, called on her to speak.

Frieda stood up in front of the class, with concentration branded on every one of her soft features, and blurted out energetically, "My grandmother told me it is impossible to have a baby without two parents! Who was Jesus's father?"

The Mother Superior's face looked as if she had swallowed a soup spoon full of *wasabe*.

She grasped Frieda firmly around the back of the neck and, without letting go, accompanied her all the way home.

When my mother-in-law answered the door, the red-faced Mother Superior shouted angrily, "Frieda is no longer welcome at St. Mary's!" She then abruptly turned around and left.

I received the news that night and was extremely worried. We had nowhere else to enroll our daughter, as she could not simply start a Japanese school in the middle of the year. Our only option was to go back to St. Mary's and reason with the administration. It was inappropriate to get mad at Frieda or angry at the school; the simple fact was that Frieda was caught in the middle of a religious discussion over fifteen hundred years old. Ezra and I tried the only thing that we thought could make a difference: presenting the school with a religiously sensitive gift.

Ezra bought one hundred yards of the best quality black cotton fabric and fifty yards of white cotton fabric from Ishii-San. I went with the truck and delivered the present to the Mother Superior directly. I was as apologetic as I could be. "Please, Mother Superior," I pleaded, "let my daughter back in school! It is the middle of the year, and she has nowhere else to go! At the end of the term, we can find a new place for her, but now it is impossible. Please accept some fabric that the sisters can use to make habits with. We are deeply sorry. It is not our intention to undermine your religious teaching. We only want what is best for our daughter."

The Mother Superior had not cooled off from her previous encounter with Frieda but made a kind concession. "I will give her one final chance," she stated with grave seriousness, punctuating the number "one" by extending her powerful index finger into the air. "One more statement or 'misunderstanding' of any kind, and she will never again set foot on school grounds. Please comprehend that I have nothing against you, your religion, or your daughter personally. Our goal here is to teach the Catholic religion, and we can't have anyone in our school that undermines our instruction."

With constant reminders from every member of the family, Frieda made it through the rest of the school year without further incident.

Frieda's rebellions assured her of more adult attention than genial Simone. I was often Simone's only protection from Frieda's hair pulling and finger squishing and inevitably she would get hurt. Soothing Simone's nerves after Frieda's spankings was particularly easy. During the bombing of Kobe, a piece of orange or egg would keep her perfectly still and quiet. I didn't deviate from what had worked. An egg brought a smile to her face after a minor injury. A more intense pain would require two or three eggs to calm her down. As she got older, her rivalry with Frieda intensified so much that I always took her with me when I left the house. It was lucky that both were never mistakenly left alone in a room together because one surely would have been dead within the hour.

The constant fighting with her sister didn't seem to affect her personality negatively. Instead of reacting violently, she helped nurture Jack's and Tony's growth every available moment of the day. When they were babies and toddlers, she carried them until they stopped crying, took them on walks in the pram, and helped feed them whenever they were hungry.

Jack, the first boy after two girls, was brought up like a prince. I took care of him like a flower in a hothouse, heating his room night and day in winter to assure his warmth and comfort. It got to the point where my overbearing concern nearly killed him. The minute I took him into the fresh, frigid air, he came down with a cold, fever, and tonsillitis. The doctor immediately operated on him to remove the infection, and afterwards he never gave me any more trouble. He grew to be a strong boy, playing sports, eating like a wolf (or his mother), and enjoying the attention everyone lavished upon him.

When he was a little boy, Jack's favorite activity was sifting through the rubble of Kobe's bombed buildings. With the other surviving children, Jack looked for toys and played hide-and-seek in the collapsed structures. When people started rebuilding, the children collected undamaged bricks for the neighbors, which were reused in new construction. Another of his postwar pastimes was to look for unused bullets or small artillery shells in Kobe's surrounding mountains. Unbeknownst to me, he and a friend collected some old gunpowder in empty soda cans. This hobby was quickly abandoned when a soda can suddenly exploded in his friend's hand, severing a few fingers.

One of Jack's favorite events was Goodwill Day. When an American aircraft carrier or British battleship arrived in Kobe Harbor, the foreign children were given a free tour of the vessel. My son was awestruck by the ship's massive size, the sleek airplanes on board, and the gigantic guns—but his favorite part of the tour was being served ice cream in the vessel's mess hall.

Both our foreign neighbors and Japanese friends regularly complimented Jack's thick blond hair, sparkling blue eyes, and the few extra kilos of muscle distributed liberally over his athletic frame. But his toothy smile—more welcoming than a warm fireplace, a glass of wine, and a milk chocolate bar presented together—compelled every mother in the neighborhood to save a daughter for him.

The first of his many match proposals came at age five. We spent the summers in Shioya, a beautiful seaside community near the house of the American Vice-Consul. The Christian Vice-Council had a six-year-old daughter who would come over every afternoon, whether invited or not, to play with Jack.

At the conclusion of the holiday, the powerful man popped the question: "Well... your son and my daughter seem to play together quite nicely. Why don't we arrange them to be married?"

Not expecting the inquiry, and not knowing whether he was serious or kidding, I answered nervously, "It is very generous of you to offer your daughter in marriage. But my son must marry a Jewish girl."

He countered quickly, "No problem. We will make her Jewish before the wedding!"

We both laughed, but I knew I would have to fend off more serious offers in the future.

Tony, the war baby, was born in excellent health, even

though during my pregnancy I had very little to eat myself. While he lacked for food early on, he benefited from my experience with the first three children. He ate plenty but never got fat, always wore a big smile, and enjoyed the attentions of the women in the house.

Tony's first love was an adopted stray cat named Minet. He wrapped the cat around his neck and wore it at all hours of the day. It even accessorized his skinny frame when he ate and slept. The furry caramel-colored scarf bordered his straight dark-brown hair and fair skin and provided a contrast to his brilliant blue eyes, which were protected by Coke-bottle glasses.

One day, I teased him, "Tony, Tony, who do you like better, me or the cat?"

With a nervous grin, Tony squeaked in a small, embarrassed voice, "I love the cat more, because I can carry Minet, but I can't carry you!"

If I didn't want to hear the answer, I suppose that I shouldn't have asked the question. But I did not get overly concerned, since soon Tony's heart was stolen away from my main competitor; this time, a white goat was the object of his affections. Ezra had bought two white goats on Awaji Island when we went there on a family vacation. Tony took his favorite goat everywhere. They hiked up the surrounding mountains after school, they played ball with his friends, and they walked together all over town.

No one told Tony the true reason for the goats' purchase, and when they maaed every morning, our next-door neighbor, the French Consul, would complain. We were not Japanese citizens, so the French Consul was very important to us. We needed to treat him very nicely in order to obtain papers for travel. Without his help, we would have trouble leaving the country for business or vacation. Angering him was a big problem, so Ezra told his mother to solve it. When the children left for school, she called the butcher, who slaughtered the animals. Before any of the children came home, the goats were cooked over a spit in the garden.

Tony arrived home and called his goat but received no answer. No one said anything. Worry etched into his face, he asked, "Ma, have you seen the goats?"

"No, Tony, I haven't seen them," I answered, staring at the floor, lying the best I could. There was no way I could tell him what we had done.

He asked the housekeeper, his grandmother, and his father but received the same answer. At dinnertime, large chunks of bony meat were placed on the table.

"What kind of meat is this?" Tony asked suspiciously, a frown growing slowly on his face.

I looked down at the table and answered, "I don't know."

A minute passed while reality soaked in. My son's face somersaulted through a few painful contortions before he jumped up from the table. "I know what kind of meat this is!" he screamed, blowing the tears that had run down his face and pooled between his lips all over the table. "I'm not eating this!" He tore away from the table and ran like a rabbit, crying in agony, all the way to his bedroom.

Frieda, Simone, and Jack echoed the sentiment and quickly followed Tony. After a few tense seconds Farida, Ezra, and I looked at each other and shouted almost simultaneously, "I'm not eating this either!" I gave the meat to our housekeeper, and we all went up to bed. The housekeeper was so heartbroken that both goats in their entirety were given away to a neighbor.

A Victorian Home in the Heart of Kobe

Once Ezra and I had made enough money, we looked to buy a permanent residence. We weren't searching for just anything with four walls and a roof; we were looking for a home.

After our family had lived in a moderately comfortable rental for four years, Lily Braha gave us some exciting news. She informed us that the house next to hers was for rent and the foreign landlord needed to find a tenant as soon as possible. Living next to my best friend was too good an opportunity to ignore, so we were the first people to see it.

The white Victorian home with green accents was not only gorgeous but also had a tremendous history. The broker explained that it had been completed by the English architect A. N. Hansel in 1896. He related that Hansel had resided in Japan from 1888 to 1918 while building a number of high-profile shops, banks, and clubhouses in the country. Among them was this Victorian residence in the heart of Kobe, which was the only building he had constructed purely for his personal use.

Mr. Stunzi, the Swiss Consul, had rented the home after Hansel left Japan. The French Consul had occupied the residence next door. Fortunately, both buildings had survived the 1945 bombings intact. The Swiss Consul returned to his home country in 1950 due to old age, and the English owner of the house needed to rent it quickly. He correctly understood that if the occupying American troops commandeered the residence, they would not pay him for the privilege of using it. And that was not his only worry. He was further restricted by the need to rent it to a foreigner for two reasons. The first was that the American forces would not kick a foreigner out of a house at that time. The second was that once the Americans left, a Japanese person would be protected by local laws. The legal protection included the virtual impossibility for a foreigner to remove a citizen from his property—even if the tenant stopped paying rent. The owner was eager to rent the house to us, and without negotiation, we paid what he was asking.

Lily intelligently kept in constant communication with our landlord. Two months after we had moved in, in late 1951, he informed her of his desire to sell it. With Lily as the intermediary, we bought the house for five thousand U.S. dollars, a large sum at the time.

From my daily involvement in business, I had learned that when we bought something good, it was always put to good use. I had also learned that when we bought something simply because it was cheap, we always got what we paid for. Every time I walked through the house, I knew we had bought something good. I knew we had found a permanent residence that would nurture our Syrian Jewish Japanese family.

David and Rafoul

Rafoul, depleted of energy and funds after his exodus from Aleppo, searched for David's office on an early Hong Kong morning. He was so exhausted from his long journey that, once he found it, he fell asleep on the building's front doorstep. David was not only extremely surprised to see his younger brother when he arrived to open the business but also was very concerned for his well-being. He immediately brought Rafoul to his apartment, gave him a place to sleep, and provided him with food, fresh clothing, and local currency.

David gave Rafoul a sales job to help him make a living. Rafoul sold stockings and other general merchandise to local Hong Kong stores and rapidly built up a customer base. When David saw that his brother was capable of running the business, he made an important life decision. David had been in Asia since the age of twenty-seven and was now forty years old. He wanted a new life, he wanted to marry a Jewish woman, and he wanted to have children. He knew it would be almost impossible to reach those goals in Asia and, therefore, moved to Milan, Italy where there was a large Syrian and Lebanese Jewish community. Our mother quickly joined him there, moving in with him.

Rafoul grew the business that David had left him. He expanded their importing, supplied a wider variety of goods to their Hong Kong customers, and also began exporting Chinese products all over the world. Many of Rafoul's old friends from Lebanon and Syria had fled religious persecution for more tolerant countries. The new immigrants needed to restart their businesses, and a few needed an agent in China to handle their buying. Some individuals Rafoul had helped leave Syria immediately gave him their business because they knew he was an honest man. Rafoul's old friends from Aleppo also helped by recommending him to businessmen in powerful positions.

Little by little, he expanded his export business to include clothing, shoes, watches, and fashion accessories. Although Rafoul's profits increased substantially over the years, he never allowed financial success to inflate his self-image. He continually donated large portions of his income to help refugees, to help the building of Israel, and to help poor people everywhere. Whenever I visited Hong Kong to renew my visa for Japan and do some buying of my own, he took me for a daily lunch at Victoria Peak, where we ate overlooking the city.

Pearls of Wisdom

Japan's population scratched and clawed their way, centimeter by centimeter, out of the bleak, hopeless nightmare they had inhabited during the war's final years and the subsequent period of rebuilding. My PX business had been successful, but we all welcomed the return of Japanese-grown food to the market. I knew there could be no long-term success without a healthy, happy group of people to work beside. Luckily, just when work on my old business was diminishing, Siyahou Zayat, one of our old friends, opened up a new door.

Siyahou, who was now residing in Italy, was thrilled when

Ezra bought a huge stock lot of transistor radios for him at a price that would allow him to reap a substantial profit. He attained the business goals of his trip very quickly and, therefore, had time to find a special Japanese gift for his wife. I introduced him to my favorite figurine carvers and jewelry makers, and he was immediately captivated by the saltwater pearls we found. Since they were inexpensive, he bought his wife five strands.

A few weeks later, Siyahou's wife shrieked with pleasure when she received the luxurious pearls. Her joy only increased when she heard the value of the jewels worn gracefully on her neck. The price was around eighty U.S. dollars for five strands, but of course Siyahou said he had spent no less than one hundred fifty for them. However, he quickly added, "Money was no object when it came to the love of his life!"

Now Siyahou's wife was quite an intelligent person. She thought, if these pearls were worth so much in Japan, why not check the price in Italy? She went from store to store, telling the same story.

"My husband went on a business trip and bought me five strands of pearls for two hundred and fifty U.S. dollars. He doesn't know anything about jewelry, though. Do you think he received a good value, or was he cheated?"

Each time, the shopkeeper's eyes gleamed with interest as he fingered the merchandise. They each declared that the price sounded high but were willing, as a favor to her, to buy them all at the cost price. She told each shopkeeper that she would consider the generous offer and return the next day with a reply.

After she discussed the day's events with her husband, they both understood that they had found a new business. Instead of selling the pearls, Siyahou went to each shopkeeper and took orders. One requested ten strands; the next, twenty; the next, fifteen; and so on. At the conclusion of the week, he had orders for over one hundred strands of pearls.

Soon afterwards, Siyahou wrote me a large order for stranded pearls because he had many interested parties. But he advised, "Lucie, if we want to make this a good business, we need a better price."

A tingling sensation of joyful anticipation ran through my veins. I went back to my supplier, but he could not fill such a big order so quickly. I convinced him to take me to his distributor and immediately began immersing myself in the pearl business. Ezra's contacts in other industries informed us that most pearls were produced in Nagasaki and Hiroshima. So I dressed in modest clothing, pocketed a substantial amount of cash, and took the train to Nagasaki. I found a resourceful taxi driver at the station and hired him to take me to the pearl cultivators in the area. The car rolled to a stop in front of an old, dilapidated wooden building with a tremendous view of the bay. A man of many years with a weathered face, extremely short hair the color of charcoal ash, and an immaculate navy-blue kimono strode confidently out to meet us. He took me around the plant, educating me in the process of pearl cultivation. He proudly explained his production methods, but was careful not to divulge any secret information. First, divers would swim to the bottom of the ocean, hold their breath, and gather strong, sexually mature female oysters. In the factory, a sphere-shaped ball of oyster shell—rounded with an electronic tool—would be injected into each oyster's womb. The oysters were then placed in small, netted cages, buoyed on the ocean's surface with bamboo floats. Here, they would be protected from predators and have time to transform a simple piece of calcium into a jewel of tremendous value.

I noticed that pearls over seven millimeters were more expensive than the smaller varieties. The man explained the reason for the added cost using an analogy I could relate to very well.

"An oyster is like a woman," he taught. "If you have a big

baby in a small woman, she has a chance of miscarrying or dying. Similarly, if you inject a big ball into a small oyster's womb, you will see the same result. The cost of finding large female oysters, or growing smaller ones to a suitable size, is passed on to the customer."

At the conclusion of the tour, I sat with two factory employees and sorted through the pearls, one by one. I was pleasantly surprised at the high quality and low price of the goods but only spent one fifth of my cash. I knew that in order to make this a long-term business, I would need to find more suppliers and give them orders as well.

The taxi driver and I became good friends as we visited numerous cultivators throughout the week. I bought from four of them, developed a supplier base, and was educated on the finer points of pearl fabrication. It was a good start and many of the relationships developed were great sources of merchandise and information in the early stages of our business.

As time passed, our extremely low prices started attracting the notice of our competition. Many international distributors approached me and asked, "How much commission are you charging for choosing the pearls?"

"Five percent," I told them truthfully.

They either laughed or yelled at me. "You do not charge five percent on pearls! People charge five percent on excess material, shoes, or clothing! But not on jewelry!"

To calm my critics, I assured them that I would raise my commission, but I never did. The truth was that Siyahou was a good, honest man who paid me right away, and the large volume of sales we were doing together made it more than worth my time. I didn't want to ruin a successful business by letting greed poison my mind, so we continued on as before.

A few years after we had begun working together, Siyahou sent me a photograph of a beautiful house in Israel. "Lucie," he wrote. "This is my daughter's wedding present! I bought it with the profits from our business!"

I wrote back, "*Mazel Tov!* That is great news! But don't get lazy! You still have two more children to buy houses for! We must continue!"

A few years later, he sent me pictures of two more beautiful houses. I wrote back, "Now you must buy something nice for yourself!"

A year after that, he mailed me a picture of a fourth house, well-located near the Israeli Knesset. "Lucie, this one is for me!" he wrote proudly.

Causing a Marriage

More than once, the trading business we did in Japan caused heartbreak on an international level. Our overseas customers often sent their sons to Japan to "learn the business." These young men would visit Ezra in his office each morning. In the afternoons, they would go out to visit various factories with the office staff and expand their understanding of Japanese business practices. In the evenings, they dined with us and slept in one of the house's guest bedrooms. Those who lived with us for more than the customary one month usually revealed that they were in Japan to do more than simply "learn the business." Some of these adolescents were ensnared in relationships their parents didn't approve of. Their fathers had sent them to Kobe, under the guise of helping Ezra, until the love for their girlfriends had faded. It was one of these amorous young foreigners who complicated the life of a sweet young Japanese woman in our employment.

We had a very wealthy English customer who was involved in the import/export and real estate business in Europe. He had four sons. The youngest one, Peter, was sent to us in Japan. His father was more interested in Peter breaking off his relationship with a lovely, albeit older, French fashion model than in any business knowledge his son stood to gain from his short visit. Peter was young, handsome, athletic, a music and art lover, and educated in the best schools of Europe. He exclusively wore clothes tailored in London or Firenze, was fluent in four or five languages, and was an amateur singer and guitar player. When he arrived in Kobe, we nicknamed him "the Prince" because he acted with the sense of entitlement and irresistible charm that one inherits from being raised in an aristocratic English family. To say the least, he was greatly in demand at the various dinner parties around Kobe.

At that time, we had an attractive young housekeeper from Kyushu. Her name was Kisako, and we called her Kisako-san. She was pretty and energetic, had a wonderful, spirited personality, and was well loved by everyone.

Peter, who was supposed to return to London after one month, kept on extending his stay in Kobe. When asked by his father when he expected to return, he answered him by saying that he still had much to learn about the business and had, in fact, began studying the Japanese language. This was all well and good, except after another month or so, Peter came to my husband crying, confessed his love for Kisako-san, and stated his wish to marry her. This caught Ezra by surprise, as men in Japan rarely cry over such issues, yet he understood that in other countries the practice was more common.

"Would you like me to speak with your father about this?" Ezra answered after a long pause.

"No, it's no use," Peter replied, continuing to weep into his handkerchief.

"Why not?" Ezra asked him.

"She will not have me. She refuses to marry a foreigner," he wailed.

"Well, you do have a lot of red hair on your head and body— like most foreigners. You have to admit that it is reminiscent of our ancient ancestors, the apes." Ezra responded, unable to constrain a hearty laugh. He put his hand on "the Prince's" back in support, and then got up to leave. "You must respect her choice and should probably look for someone else to marry."

Apparently this is what happened: after dinner, Peter would go out on the town, as many young men would do. Kisako-san would steal out of the house and meet him. Together they would walk, hand in hand, through the many narrow lanes of the town, visit the parks where other romantic couples met, or go to a coffee shop to talk. On Kisako-san's one day off during the week, they would secretly meet in Kyoto and other beautiful places to visit various temples, gardens, and museums. It was quite a romance. It was also true that Kisako-san's knowledge of English improved relative to Peter's mastery of Japanese. No one knew of their clandestine activities until Peter's confession.

Peter's heart was broken, but he returned to England and resumed a life of luxury and splendor. When he received no response to his many letters to Kisako-san, he would write me to ask about her. The news was not in his favor. Not long after Peter's departure, Kisako-san's parents got wind of the situation, told her to leave our employment, and had her move back to Kyushu. Her parents quickly arranged a marriage to a young man from their village. A year and a half later, Kisako-san gave birth to a daughter whom she called Haruko because she was born in springtime. Another two years went by, and Kisako-san had a son named Osamu. By the time she had her third child, Peter knew he had no chance and had to give up. It was only then that the letters stopped coming. He ended up marrying a beautiful young lady whom his parents did, in fact, approve of. But his heart was always with Kisako-san in Kobe.[59]

---

59 Story as written by Tony Choueke with a few omissions, additions, and changes.

The Rat

"If you associate with kings, you become a king. If you associate with rats, you become a rat." This Arabic proverb delivers a message that would have saved us many a headache had we heeded its warning.

Sigmund's unsuccessful attempt to steal our customer, Joe Dahab, only increased his irrational jealousy towards Ezra and the rest of our family. Ezra and Sigmund continued to share many meals together each week, not because they were the best of friends, but because they were cut from the same cloth, although Ezra was the rise, and Sigmund, the run. They spoke the same languages, had the same friends, knew the same jokes, and most importantly, were born in the same place. Growing up poor in the Middle East had shaped their intellects, priorities in life, and—most evident to outsiders—their business acumen. In postwar Japan, they had both managed to carve out substantial financial niches benefiting the local Japanese and the foreign importers abroad. But while Sigmund accumulated more wealth than almost anyone we knew, he rarely spent anything. Instead, he was always focused on others' income streams, hoping to divert them into his own wallet.

Whenever a business deal was discussed, tiny grey hairs stood at attention in his oversized ears, an adaptation that allowed him to scamper in on any financial arrangement nearing completion.

One evening, I was entertaining a nice woman who had been distributing our pearls in Germany. I still harbored a deep hatred of German policies toward the Jews before and during the Holocaust, but I rationalized that it was better to use her money for good instead of making a political statement. Refusing her business would only make her buy from someone else, which would not do anything to improve the lives of any Jew who had suffered. From our experiences in

Japan during the war, we understood that some Germans were sympathetic. At the same time, we understood that many still harbored intense anti-Semitic beliefs. From the conversations we had together, I was confident that this woman considered me an equal and a good business partner.

I took my customer to dinner at the Kobe Club, a country club for foreigners with a good restaurant, swimming pool, movie room, and bar. We had just ordered dinner and were discussing a selection of pearls on the table when Sigmund wandered over, quite drunk. He had been invited to the club by a member, and had concluded his meal, but his hunger was obviously not sated. The buyer and I were occupying the only two chairs at our table, but he happily grabbed one from another table for himself.

To my horror, he tossed his chair right next to my buyer, leaned his briefcase against it, and plopped down. He started talking loudly in her ear and gesticulating wildly. As he ran through the well-worn jokes and witty remarks he often rehearsed for such occasions, we were slowly asphyxiated under a cloud of pungent, inexpensive cologne. A tightness in my customer's face slowly intensified throughout the interruption, but she was able to maintain her composure and dodge as much of the hot air gushing out of his throat as possible.

Sigmund, noticing the pearls on the table, arched his greying eyebrows with interest. "Did you come to Japan to buy pearls?" he prodded my dinner guest.

The German buyer smiled politely and answered, "Yes, I did. I came to work with Lucie on a collection of saltwater pearls for my customers."

Sigmund guffawed incredulously at her response. "Why are you going through Lucie?" he asked.

"Well..." she paused, visibly embarrassed, quickly glancing at me. "Lucie is my representative here in Japan to help me buy the line."

Sigmund reached into his ample briefcase and pulled out a

business card. He presented the information to her in an overly dramatic fashion: tightly grasping the sides of the tiny card in his large hands, outstretching both of his arms, and delivering a humungous smile that showed off his gritty yellow teeth. "Here is the best source of saltwater pearls," he carefully enunciated with a fake charm so nauseating that it overwhelmed even the cologne. "This man has been a friend of mine for many years. He grows the oysters himself, and by going directly to the source, you will save the money that Lucie charges you for her services."

Flabbergasted by his bold attempt to hijack my client, I shifted nervously in my uncomfortable chair. I tried to decide whether to leave the table and run to Ezra or strike him as hard as I could in the face. In a controlled hyperventilation, I slowly calmed my anger and regained my wits. I knew Sigmund could not get a better price than I could because I was working with four very good cultivators. He was working with an expensive distributor, regardless of what he claimed to my customer.

Finally, Sigmund seemed to tire of our company. He had done what he had come to do. He sprang up quickly from the table, ignoring the fire burning in my eyes, and made a clumsy exit, disregarding a few tables that jostled under his contact on the way out. The three glasses of wine he had gulped down, which would be added to my bill, were a small price to pay to get rid of him.

The extent of the damage done at dinner was only fully realized a few days later. My regular order was reduced by half! I was livid, but there was really nothing I could do. I continued to communicate with my buyer, giving her the best service I could. My orders quickly returned to—and surpassed—previous levels when Sigmund shipped her a few thousand dollars of distressed, low-quality pearls.

I ignored Sigmund completely during his many weekly visits to see my husband and warned Ezra to tread carefully in any dealings with him. However, it was only a few short weeks until he struck again.

Roasting the Chicken in its Own Fat

Aside from a few missteps, our progress in business lunged rapidly forward. The money brought in from the pearl sales, although a substantial sum, was merely a drop in the bucket when the gains were pooled with the profits from Ezra's export business. A novel problem reared its head: we needed to find a way to reinvest the money we were making. Fortunately, making the money was much more difficult than finding places to keep it.

Through our acquaintances in the synagogue and Kobe Club, we became friendly with an American manager from the Lockheed Aircraft Company. He had moved to Japan together with his wife to supervise the building of airplanes in the Kobe area. One Saturday, they came over for lunch and related that, as foreigners in the country, they were having trouble finding someone who would rent them a nice home. The wife complained that the company paid all their expenses abroad but did not help them find a suitable place to live.

"Where do you want to live?" I asked the wife sympathetically, seeing an opportunity for all of us.

"If I had a choice, I would love to live in Shioya—by the seashore. But we couldn't find anything available," she exclaimed, exasperated.

"How long are you planning to stay in Japan?"

"A few years! That's why it's so important we find a nice place!"

"Well..." I offered with a smile, "we can build you a house by the seashore. We only need to ask your patience, since it will take us half a year to complete."

I knew nothing about building houses, but I knew a good opportunity when I saw one. These people had a company paying them in strong U.S. dollars, and their rental payment was a business expense. Therefore, they could pay a good rental rate and would end up passing the expense onto their company. Additionally, since Ezra and I would set a competitive price, they would spare their company some of what they would have to pay for a suitable alternative on the housing market. Most importantly for us, the arrangement would create a destination for our excess cash: in an investment that would immediately bear fruit.

Benefiting from low land prices, Ezra was able to buy a suitable plot in only a few weeks. He then quickly negotiated a price with a local architect and offered the builder a bonus for early completion. In less than the time we had promised, the house was ready for our tenants.

Renting to our friends went incredibly well, so much so that when they told us more Lockheed employees were on their way from America, we immediately bought three more houses in Shioya—two for renting and one for ourselves. Each house was put in the name of one of our four children, giving them each an investment to propel them to future success.

My property management philosophy can be best explained by the Arabic saying, "Roast the chicken in its own fat." It explains that while preparing a chicken, one should use the animal's own fat in order to bring out the best flavors in the meat. This advice was not only meant to be applied in the kitchen. After the houses were built, they could only command a top market rent, year after year, if they were properly maintained. A portion of the rent, or "fat," from the property was spent to make any improvements or repairs needed. In this way, the house, or "chicken," was kept in immaculate shape using the "fat" from the property. In short, the tenants paid for their own building's upkeep. The remainder of the rent was used by our family to buy actual chickens, chicken fat, beef, and other food for the kitchen.

On many afternoons, when the chicken, earned through our labors and investments, had finished cooking, Sigmund showed up with a healthy appetite. He would use the lunch or dinnertime to hammer Ezra for hours about properties in the area. Sigmund shared information on the properties he had considered buying but ultimately rejected for one reason or another. Ezra would talk about land he was currently reviewing or deals he was in the process of closing. One by one, these deals fell out of escrow as a mysterious foreigner found creative ways to complicate the agreements. Unfortunately, it did not take long for Ezra to forgive him, and soon Sigmund scampered back into our house.

"A ship can only have one captain"

Even though I had written to Mama a few times in 1946 detailing the changes in our family, I was unable to visit for another eight years. After the war, the immediate reason had been our lack of finances, but even once we had accumulated some money, travel had been impossible because I had four small children to care for. I was finally able to visit on the way back from settling Frieda into her American boarding school.

Mama was living in Italy with my brother David when I experienced the surreal reunion fifteen years after our separation. Her youthful features and bright skin color had been washed away by a number of difficult years. Sad but unaffected, I understood that my beauty would share the same fate when age came to claim it. We slept on the same bed together in my brother's house but spoke little about the past. Our first night's conversation proved that the future and other family members were the only suitable subjects for continued civil communication.

"How is it being married to Ezra?" she asked sensitively, displaying a tiny probing smile. Joy danced cautiously in her eyes. "Are you happy?"

I understood that she was satisfied with her match. My husband was a successful man who had kept me safe through recent horrifying world events. The picture I gave her of our four beautiful children only enhanced her confidence in the decision.

I was not ready to forgive her for throwing me out of the house into the arms of a man I had hardly known. I answered in the kindest way I could while still being unable to extinguish the fire of disappointment raging in my core. "Let's not talk about the past," I replied glumly. "I will only say that I will never do to my children what you did to me. You forced me to marry. You didn't give me enough time. You should have left me alone for a few more years. Also, don't forget my only wedding gift. I received his mother for the last fifteen years. She has been criticizing me every day since."

My mother started sobbing and pulling her brittle graying hair. "I didn't know she would go with you to Japan!" she cried. "But I still think if you were in my position, you would have done the same. The choice I made was the best for the family. God willing, you will never be in that situation with your children." She kept crying, and I cried with her. We lay side by side in the same bed, spilling and commingling our tears late into the black night.

I spent only a few days with her in Italy before I had to return to my children. She occasionally cursed my mother-in-law for the difficulty she gave me. But my touch and my words were icy with indifference. "Curse her or don't curse her," I said. "It is all the same. It is too late... It is just too late..."

"Send me Simone," she requested hopefully before I left. "I will find her a good husband."

I stayed silent, knowing that we had experienced enough difficult matches between us for at least one lifetime.

I promised to see her again soon but explained she couldn't live in Japan. Farida, after one of our recent arguments, had exclaimed: "A ship can only have one captain!" My mother and I would have to meet somewhere else.

Mr. Konosuke Matsushita

In 1962, I was given the honor of attending a meeting with Mr. Konosuke Matsushita, a very wise businessman and head of the Matsushita Electric Industrial Company. Today his organization is one of the world's largest manufacturers of electronics and is known as Panasonic Corporation.

I was attending the meeting at the request of Reyna and Aron Roza, Syrian Jewish friends of ours who owned a large electronics company in Mexico. Ezra and I often helped lubricate business transactions between our foreign friends and our Japanese countrymen. This helped our friends source innovative products and helped our suppliers find new sales outlets for their goods. I was not there to add to my friends' knowledge of electronics, as they were already experts in their field. I was present simply to use my knowledge of working and socializing in the country to help make a good impression on the supplier.

Japanese inter-company business etiquette calls for employees in similar corporate positions to communicate with one another. For example, an accounting manager of one company would speak to an accounting manager of another, a sales manager of one company would speak to a sales manager of another, and a vice president of one company would speak to the vice president of another. Since the Rozas' were the bosses of their corporation, it was natural that they would meet directly with Mr. Matsushita.

I was conflicted before meeting one of Japan's most influential businessmen of the twentieth century. I knew that Mr. Matsushita had to push himself from a very young age to build such a successful enterprise. He had started the business in a basement, and had personally developed the company into a dominant electronics manufacturer. Even after the Allies meddled in Japanese businesses following World War Two, he was able to keep his company profitable and grow the business to incredible proportions. I was excited and deeply honored to be given the chance to meet such an intelligent and hardworking man.

However, I didn't know where my loyalties should lie. Could I negotiate with such a revered man in a way that satisfied both parties? Would I disappoint my friends from overseas? I simply couldn't make up my mind regarding which side to support if the negotiation became difficult.

Luckily, the meeting went very smoothly. Mr. Matsushita's very large smile, calm demeanor, and charming personality relaxed all of us right away. I was impressed that a man with over twenty thousand employees could take hours out of his busy schedule to entertain us, invite us into his home, lend some insight into his many interesting life experiences, and discuss the challenges present in the Mexican marketplace. He reviewed various details essential to creating a strong foundation for a long-term business relationship before putting a complex agreement in place. I could immediately see why he was successful. He was much less concerned about the price of a specific product and much more concerned with the viability of the partnership. He expressed his wish for both sides to make money and grow together in the foreign market.

I was thrilled when the relationship between our industrious Japanese neighbors and intelligent foreign friends resulted in a long lasting, mutually beneficial, and profit generating business.

Dance Partners

They say that "time heals all wounds," and a few years after the death of his goat, Tony found a new love—although this time, the identity of the wily being that stole his heart was a secret. Tony would leave every afternoon on a mysterious journey and not come back until evening. His favorite food changed suddenly from cheese *sambusak* to *mechshi gazar*, stuffed carrots. This did not escape notice because *mechshi gazar* is very difficult to prepare. We needed to carve out the middle of the carrot while it was still hard and brittle, stuff it with meat and spices, and then cook the fragile vegetable and meat concoction slowly in a broth for a few hours. Tony would tell us to keep the carrot shavings for him in a bag. That very day, he would disappear with the extra carrots, often arriving late for the very dinner he had requested.

One Sunday, Tony invited me to come with him on this most secret mission. I jumped at the chance to discover my new competitor. After a twenty-minute drive, we arrived at a horse farm. I watched from a distance as Tony fed the horses, cleaned out a stall, and brushed the auburn coat of his favorite animal. To my surprise, he then asked me to get on the horse. I declined but watched contently as he rode beautifully around the compound.

On our way home, Tony slyly unloaded the question that had been burning in his mind. "Mom, I want you to buy me the horse!" he demanded confidently.

We argued over the intricacies of horse ownership for a few tense moments before I impatiently put an end to the debate with an aggressive answer to one of his wonderfully simplistic solutions. "Tony, are you crazy!?" I demanded. "A horse can't live on the second floor of a house!"

Tony stayed quiet for the rest of the ride home. I knew the silence between us would last for a while.

Surprisingly, though, he didn't drop his new hobby. He went horseback riding every day and learned how to take care of the animals professionally. After riding for a few years, he learned how to jump the horses and began to win equestrian tournaments. This was no small accomplishment as the sport was popular in the country. This was partly due to Tokyo born Colonel Baron Takeichi Nishi, who won a gold medal in show jumping at the 1932 Los Angeles Summer Olympics.

Ezra and I were proud of Tony, but we wanted to nurture other sides of his creativity. No Choueke had ever become self-sufficient riding horses.

One afternoon, Tony came home extremely depressed. The end of the school year was approaching, and he had been chosen for an academic award. The honorees were given the distinct privilege of singing their home country's national anthem in front of the school. However, a complicating factor was that the song had to be performed together with a parent.

Tony was upset since we were stateless, and he didn't have a country to use as his nationality. I went to the synagogue, borrowed the Israeli flag, and brought it to school. I planned to hum along with everyone else and help Tony through his commencement ceremony.

When the graduation began, I was disturbed to see how I had misread the situation. There were many people in the audience and each award winner, accompanied by a parent, sang a carefully practiced duet in front of the entire school. I watched in horror as the English national anthem, the Canadian national anthem, the German national anthem, and the Japanese national anthem were all sung with absolutely no help from the audience. Then Tony's name was called and I accompanied him onto the stage. His skin took on a sickly violet color as he focused his attention on the floor, closed his eyes, and sealed his mouth until the entire nightmare had ended.

I surveyed the audience quickly. Fortunately, Lily Braha seemed to be the only Jewish parent in the group. I dredged up the old Hebrew songs from the recesses of my Aleppo school memories and began to sing as the Israeli flag climbed up the flagpole behind me. I confidently belted out the Hebrew words I knew to the melody above the sounds of the un-tuned piano. I didn't know the first few lines, so I just began with the part I did know: *"Nefesh Yehudi homiya Ulfa'atey mizrach kadimah Ayin l'tzion tzofiya Od lo avda tikvatenu..."* When I ran out of Hebrew words in my limited vocabulary, I began filling them in with Arabic phrases. For a full three minutes, I sang just as I did as a little girl in the Allianz Aleppo choir.

I noticed Lily Braha running out of the room to avoid exploding with laughter from my Arabic-Hebrew song. But strangely enough, everyone else began humming along with me. The kindness of the audience encouraged me to sing louder and louder. When I had finished, everyone gave us a standing ovation. Tony, after a few moments of indecision, lifted his head, opened his eyes halfway, and peered self-consciously at the raucous crowd below. He was obviously surprised that he hadn't been kicked out of school. The audience still hadn't sat down when the master of ceremonies reclaimed the microphone. It was an incredibly emotional moment, knowing that I was in Japan, in front of a German, French, Canadian, American, English, and Japanese audience, all applauding the creation of the State of Israel. I hoped that next time they would hear the national anthem from someone who actually knew the words.

The boys' high school would organize frequent dances, where the girls would pester Jack to be their partners. He refused because he was too shy to hold their hands, and more importantly, he didn't know how to dance. The problem came to my attention only when I hosted a party at our house. In between serving overflowing plates of Syrian food, I watched my son fend off one girl after the other.

From the movies we watched regularly, it was clear that every true gentleman, and therefore my sons, needed to know how to dance. It was also clear that, because of Ezra and Farida's conservative Aleppo upbringing, the responsibility to teach them was one uniquely suited to my talents. I waited until the party had finished and called my boys downstairs. I kept the gramophone playing, told Jack to hold my left hand, and placed his right hand on my waist. We slowly reviewed the steps to the fox-trot and the cha-cha. In the days that followed, we learned the waltz and the tango. When Jack was tired, Tony became my partner. Before every party, I made sure Jack practiced with me to increase his confidence. In truth, it made me happier than it made him. I had finally found a dance partner Ezra wouldn't object to.

A school friend of Jack's introduced him to the movie business. The Japanese movie studios often needed Japanese-speaking foreigners to appear in their films. Jack's good looks won him quite a few acting roles, and he was able to find Tony work with the studios as well. They made an early departure from the business when a few companies tried to cast them as German soldiers in war movies. But they always treasured meeting Marilyn Monroe and Caroll Baker at the Oriental Hotel.

Jack loved cars and motorcycles of all kinds. My co-worker, Masse-San, had a son who had been a kamikaze pilot. He was shot down during a mission and had spent over twenty-four hours in the ocean before being rescued by a passing ship. As he was also an expert mechanic, he became a good friend and mentor to Jack, and taught him everything from changing the oil to repairing an engine.

Simone finished her high school education and, due to her high class standing, was accepted at every college to which she applied. She wanted to go to McGill in Montreal, but I forced her to attend Barnard in New York because it was closer to a Jewish community. Disregarding the schools' respective educational advantages, I thought that sending my daughter from Japan to Canada didn't seem to increase her chances of finding a Jewish husband. And every time I visited, my main goal was to drag my daughter into Brooklyn and quickly find her a match.

After the completion of a bachelor's degree in economics, Simone was eager to work on Wall Street. Even though I was thrilled that she wanted to enter the business world, I knew that Wall Street was a difficult place for a twenty-year-old. I decided that Simone would have an easier time meeting a husband if she stayed in university. So, we made a deal. Simone agreed to stay in university and study something feminine, like interior decoration, and afterwards I would support her decision to make a career for herself on Wall Street.

Before I knew it, I attended her graduation from Columbia University where she had earned a master's degree in literature with full honors, not interior decoration as we had discussed. My husband and I cried on the phone together afterwards, but for two different reasons. Ezra was fiercely proud of his daughter's intellectual accomplishments. I was incredibly worried! After the Western education my daughter had received, I feared that finding her a compatible Middle Eastern husband would be a difficult task.

When Simone went to work on Wall Street, I didn't get involved. I didn't understand why stocks rushed up and down at a moment's notice based on abstract economic news involving international currencies, commodities, and the whims of investors. I only understood the inherent conflict of interest in public companies—the consequence for a company truthfully reporting bad financial performance was the loss of a job or assets for those employed there. And I was sure that if an investment was doing badly, no matter how well we read a company's fake financial reports, we would be the last to know.

While my three younger children were under closer supervision, my eldest was strongly independent. My beautiful Frieda's first suitor presented a difficult challenge. She was at school in New York, when Ezra and I were approached by an acquaintance at a Kobe dinner party. He ambushed us with a proposal most Aleppan parents appraise for some time. "Your daughter Frieda," he asked in a low voice with a smile too wide to be misconstrued as polite, "what size dowry does she come with?"

I laughed nervously and answered quickly before Ezra had a chance to enter the conversation: "Our daughter Frieda is only fifteen and too young to get married."

The man's smile vanished quickly. He was obviously

unprepared for a long conversation on the subject. "Well, I don't understand. Your daughter and my friend's son have been dating and are at the point of being engaged. But before proceeding with the engagement, the family wants to know the dowry amount. What does Frieda come with?"

"I know nothing of what you are speaking!" I answered bluntly.

"Well these are the terms: the family wants fifty thousand U.S. dollars, and the cash must be in the bank before any wedding is to take place."

My polite smile spontaneously transformed into a scowl. The words formed were slow and deliberate: "First of all, we do not have that kind of money. Second of all, my daughter is too young to get married! I thank you very much, but we are not interested!" I shook my head in utter disbelief and dragged Ezra away before any argument erupted between them.

The next morning, as soon as we had gathered the information we needed from our American social network, I received the call from Frieda. "Mom!" she gushed, her voice cracking from apprehension and excitement. "I met someone..."

I didn't let her continue. "I know," I answered somberly, "but we cannot help you. His family is asking for a fifty thousand-dollar dowry."

Frieda stayed silent as I relayed the events of the past few days. She soon hung up, sobbing. My heart broke for her, but I was proud when she quickly ended their relationship. She said, "If it's money you want, you need to get it somewhere else!"

Building a Home

It had always been a dream of our community to create a permanent synagogue in Japan. Fifteen years after our previous synagogues had been destroyed in the American air raids, the community worked towards making the dream a reality.

After World War Two, we had all been using a large furniture warehouse, converted into a community center, for our daily prayers. Upon the community's request, Rahmo Sassoon, Isaac Djemal, and Edmond Sassoon, who shared ownership of the plot on which the community center stood, charitably agreed to sell the land at a low price. Ezra joined an eclectic group of European and Middle Eastern Jews all eager to contribute to the project.

Despite the significance of a few large donations, the intrinsic beauty of the future synagogue would be firmly based on the community that contributed in order to build it. The fact that it took contributions from everyone to mold the dream into a reality was infinitely more powerful than reaching our goal with a donation from one or two members. In effect, we created a congregation of synagogue owners who could pray at the synagogue they had all built together.

The synagogue plans included a second-floor apartment, among other practical additions. The apartment would be used as an incentive to convince rabbis or scholars to remain in Japan with our congregation. The visiting intellectuals could live rent-free in exchange for running the prayer services. Alternatively, when the synagogue was low on money, the apartment could be rented out to help subsidize part of the community activities.

The construction was completed around 1970, and the synagogue was named Ohel Shelomo in honor of Rahmo Sassoon's father.

The challenge in forming a synagogue is not only present in raising the money for a building, but more so in filling the building with prayer, Torah study, *mitzvot* (good deeds), and charity. Thank God, in addition to having the financial resources, we were also given the intellectual resources to fill the synagogue with what it required. Victor Moshe, Albert Hamway, Jacob Gotleib, and others led our congregation for decades.

In contrast to Kobe's earlier Jewish residents, most Jews

who immigrated after the synagogue's completion were single men, from less religious backgrounds, in search of business opportunities. The community valued these important additions, but remained orthodox in style. The synagogue became an island of familiarity in a serene, foreign sea.

The Underfunded Charity

Not all projects undertaken by the Kobe foreign community were as successful as intended. A prime example involved our plans to help some refugee groups in the Middle East. Sigmund was not personally fulfilled by his ever-growing bank account alone and decided that he needed to add an act of charity to his substantial list of financial achievements. He thought an international aid fund would complement our existing efforts quite nicely and made an announcement at a neighborhood meeting to jump-start the project.

Dressed in his finest suit and sipping a glass of expensive brandy, he fingered the long strands of his unkempt beard, stood up slowly to create suspense, and brayed loudly to all in attendance when the meeting had reached a suitable climactic moment: "Ladies and gentleman, it was not long ago when international organizations sent funds and resources to Japan at a time when we did not have the means to help ourselves. Now, thanks to the prosperity of our adopted home, we finally have the ability to help others. I propose we set up an international charity so we can shine a bright light to help our brothers and sisters lost in the shadows. In order to demonstrate my enthusiasm for the project, I will match every contribution."

When a substantial amount of donated money was sitting in a bank account, it was time to approach Sigmund. Two community leaders visited him at his office to communicate the good news and collect on his pledge. An employee quickly ushered them into a room where Sigmund sat in an overstuffed navy-blue leather chair behind a polished oak desk.

After a quick exchange of pleasantries, Sigmund broached the topic of discussion. "How much money have you collected?" he asked in a cool, relaxed tone, although his left eyebrow arched higher than his right betraying his interest.

"We raised ten million yen!" they replied proudly.

"Wow, that is really incredible!" he declared with a mischievous smile slowly growing on his face. After a pregnant pause, he continued, his mind dancing joyfully through the calculations. "So, ten million yen is quite a lot of money. It is more than enough to do some good in the world! Don't you agree? If you already have ten million yen in the bank, you obviously don't need any money from me! When you need the money, I will give it to you. But for now, I will keep it!"

The money contributed was sufficient to get the charity running and enabled the community to help many people. His contribution would have enabled us to have a broader reach; nevertheless, as much as I hated to admit it, I must give credit where credit is due. Sigmund's trickery had finally resulted in something positive.

Womb of Diamonds

After the war, my mother-in-law and I had finally drafted a nonaggression pact of sorts. Neither one of us conceded that the other had any valid points whatsoever, but for Ezra's sanity, we agreed to disagree, semi-agreeably.

It became clear that our spats were not producing a clear favorite between us. We realized that the only thing we were accomplishing was slowly turning Ezra into a crazy person. Without a formal agreement, or even the exchange of words, we intuitively cooperated to limit our aggression—not for the benefit of each other but for the man we loved.

A short two weeks after our unspoken truce began, my mother-in-law was obsessively complaining about our life in Japan. "There are so few people here to play cards with! There is no kosher food! No one speaks Arabic! In Aleppo, I was always busy... Here, I have nothing to do!"

We had quite a few guests over, so Ezra and I remained silent. Furthermore, neither one of us had saved up any desire to jump into a fresh argument. Our old friend Rahmo Sassoon was the one to give her a new perspective on life.

"*Um* Ezra," he said kindly, "next week, I am returning to the Middle East to get married. I will happily escort you, carry your luggage, and buy you a one-way ticket if you truly miss Syria that much."

Farida, for the first time since we had met, was at a loss for words. Thirty seconds later, amongst a keenly interested and breathlessly silent crowd itching to hear a response, a beautiful serenity swept over her entire countenance. She muttered to herself, "Am I crazy?!"

She then answered Rahmo happily: "My house is in Japan! My only son is in Japan! My grandchildren were raised in Japan! Japan is my home! And whoever doesn't like my company," she paused to glance in my direction, "can leave!"

Ironically, it took the offer of a return to the land of her birth for Farida to finally realize all the blessings she possessed in her adopted country. The arrival of the knowledge brought her happiness and peace. We never became friends, but we became tolerant of one another.

As the years dragged on her body, she accumulated various ailments. She screamed at night, lost her ability to sleep, suffered from daily headaches, and lost her appetite. She hated visiting the hospital, but I would take her there three times a week to receive sleeping medication. We were happy to keep her at home as long as we thought there was nothing seriously wrong with her. But, one day, after twenty-two years of living together, I could no longer rule that out as a possibility.

In the youth of our relationship, Farida had known I was pregnant on the first day I couldn't eat. At the conclusion of our relationship, I knew she was dying on the first day she couldn't smoke. She complained pitifully about not being able to taste the tobacco, and I took her directly to the hospital. The Mother Superior, director of the Catholic hospital, confirmed my grave diagnosis. She sullenly explained, "Lucie, you can't buy years. When it's your time, it's your time. She needs to stay with us now."

Farida became extremely dispirited upon her move to the hospital. She felt utterly abandoned. At first, she would turn to face the wall on our daily visits. We were also depressed but knew that we could not give her the care she needed at home. We visited for long hours every day and brought friends with us to inject the room with some cheer.

The Mother Superior was extremely kind to her, and their only arguments were germane to smoking. My mother-in-law claimed it was her only joy, even though she could no longer taste it, and kept lighting up during her two-month stay. Nonetheless, she always politely waited until her new friend had left the room.

One morning when we arrived, Farida was staring up at the ceiling. Something was very wrong. Her deliberate breathing seemed more painful than usual, and there was an eerie dryness to her eyes. The life, the luster, the vigor, and the animation had ebbed out of them, like an empty stretch of beach at low tide. Nothing but the flat horizon remained.

With our close friend Mrs. Mattuck by my side, I leaned over Farida as tears flowed down my face, dropping at irregular intervals on her bleached polyester hospital gown. My memories gripped me by the shoulders and whisked me away, to the days when she had studied the coffee I had made in my mother's house, to my wedding day, to our ocean voyage, to the children we had raised, to the war we had endured, to the poverty we had emerged from, and to our present success. I realized that the twenty-two years I had spent with her were seven more than I had spent with my own mother. I realized that she was an irreplaceable part of my life, and I wasn't ready to let go. I realized that all her complaints, taunts, and torments were the tools she used to mold an immature, impractical girl into a capable woman, wife, and mother.

I finally understood why she had plagued me incessantly with the hurtful comments: "You eat like a wolf and sleep like a marmot (a hibernating rodent)," "The money my son gives you flows as freely as a river from your pocket," and "What little you had with you on your wedding day, you gave back." The last one had especially stung. It referred to the gold bangles with my initials on them that I had worn to my wedding. The following day, I had given them to my sisters, hoping the jewelry would bring them luck in finding husbands.

What my mother-in-law was saying, in the way only she knew how, was that I came from my family with nothing but youth and energy. Therefore, I needed to use those tools to create something where before there was nothing. With the tears coursing down my cheeks, I realized together we had accomplished just that.

Farida seemed to notice me in the room for the first time. She rotated her fragile frame towards the both of us. The wrinkles on her emaciated face had deepened, her thinning hair had become as white as the top of Mt. Fuji, and her piercing blue eyes were muted to turquoise. She saw me crying over her and lifted a malnourished, bony finger towards Mrs. Mattuck. "This girl here..." she said slowly and painfully, taking a feeble breath in between each word, "gave me four beautiful children... She has a womb of diamonds..." She exhaled laboriously and shuddered in the grasp of a deep, unrelenting cough, while collapsing back into her initial position.

I stopped crying suddenly due to shock. It was the first nice thing my mother-in-law had ever said to me. I looked at Mrs. Mattuck, drawing an arm across my face in a vain attempt to mop up the pools of moisture streaking thick lines of mascara across my face. "That's not a good sign," I whispered, sadly shaking my head.

"No, it isn't," Mrs. Mattuck replied soberly. "It definitely isn't."

At five o'clock the next morning, Farida passed. Ezra was by her side, while the Mother Superior, Lily, and I held hands in the waiting room. Lily and I were too afraid to join him, so we waited while Ezra spent a few last moments with his mother. I began sobbing uncontrollably, with Lily looking on in disbelief.

"Now you are upset!?" she exclaimed, cracking a mischievous smile. "You *really* want her to come back?"

After a moment of silence, she teased me again. "You *really* want her to come back? Then keep crying—it will surely happen!"

We both embraced and sobbed on each other's shoulders. A few minutes later, Ezra stumbled to the car as white as a roll of cotton sheeting.

The Jewish cemetery had recently been moved from Yokohama to Kobe's Lake Futatabi due to a highway that needed to be built. Farida was the first person buried on the small parcel of land perched in Kobe's serene heavily wooded mountains. Ezra purchased three adjacent plots at one time: the first one for her, the middle one for him, and the last one for me.

Advising My Subjects

We married off all four of our sons and daughters. None of the children took our advice on whom to choose as a partner, but each found someone who best suited them, for better or for worse. I felt accomplished in giving them a gift I never had myself: the choice of a partner and direction in life.

It was easy for me to assume my new title of "mother-in-law."

I knew exactly how to treat each of them, since I had the perfect template to betray. Whatever my mother-in-law did to me, I would do the opposite to them. From my studies, I knew that a good mother-in-law happily closes her eyes to anything her daughter-in-law does. Any overeating, oversleeping, or lousy cooking would be ignored completely. Any mistreatment of my grandchildren, such as under-bathing, underfeeding, or neglecting them to go shopping, would be "corrected" when they were left alone with me. A son-in-law would be given even more allowance for error if he was supporting his wife and children. While I didn't demand too much, I didn't obsessively prepare for their periodic visits. I told my in-laws, "The most precious things I have are my children, and you already have possession of them. More, I cannot give."

One of the benefits of my children choosing their own spouses was that I didn't have to push them to have sex.

But if anyone was making me wait too long for an addition to the family, I would give him or her face-to-face advice, which proved to be quite efficient. Since Frieda married approximately eighteen years before my other three children, my grandchildren were fairly spaced out in age. Luckily, I was able to torture and advise both my children and grandchildren, when they came of age, regarding these crucial but delicate issues.

And as my mother-in-law pestered me, I was able to torment my subjects to do my bidding.

My first suggestion, after six months of marriage, was detailed enough to warn the women in my family not to keep me waiting forever. I instructed them privately, "After making love to your husband, don't go to the bathroom! Just lie in bed the entire night, as still as possible! Then you will surely get pregnant!"

If one year later there was no evidence of progress, I would have to get more in depth. "Have you been to a doctor?" I'd press. "Is there anything wrong with you?"

A demure "No" would automatically prompt further intrusive advice by way of example. I'd exclaim, "I had my first child at seventeen, and I was a grandmother by thirty-five! What are you waiting for?"

Sometimes they were bold enough to answer, "I am not waiting."

I'd only insist once again, "Then there must be something wrong!"

At that point, they were usually intelligent enough to keep silent.

If six months later there was still no action, I'd press nervously again, "Have you been to a doctor?" If she persisted that she was healthy, I would start working on the husband. This was done publicly or privately, depending on what I thought would work best.

I'd accuse him directly: "If there is nothing wrong with the field, then there must be something wrong with the planting! Do you need me to take you to the doctor?"

When he assured me, "There is absolutely, positively nothing wrong with the planting!" I'd leave him alone until my next visit.

Thankfully, I never had to dive any deeper before the required results were produced. My children, in-laws, and grandchildren were quick learners.

Once they were pregnant, no more face-to-face discussions were necessary. A little pregnancy advice communicated over the telephone was all that was needed. And I made sure to advise them of all the important superstitions, like dropping my grandchildren's shriveled umbilical cords on the floor of the biggest bank of the city.

Apparently, my advice was well received since we added grandchildren and great grandchildren to the Choueke tribe by my sixtieth birthday.

My Business Partners

From the mid-seventies to the early eighties, Kobe became a city better known for its beauty as a tourist destination instead of as a necessary stop for traveling businessmen. Like Aleppo textile traders of the 30's who replaced their English and Italian business contacts in favor of those that handled lower-priced Japanese goods, other Asian countries began to compete more fiercely in the global textile marketplace. Many importers expanded their buying to countries like Korea, Hong Kong, China, and Taiwan, and reduced the orders earmarked for our Japanese suppliers. Ezra was still able to maintain a good business by refocusing his attention on high-end complex fabrics and finished goods, but many of the foreigners residing in Kobe relocated to more dynamic business environments.

The ever-changing winds of business resulted in other economic problems in America and Europe. These difficulties affected our customers, which in turn affected our payments. There were a few situations in which we had to resort to creative means to insure our collections. An acquaintance of mine from Europe borrowed twenty thousand U.S. dollars' worth of carved coral figurines on credit. He assured me that once he had sold the goods, he would send me the money. I had a standing agreement with all my customers that if they were unable to resell the merchandise, they simply had to return it. However, after two years, I had received nothing in return but silence. I called him on a few occasions, but each time I delivered a loud "Hello," the phone line inexplicably went dead.

On my next business trip to Europe, I located the man's home from the return address used on his written correspondence. I hired a room in a nearby hotel and called the house every hour. Finally, after half a day, he answered the phone, and I hung up without saying a word. I walked purposefully to his house, pounded on the door, and stood to the side of the peephole so I couldn't be identified from the inside. The door squeaked open on rusty hinges, revealing only a crack. I quickly shoved my foot into the space and pushed inward with all my strength. The man immediately recognized me and reluctantly let the door swing open.

"L—L—Lucie," he sputtered. "H—H—How are you? Why didn't you tell me you were coming? I would have prepared for your visit!"

I chose not to engage in unnecessary conversation and demanded, "Where are my figurines?"

Before he could answer, I spotted most of them proudly displayed on his mantelpiece. I walked straight over and unzipped my suitcase, wrapped up each piece in a separate *furoshuki* (a small multi-purpose Japanese cloth), and counted them twice. "There are three missing!" I accused. "Where are they?"

"Lucie, I-I-I already sold them. I am only waiting for the payment. In fact, I have a customer coming to look at the rest of them tomorrow. Can't you give me a few more days?"

"No!" I purged adamantly. I quickly collected my items and stormed out the door.

On the return flight to Japan, I had a moment of clarity and began scolding myself. "Why am I being so short-sighted? Why give credit to people I hardly know, when my children need money to begin their independent lives?" From that point forward, instead of only helping other people get rich, I would help my children with their businesses. That way, either the merchandise or the capital would stay in the family.

I realized that with Frieda and Tony in Los Angeles, Simone in New York, Jack in Mexico City, and Ezra and me in Japan, we now had the opportunity to establish an international trading business in which our family would be the compelling choice over any other supplier. Before, pursuing a customer like Macy's was an impossibility since we didn't have anyone to import the goods and service the organization on a daily basis. But now Ezra and I had four loyal, intelligent, energetic partners who could manage the importation, distribution, and sales in the West, while we managed the buying in the East.

Because the pearl and jewelry business I was doing with Siyahou involved only Europe and the Middle East, this was a natural starting point for our business in the United States. I gathered my best goods, partnered with Frieda, and visited all the jewelry stores in Beverly Hills, downtown, and other areas populated with potential customers. Our prices were so low and Frieda was such a good communicator that we soon were selling throughout the United States, Canada, and Mexico.

Jack was interested in electronics and Tony was enamored with fashion. We not only sourced products and fabrics for them in Japan, but also expanded our buying to other countries. I visited the Canton Fair in mainland China for the first time in 1978. I was pleasantly surprised with the important positions women held in Chinese companies, and conversed easily with them in English, Japanese, French, or Arabic—depending on the language they spoke best. We soon established great relationships with many factories and starting shipping their products around the world. Among our customers were small, but quickly growing, companies named Target and Wal-Mart.

Working with my children was periodically difficult but was immensely more rewarding than working with anyone else. Instead of only receiving an accounting sheet with figures on it, I saw my profits in action every time my grandchildren came to visit.

My Pearl

My respect and fondness for Rafoul enabled him to change a fundamental problem with my life: the reluctance to forgive my mother for marrying me off against my wishes. On one of my buying trips to Hong Kong, he discussed her decision with me over dinner. I had known the reason my mother had sent me away before we discussed it. But I realized then that, despite what your heart tells you, sometimes you need to hear the same thing from someone you respect before you start to believe it. I wished she could have given me more time, but there was nothing I could do to reclaim the past or my childhood. The only question was how I would spend the future. Would I be upset forever at Mama's decision or a willing participant in her remaining years? I unearthed inspiration from an unlikely source—something I saw quite often yet had never before equated to anything spiritual.

The simple oyster has an ingenious solution to cure an infection or control a foreign particle invading her core. She does not eliminate the malady but covers it delicately with luster. The first layers wrap the intruder in a translucent orb; the next bury all virulence with a pleasant luminescence; and the final coats create nothing less than a majestic, incandescent jewel. Like the oyster, it took me years to convert my pain into something beautiful. The difficult event catalyzed an understanding of Mama in the depths of my soul—an understanding of the strong decisions she made to keep us alive, and an understanding of where my tools for scraping through life were forged and sharpened. More importantly, by forgiving her I finally had something valuable to give in return.

On that same trip, I opened a Hong Kong bank account with Rafoul as the cosigner. I deposited money regularly into the account, and my brother sent it, with his much larger contribution, to support my mother in Argentina. After she had worried for over fifty years about money, we wanted all of her financial needs to be well covered.

Health Challenges and a Way Out

In his late seventies, Ezra started slowing down. A myriad of health problems kept him from going to the office regularly, and even more problematic was the slipping of his memory. He had never had a strong accounting background, as he had learned business on city streets and country roads. His virtually photographic memory had compensated for this, allowing him to remember what each customer owed him, what he owed each supplier, and everyone's phone number so he could call to check on either event. Even with the waning of my husband's abilities, I was reluctant to close the office. I wanted Ezra to have some incentive to get better, something to stimulate his interest.

The diminishing of Ezra's abilities opened the door for dishonest individuals. Almost all of our employees maintained their loyalty to us, but a few started to bleed the company for all they could. The most common trick was for a crooked employee and a supplier to go into business together. Ezra would buy ten thousand pieces of a product, but the supplier would only deliver five thousand. To cover up the shortage, the thieving employee would sign that ten thousand pieces had been received in the warehouse. Ezra would end up paying for an extra five thousand pieces, and the extra money would be split between the two perpetrators.

Soon, the stealing was so frequent that our company was not profitable anymore. Ironically, the more orders we received from customers, the more money we would lose. We had to start dismissing our honest employees, thereby decreasing our operational costs, to cover the money that the robbers were stealing. We fired half of our staff, occupied the top floor of the office, and rented out the bottom. Nevertheless, we still couldn't make money and needed another option.

On one of the rare days Ezra managed to get to the office, a real estate broker walked in with an answer to our problems. The broker asked Ezra if he was willing to sell the property.

Ezra instructed the broker to discuss the matter with me and led the man over to my desk. Ezra spoke in Arabic so only I understood: "This man wants to buy our building. See what he will pay for it."

I answered Ezra right away in Japanese so the broker could comprehend my answer. "No! I like this office, and I don't want to sell it. We have been here for many years, and all of our customers know our address!"

The broker and I negotiated his original offer of $1,000 US Dollars per *tsubo* for over a month. Finally, I wrote "$75,000 USD per *tsubo*," on a piece of paper and signed it. I explained to the broker, whom I felt sorry for, that I had no intention of selling our office. I wanted to keep it for my husband and my two sons. But if they paid me the admittedly outrageous price scribbled on the paper, I would agree. I was more surprised than anyone when the developers, who secretly owned the rest of the block, approved the deal. We moved our offices into a friend's building.

Ezra's maladies did not improve, and in the early eighties, he gave up going to the office altogether. His biggest concern was finding an honest man to take over the care of his remaining customers. He transferred a lot of his accounts to Albert Hamway, a religious member of the Jewish community, but soon afterwards Albert decided to leave Japan. Ezra then decided that Dawud Nasri, a Muslim friend, would be the best representative to service his old customers. Recommending a Muslim man to work with our Jewish customers caught some of them by surprise. Relatively quickly, though, they realized he was a good, knowledgeable, honest man and contracted him as their agent. Ezra believed it was not enough to find the best Jewish, Muslim, or Christian for the job. He had to find the best person for the job. Pairing an old customer with an agent unfamiliar with the product would have dire consequences for everyone involved. By recommending Dawud, he gave everyone he worked with the best opportunity to succeed.

Our House—A Foreign Icon in the Heart of Japan

When we closed the office, we realized the full extent of the theft that had been taking place. Our accounting books stated that we had hundreds of thousands of dollars of merchandise available, and I was eager to sell off everything remaining in the warehouse to recoup some of our investment. However, I was shocked to find our warehouse completely empty. Everything had already been stolen. I did not sit and lament over our misfortune. I knew that with the loss our business had taken and the loss of Ezra's ability to work, we needed to find a new source of income for ourselves.

There is a proverb that explains that one of the worse things that can happen to an elderly person is to take from his children in order to live. Our children needed money to build their support system and did not need their income sapped by their parents. As Ezra was almost completely bed-ridden, the financial failure or success of our family now rested squarely on my shoulders.

I initially focused on my pearl business and spent my extra time hanging, accommodating, and cataloging the art-works we had collected over our lifetimes. By 1980, we had decorated our residence with countless foreign and domestic artifacts. We entertained less but continued having three or four large dinner parties a month, during which our guests would demand a tour. As I expounded upon all the interesting details wrapped up in our possessions, I would capture their imaginations and make an impression they didn't soon forget. They would write many letters thanking me for the insight into our unique foreign experience in Japan. This was not the first time I had been alerted to a public interest in our home. We had begun receiving letters and commendations only nine years after we had moved in.

July 23, 1960

Kobe City Hall
Kobe, Japan

Dear Mr. Choueke:

Your house was designed and built on September 29, 1896 by the late A.N. Hansell, an Englishman. He lived in Kobe at that time and worked as one of the best architects here. He built many excellent buildings. Among his works were the then Kobe Foreigners Club house and Hong Kong Shanghai Bank building. Unfortunately, however, those buildings were lost in the war.

I am now studying the history of Japanese modern buildings. I have found out that your residence was built by the late Hansell as his home after contacting his daughter who lives in Monaco now. On my investigation of the old wooden buildings which now exist in Kitano-cho or Yamamoto-dori areas, I have found out that your house is the best one there.

Your house fortunately escaped from war damage and we are proud of having such an excellent building as yours. Therefore, it is our earnest desire that you will take good care in maintaining your house, taking its significance into your consideration.

Yours Sincerely,
Katsuhiko Sakamoto
Member
Modern Buildings Survey Committee
Japan Architecture Association

When we bought the house, we knew it had been built by the English architect A.N. Hansel, but we did not know the extent of his work in the Kobe area. Among the high profile shops, banks, clubhouses, and other popular structures in Kobe that Hansel had designed, some of his more prestigious assignments were Doshisha University, Heian Women's Graduate University in Kyoto, and Pool Women's Graduate University in Osaka. We appreciated that out of all the well-known projects completed by the architect, the house we lived in was the only building in Japan constructed for his own private use.

We loved Hansel's creation, raised our children inside, and preserved our family memories together with his masterpiece. In our minds, and in the minds of our guests, the legacy of Hansen's Yamomoto-Dori residence became fused with our contribution to Kobe. In addition to filling the house with our cultural identity and family pictures, we created an icon of international culture in the heart of Japan. We installed elaborate Italian chandeliers in every room; filled the space with authentic French and English furniture; warmed the floors with Persian and Chinese carpets; kept track of the time on German clocks; stored multinational wines in the cellar; filled the air with French, Arabic, and American music playing on the gramophone; dressed the tables with cloth embroidered in Belgium; served drinks in glasses from the island of Murano; reclined on hand-sewn Mexican cushions; decorated the mantelpieces with delicately carved Indonesian coral; and served Middle Eastern dishes to our international visitors.

Of course, a representation of the world's luxuries to our foreign guests would be incomplete without an underlying artistic theme from our adopted country. Japanese art beautified our downstairs rooms, which featured various ivory pieces exquisitely carved by local masters, hand-painted screens accented with gold leaf, glowing jade figurines, and intricately detailed porcelain bowls and vases.

Tony, over a period of thirty years, compiled an extensive collection of Meiji Era wood block prints which blanketed almost every wall. The artworks depict the foreign presence in Japan against the backdrop of significant national events. Some of the earliest prints were created in the 1850s upon the arrival of Commodore Matthew Perry, an American who opened up Japan to international trade. Others, from the 1850s to the 1920s, depict trading vessels arriving from England, France, Spain, Portugal, and Scandinavia. Many paintings recreate scenes of foreign traders mixing with the Japanese for business purposes. These prints are full of informative content, such as how someone from Holland dresses, what the country's flag looks like, and even how to speak a few key Dutch phrases. I showed our guests how the artwork contained both the *kanji* symbols for a word and the Dutch pronunciation in *kana*, teaching a Japanese person to communicate with a foreigner from Holland. All the artworks were created by Japanese, and the captions are meant to educate. Therefore, a modern Japanese man can study the local attitude towards foreigners in the 1800 and 1900s. A foreigner, even if unable to read the explanations, can achieve a clear understanding of how the Japanese population first perceived them.

Tourists, architects, painters, and scholars kept writing us, hoping to gain access to the house. For forty years, I had been busy with our businesses, but when we closed the office, I would occasionally give free tours to groups from local universities. Word of mouth increased our popularity until hundreds of requests were rolling in. At first, I didn't mind giving the tours in my spare time, but the increase in foot traffic brought an increase in the required cleaning afterwards. People's shoes would dirty the rugs, cigarette ash would stain the tablecloths, and fingerprints would smudge the windows. I decided to suspend the tours, but to my surprise, people kept taking photographs of the house from the outside. Interest didn't diminish but seemed to shoot up exponentially.

An Injinkan Museum

One morning, I was walking toward the train station wondering what business I could start to cure our financial inactivity, when I saw a sign for an *injinkan* (foreign) house. I immediately became curious when I saw a line of people waiting to enter a rundown foreign residence. I took my place in the queue and inched forward with a number of tourists from Tokyo, Osaka, and other cities. As I waited for my turn to enter the dwelling, I spoke to a few of the Japanese customers who told me that they were interested to see how the foreigners lived. Upon entering the house, I was extremely surprised when they charged me one thousand yen. I couldn't believe the amount of money they were asking to merely view the residence. I paid the entrance fee and walked around a house far inferior to ours. The owners of the foreign residence did not offer a guided tour but simply directed people around the house with the use of ropes. Strangely enough, the tourists seemed to enjoy the window into another world. They couldn't believe how large the rooms were, they marveled at the strange toilets, and they even enjoyed looking at the large family portraits.

At the conclusion of the brief visit, I ran home ready to start my own *injinkan* museum. On the way, I laughed out loud at myself. Here I was, giving free tours of our historic residence, while others were charging one thousand yen per person to look at a recently built, third-rate foreign shack.

The housekeepers and I set up the house as if we were expecting guests. We set the dining room table with our best Noritake china, crystal glasses, and a full complement of silverware for a proper English multicourse meal. We put up signs that explained the origins of our artworks, valuables, and family. Before opening for business, we put a desk in front of the entrance, hoisted our families' flag, and put a price list in front of the door.

I was not interested in merely competing: I wanted to make our *injinkan* house a rousing success. Instead of charging one thousand yen per person, I charged five hundred and offered any group over four the price of three hundred. The other *injinkan* house opened at eleven o'clock, so we opened at nine. Immediately we started receiving a few hundred guests every day. I would give group tours, take pictures with the tourists, and entertain them the best I could.

Listening to the Customer

At the conclusion of the tour, I took a picture with each of my guests. I then invited them to spend as much time at the residence as they wanted, before leaving them to take the next tourist group through the house.

Many expressed disappointment that I didn't sell any souvenirs that they could take to their hometowns. Giving my customers what they wanted gave me an invaluable opportunity to grow the business. I started by asking the simple question "What do you want to buy?" They answered, "We want to buy pictures of the house." So, I took some pictures, went to a postcard maker, and ordered twelve hundred pieces of each. Only a few weeks later, I ordered two thousand more and was soon ordering five thousand pieces at a time. My guests were still looking for more goods to buy, so I expanded. I put tables in the hall and began to sell miniature family flags and scarves. To fill up the extra space, I displayed all the remaining samples from our trading days. When everything sold very quickly, I bought more tables and contacted Ezra's old Japanese suppliers. I made tablecloths, mufflers, bags, shirts, jewelry, disposable cameras, pens, and even transistor radios with the Choueke name on them.

When those were selling regularly, I had another idea. People were coming to see our foreign house, so we should sell foreign products. Tony started shipping me fashion bags, manufactured for the European market, directly from his Taiwan factory. Jack's wife started shipping me embroidered dresses from Mexico. Frieda started sending me jewelry from the United States, and Rafoul's friends started sending me low-priced watches from Hong Kong. Our guests were amazed at how low our prices were, and I explained several times daily that we brought everything directly from the factory. The watches particularly sold very well, and soon I was ordering five thousand pieces every few months.

The media started to notice the museum and we appeared in magazine articles, newspapers, city tour books, and on television. I began seeing my own face around the city in various publications but didn't mind as long as it improved our business. The flow of customers grew to eclipse one thousand a day, and every morning a long line of people formed in front of the house. To satisfy the demand, I started opening at eight in the morning and closing at six in the evening.

My next idea was also brought to me by my customers. In between waiting in line, seeing the museum, and taking pictures, they got hungry. They kept asking our staff if we had anything to eat. Again, they pointed me in the right direction. "We want cakes, cookies, or bread from your country," they said. I knew the concept was a good one, but I needed to expand our staff in order to supply such a large number of guests with food.

We started by making chocolate cake, sponge cake, and *baklawa*. When our cakes started selling out before noon, we added more choices. I imported ingredients from the United States to prepare *mahmoul* and other Middle Eastern cookies, as well as spinach-or cheese-stuffed filo dough shells called *sambusak*. We also sold packaged pistachios, almonds, and cashews. The larger variety and quantity of food did not make it last longer. When word filtered through the city that we were making freshly baked goods every morning, the line grew even longer. Aside from the tourists coming to see the museum, we had regular customers who wanted to eat the cookies for breakfast, and our business grew once again. We even started shipping our baked goods to Yokohama, Tokyo, Hiroshima, and Hokkaido.

I understood that our kitchen's capacity was at its breaking point. During the day, the kitchen temperature would cruise close to forty degrees Celsius, and anyone entering would spontaneously break out in a heavy sweat. To increase our foods for sale, I contracted with our friends to produce the rest. Simon Elmaleh, a good friend of ours from the synagogue, delivered fresh pita bread every morning. The Morozoffs, our Russian friends, delivered freshly made chocolates directly from their factory. Frendlieb, a German bakery in Kobe, delivered European freshly baked cookies. Everything, except for the chocolates, was sold in Choueke cellophane bags to advertise our brand name. No matter how much we produced, our guests were waiting to buy them before the foreign delicacies could even be packed.

The next idea came to me while walking around Kitanocho. Many people were advertising to do weddings at very high prices. I said to myself, "Our house is beautifully furnished and historical, and the garden is a perfect place for a wedding." So, we started advertising our house as the premier local, foreign wedding destination and got into the wedding business. Mr. Burke, an American friend of ours, would do the wedding in the Buddist, Shinto, Protestant, Jewish, or Catholic style, providing an international touch. His Japanese wife would translate the wedding speech so everyone understood. I would join the wedding festivities and take photographs with anyone who wished. I noticed that, similar to weddings in other countries, the boy's mother was usually unhappy, and the girl's mother was usually overjoyed.

On the days considered lucky for weddings, we would have two or three services. We did not want to cook the wedding meal, so we contracted with a Pakistani man to provide the catering at another location. Tony shipped a Rolls Royce Silver Shadow to Kobe for the purpose of stylishly shuttling the couple from the museum to the restaurant. The wedding events were so festive that we provided twice the regular number of cookies and cakes to accommodate all of the visitors' appetites.

A Distinguished Visitor

One afternoon I came down after lunch, and a strong man dressed in loose-fitting black clothing entered the house. I could not hear the conversation between him and Ayako-San, but it appeared that there was an imminent event of great importance. He looked around the house quickly and then strangely began hurrying some of our guests out of the museum. I wanted to go speak to the mysterious gentleman and ask him why he was bothering my customers, but his deliberate movements kept me silent. When I peppered Ayako-San with questions, she told me to let him do what he wanted and keep quiet until later. The man cleared the house and quickly disappeared. Less than one minute afterwards, a tall, nice-looking Japanese man walked into the house. He was wearing a navy-blue Western suit, a matching tie, and gold-rimmed spectacles. One security guard led him in, and another one followed directly behind him. A pretty young woman and an older woman entered next, each in an elaborate kimono. They were also accompanied by two security guards each. I knew I had seen them all before but could not remember where for a few seconds. Suddenly, it hit me like a rock falling out of the sky. It was Prince Mikasa, the brother of the Emperor, and two of his relatives. I knew that it was an incredible honor to receive a visit from any member of the Imperial Family. If I had known that even one of them was coming, I would have prepared for weeks. With the three of them suddenly entering the house all at one time, I was a bit embarrassed for not having been more ready to entertain.

I knew that Prince Mikasa was a very powerful, handsome, worldly, and intelligent man. I had heard rumors that he was a student of Middle Eastern religions and a defender of the Jewish religion in political circles. I gave them all a private tour of the museum, careful to be as respectful as possible. They said very little to each other but looked at the house with great interest. I started speaking to Prince Mikasa in my most respectful Japanese, and to my surprise, he answered me in English. He told me, among other things, that he had been to Israel and was very familiar with the Jewish religion.

During my tour of the museum, he explained that they wanted to build a new house and were looking for new architectural ideas. He especially liked the aesthetics of the fireplaces and chimneys. I commented that there was a fireplace in every room and that the chimneys of the upper floors were connected to those on the lower floors. I explained that they were a prime example of traditional English brickwork from the Middle Ages.

I was so nervous around the presence of Japan's most revered family that I barely noticed all the photographs being taken. While I was showing them the garden, helicopters flew overhead, snapping shots of everyone. My famous guests stayed for only thirty minutes, and I gave them all the presents they would accept on their way out. I bowed low to Prince Mikasa, and he shook my hand in thanks. He was really a very charming man. Soon afterwards, he also visited the synagogue.

I was completely unprepared for the repercussions of such a visit. Two days later, we appeared in various newspapers, and news of our museum apparently circulated like a raging inferno. We started receiving three thousand and occasionally four thousand visitors per day in the peak season. I gave the tour close to seven hundred times a week, and in addition to the standard questions about me, they would always ask me for a bunch of new material.

"Where did Prince Mikasa sit?"

"What was Prince Mikasa's favorite part of the house?"

"Which souvenirs did the Imperial Family buy?"

I patiently discussed their visit in great detail. To answer the last question, I told them that we obviously could not accept money from the Imperial Family, but happily showed them the gifts we presented. I knew the Prince and the Imperial Family were loved by their subjects, but I was extremely surprised at our guest's curiosity—even years later. Our newfound publicity brought various Japanese celebrities and television personalities to the museum. I would be sure to take pictures with each of them and put them in our photo albums. The celebrity sightings and pictures brought even more guests to the house.

I was working like a crazy person all day long, three hundred sixty-four days a year, but I enjoyed myself. The only day we closed was on Yom Kippur, the Jewish day of repentance. I had the pleasure of meeting millions of Japanese citizens and became a minor celebrity in my own right. Whenever there was an ebb in the flow of visitors, I would concentrate on selling the goods in our retail area. I would start by trying to sell the pearls and jewelry from Frieda. If the jewelry was too expensive, I would next show them the watches from Hong Kong. If the watches were too expensive, I would show them the shirts, dresses, fashion bags, and scarves. I often wore our best-selling clothing and demonstrated five ways a woman could use a scarf: around the neck, in a jacket pocket, as a colorful belt, as a hair tie, and under a jacket lapel to inject some color into a dull outfit. If the fashion items were still too expensive, I would show them the cookies and postcards. After I had practiced for a few years, almost every person leaving the museum had a Choueke souvenir bag in hand.

I believe it is never too early in life to begin working, so when my grandchildren came to visit for the summer, I took advantage of the new additions to my staff. My new employees ranged from age five to age eleven. I sent my beautiful granddaughters to invite the passing tourists to enter the house by repeating, "*Irashaimase* ("Welcome")," and, "*Ichiban injinkan* ("Number one foreign house")," with their Mexican and American accents. I stationed my grandsons behind the front desk to collect the admission fees. I paid all my grandchildren handsomely, so they could make plenty of trips to Daimaru Department Store, where they bought the latest toys.

In the Public Eye

The museum was a very rewarding pastime, but there were some challenges along the way. Neither Ezra nor my children liked their house being opened up to the public. They were angry at me for selling their privacy. We even argued about it one day.

"Mom," my children criticized, "why do we need to have so many people in the house all the time? You need money, we'll give you the money! It doesn't feel like a home anymore! It feels like an office!"

I yelled back in frustration, "What shall I do with myself!? You are all grown up! It is just your father, me, and some help around the house! I need something to do with my life! I can't just sit around all day, play cards, and talk on the phone."

Yet some days, I became annoyed with our public life as well. One morning, I got out of the shower and wrapped a white towel around my body. The bathroom door suddenly swung inwards, and a strange man peered in.

"What are you doing!?" I shouted at him, still partially naked.

"I paid the ticket, and I'm seeing the house," he answered, obviously shocked but unsure what else to say.

"This is not part of the tour!" I shouted and slammed the door in his face.

Unfortunately, this comical event took place more than once. My grandson David, at age twenty-two, was a tall, strong, and good-looking boy. He had finished taking a shower and had just wrapped a towel around his waist when an ancient woman walked into the bathroom. She looked at him for a few seconds and then proceeded to tour the rest of the bathroom, while he was still inside. She walked slowly around him, peered at the sink, inspected the shower, and left without saying a word.

Needless to say, we developed a solution to solve this problem. We strung thick ropes in various parts of the house, restricting public access. Occasionally, we would have other challenges. Sometimes drunk men would pay the admission and fall asleep on one of our couches for a few hours. Ezra, who was bedridden, was the only man living in the house, so often we would let the drunkard sleep. We were all too afraid to disturb him. A few drunks kept returning and sleeping later into the night. Finally, we contacted the police, who gave us a direct line to the station in case of further trouble.

A difficulty of dealing with the public daily is that one often encounters many people who lead very difficult lives. I tried very hard to make sure everyone felt welcome in the museum. Every blind, deaf, mute, or otherwise physically handicapped person was let in free as my guest. It was especially sobering to see the victims of the atomic bombs, whom would often cover their faces with scarves to hide their scars. Some had part of their faces burned away, some were bald on parts of their heads, one woman was deformed so badly that half of her nose bone jutted out of her skin, and some were almost bent in two from the effects of radiation on their bodies. I made it a priority to personally escort my most welcomed guests around the museum, but their plight greatly saddened me. I was in the war as well and know it was only luck that separated those who had lived from those that had died.

The true beauty of the museum crystallized amid the surrounding, buzzing chaos since the business's most stringent demands also provided an invaluable benefit. The museum consumed my time, like a hungry wolf digging into a goat carcass. The more money I wanted to make, the more visitors I needed to attract, the more products I needed to sell, and the more tours I needed to give. Fortunately, the harder I worked, the more I needed to stay home. We ran the only *injinkan* house that was owner-occupied. Through this setup, I could run a business and be close to my husband throughout the day. I ate breakfast with him every morning, ate lunch with him every afternoon, and relaxed with him in the evenings after the museum visitors departed. At first we ate at a table in the bedroom, but later, when he could no longer get up, we ate at his bed. Ezra wanted me with him all day, but there were only so many hours I could watch Arabic television. I was happy to escape our bedroom into the bustling action downstairs, and I was happy to escape the bustling action downstairs to review the day's happenings with my husband.

Ezra usually had friends and old customers visit during the day. After the museum closed for the evening, we would all first have a coffee, then have a whisky, and finish with a good meal together. Ezra didn't like the museum, but at least it gave us something new to talk about. Before retiring for the evening, I summarized the totals of people and goods sold that day. We laughed or complained together, depending on the numbers, as we drifted off to sleep with Arabic music playing softly on the television.

The Hangover

Just as grapes take years to ferment into a fine wine, by the eighties our lifetime of tireless work spent cultivating our fruit of the vine produced the long-awaited, intoxicating effect of a job well done. Action continually pulsed through our home as our children achieved success in their lives and visited often. Ezra remained in good spirits despite limited health problems, and the museum filled much of my time.

Yet with the ending of one decade and the beginning of another, there came a harsh hangover that drastically altered my view on life. Our first loss was felt on an international level. On January 7, 1989, The Showa Emperor passed from the earth. It was a moment of great sadness for everyone in Japan. The citizens of Kobe closed their shops, unfurled black flags, and went to the shrine to pray. We closed the museum for one week. Many were surprised we reopened so soon, even though I didn't charge admission, but the truth was that I needed to talk about the Emperor, a man who did so much for us personally. I told the museum guests how he had provided us with stable rations through World War Two even though the entire country's population was suffering from a lack of food. I told them how he had saved all Jews in Japan from certain extermination. I heard how The Showa Emperor and the government were approached repeatedly by the Nazis, who pressured to kill us all. Thank God, they saved us through astute diplomacy.

We understood that compared to our peers in the Middle East and Europe, we had lived a very good life in Japan, which was largely due to the Emperor's benevolence as a leader. We gave money to all of our museum guests who were on their way to the famous Shinto Ikuta Shrine. Each honored him on our behalf with a donation and a vigorous ringing of the temple's large bells. In order to provide our own personal thank you, we conducted a Jewish prayer service for him in the synagogue as well.

I had been speaking to Mama every day while she prepared her papers for an upcoming visit. I had finally managed to compress or jettison most of the childhood anger that had still stained my soul. I was eager to see her again, eager to further mend our relationship, and eager to give something back. It was one week before her scheduled flight when I received a call from David.

"Mother fell on the way to the bathroom," he explained sadly. "She is in the hospital with a broken hip."

I could not go to Argentina, as Ezra's health was deteriorating. The only option was to pray and wait in horrid, itchy suspense for David's phone call.

The next day, with excruciating pain in his voice, he told me that mother had passed of a late-night asthma attack during her recovery from surgery. Tears ran in interminable streams from the corners of my eyes, and I dropped the phone without saying goodbye. I tore my clothes and sat on the floor for ten days after her death. I couldn't go to the funeral but visited the synagogue often, looking for an answer, or perhaps a reason.

Weeks later, as the pain dulled, I understood that her passing in itself was not sad. She had lived almost one hundred years, although she would never admit to any age older than sixty. She was well-cared-for by David and Moise, and given freedom from financial worry by Rafoul, Ezra, and me. Before passing, she understood that her time was approaching. She knew the place she belonged, and it was not in Japan with me. She personally prearranged her funeral in Argentina, buying herself the best plot of land, the best headstone, and the best casket available. Although she came to the Earth in poverty, she left it in style. Everyone agreed that she was among the most chic in the entire cemetery.

The only tragedy was present in our inability to completely resolve the past. That was a road I would now have to travel alone, understanding that my mother, and whatever I loved or hated about her, was woven into the fabric of my body and soul.

Driving Alone

It was difficult to prolong the grieving for my mother when my husband's health was failing rapidly. Ezra's tremendous strength was derived from the challenges he had overcome, but the efforts expended to overcome them had worn on his health. The daily aggravation took a toll on his health, giving him migraine headaches, and eventually the more serious Alzheimer's disease. The state of his mind and body permitted him only the simple pleasures of eating, watching television, and playing cards. Dr. Ishigami, our family doctor, came to check on his progress daily, repeatedly insisting that it was the least he could do since Ezra was like a father to him.

One afternoon I entered our bedroom for our usual lunch together and called out his name. I received no answer so I assumed he was asleep, but when I glanced at his face I immediately knew there was a problem. Ezra's skin was as pale as polished ivory, and his big blue eyes stared unblinking at the wall. He obviously did not recognize my presence or hear the sound of my voice. I immediately called the Mother Superior, and an ambulance took him directly to the hospital.

The Mother Superior advised that Ezra had had a stroke and would need to stay in the hospital from then on. Ezra objected, vehemently insisting on going home. We solved the problem by moving another bed into the hospital room. I slept there every night, watching his body and spirit atrophy in front of my eyes. The most excruciatingly difficult days were the ones when he couldn't remember who I was. I cried often in helpless sadness. The past years had taught me that ingenuity and effort could improve almost everything in our lives. With this sickness, there was nothing I could do but sit and watch the man I love disintegrate.

Ezra had been in the hospital for over three months when the Mother Superior advised me to call our family together. In less than twenty-four hours, Frieda, Simone, Jack, and

Tony returned to Kobe. This was our first complete reunion in over thirty years. We all solemnly drove to the hospital and were in a state of subdued joy when we saw Ezra awake and coherent. Seeing everyone together brought a weak but captivating smile to Ezra's face. We spent a criminally short time together as a family before Ezra spoke to each of us privately.

"Lucie," Ezra mouthed deliberately, his face wrinkling with concentration, "I love you... Take care of our children." I walked out of the room sobbing, managing only a nod in reply.

Tony and Jack approached the bed together. "Boys, I want you to take care of your mother," he said slowly, draining his remaining energy. A peaceful thought relaxed the skin bunching up around his eyes.

"Don't worry, Pop!" they answered with energetic confidence and all the joy they could forcefully display. "Don't worry."

Ezra passed away the next morning, and according to Jewish custom, the funeral proceeded almost immediately afterwards. A crowd of mourners packed into the synagogue for the memorial service. I had forgotten the many friendships Ezra had accumulated over his ninety years until I surveyed the Jewish, Japanese, Protestant, Catholic, and Muslim families paying their respects.

I was particularly touched that Dawud Nasri, a pillar of Kobe's Muslim Community, had shown up for the prayer. It was not safe or diplomatic of Dawud to do this because he was one of the most respected members of the mosque.

The funeral service and the surrounding events whirled around me like a powerful typhoon's wind. They interred my husband next to his mother at Lake Futatabi, leaving the final spot for me. I imagined that my mother-in-law was happy to have her son's company all to herself again. I also imagined that she was in no hurry to receive me in heaven. I would let them have a few years together before I interrupted their peace. I closed the museum for one month, ripped my clothes, and sat crying on our hardwood floors.

I felt alone and conflicted. I did not regret Ezra's death, since he had been in pain and confined to a hospital bed. I knew he was en route to a better place. I missed my partner of fifty-nine years, and all that we had accomplished felt hollow without him. It felt as if Ezra had helped me build a Rolls Royce and left before we could drive it together. No matter how materially rich our life had become, riding in the car without him felt unfulfilling. My only comfort was in the voices of our children. In them, I could hear the echoes of our past and see our future.

I tried to work through a haunting depression after Ezra's passing. I threw myself into every aspect of the museum, and we continued our reign as Kobe's premier *injinkan* house. Just when I was beginning to appreciate life again, Rafoul passed away. In less than three years, I had lost the mother who had raised me, the husband who had nourished my development, and my brother, the individual I most respected. Sadness enveloped me like a thick fog, but luckily the predictability and regularity of work in the museum warmed my heart with a powerful, all-encompassing distraction. I was able to immerse myself in something immortal and safe: our house that stood proudly in the same spot since 1896.

A Loss I Could Respond To

I was shaken from a deep, comfortable sleep into a dark nightmare. Terror paralyzed every muscle and sinew in my body, leaving only my eyes to watch the sudden explosion of unrestrained chaos around me. Cataclysmic tsunamis of shock waves, invisible to the naked eye, shook, rattled, jolted, and shoved our fragile house with an accompanying cacophony of destruction. Windows shattered, wood splintered, family valuables crashed to the floor, and when the ceiling started to fall, I pulled my bedcovers over my head, preparing for the end... Suddenly, everything stopped, leaving only a deafening, completely saturating silence. My mind shouted question after question: "What happened?" "Am I alive?" "Is Catalina alive?" "Did many others survive?" "Is everything we own reduced to rubble?"

We were all dealt a devastating blow by the Great Hanshin Earthquake, magnitude six point eight on the Moment Magnitude scale, which struck Kobe early Tuesday morning on January 17, 1995. Over five thousand people died, over twenty-five thousand people were injured, over three hundred thousand people were left homeless, and over two hundred thousand buildings collapsed.

I lay in bed hiding under the covers until long after the mayhem stopped. Surprised to be alive, I slowly got up and nervously rummaged in darkness through the fallen debris. Once I found my shoes and a heavy coat, I tried to exit the house quickly. As I opened up my bedroom door, plaster crunched underneath my feet, and I noticed fractured roof beams exposed like a haunting skeleton on the ceiling above. As the sun was rising, I made the short trip to the stairs in disbelief. I could see gaping holes in the side of the house where our brick chimneys had been severed from the building and lay in thousands of pieces on the street below. I gingerly walked down our intact staircase, careful to avoid the shattered glass and fallen picture frames that littered the floor. Downstairs, chunks of plaster, expensive Satsuma vases, fragments of irreplaceable porcelain dishes, decimated grandfather clocks, damaged wood block prints, window glass, and wooden stakes protruding at irregular intervals formed a complex obstacle course on our house's bowed floors. I met up with my companion Catalina, who had been calling my name, and spent the morning in the freezing garden.

We sat for a number of hours collecting ourselves, surveying the damage, and flinching from a number of violent aftershocks. We then collected the food and water we had left and designated an area of the garden as a bathroom. We also started a fire with some of the house's splintered wood to combat the cold. I jumped when the phone rang and ran into the house to answer it. Tony was in Taiwan and obviously relieved to hear my voice. Right before the phone went dead, he told me that he was on his way.

Fortunately, one of the areas built well enough to withstand the earthquake was Kansai Airport, and Tony was able to land in Osaka that night. The Hanshin Expressway had collapsed, and he needed to wait until the following morning to traverse the ninety kilometers to our Kobe house. The taxi drivers couldn't navigate through the crevices in the damaged streets, so he bought a bicycle and rode west for half a day through the decimated city until he found his way home. I waited outside for many hours until I saw my son. Like in one of those Western movies, he materialized out of the dusty afternoon—a cowboy rescuing a damsel in distress.

We walked over to a friend's house and spent the night on the first floor of a mostly intact concrete building. Twenty or so people, homeless like us, smoked and solemnly discussed their problems late into the night. I could not sleep in that depressing environment again and became impatient to start repairing the museum. The shock of the catastrophic event had worn off, and I actually missed my busy lifestyle. Once my mind cleared, rebuilding was an easy decision. Giving up on the museum was giving up on my independence. Quitting could only lead to two unacceptable courses of action: leaving Japan and burdening my children.

Tony and I started removing the fallen ceiling plaster, shattered glass, and broken antiques from the house. We started with my downstairs office and used the space as our bedroom every night. With every severe aftershock, my office's strategic location allowed us to quickly escape to the garden. Tony covered the broken windows with newspapers, preventing the freezing winds from disturbing our sleep. The

City of Kobe distributed food and water on most street corners, but we were without the luxuries of gas and electricity.

The biggest obstacle to repairing the museum was that no one in the country was qualified to fix all the residence's structural problems and cosmetic details. The government generally declined to use foreign contractors for rebuilding projects, but in the case of our house, they made an exception. In order to fast track the repair of one of Kobe's unique treasures, they not only found some English contractors who could complete the work but also helped pay for the reconstruction. Geary and Black, Limited,[60] and George Cook and Sons, Limited,[61] were two English companies, among others, that helped in the restoration efforts.

Our international crew took one year to repair the museum. In the beginning, it was difficult to make progress since large portions of Kobe's manpower were diverted to rebuild the roads to Osaka. But once the intercity roads were reconstructed, the repairs progressed much faster. To commemorate the completion of the tremendous project in the fall of 1996, we held a rededication of the Choueke *Injinkan* to thank everyone for their help.

The guest of honor at the elaborate ceremony was Prince Edward, the Duke of Kent, grandson of King George the Fifth and member of the British Royal Family. In addition, we had the privilege of welcoming the Mayor, many important dignitaries

---

60 http://www.rodneyblackdesignstudios.co.uk/japan.htm.

61 George Cook and Sons, Limited advertises on their website that some of the houses "outstanding features were the large plaster cornices and ceiling roses." They replicated "the moldings in fibrous plaster" and replastered "the walls after... structural repairs were carried out." They explain that the entire process "was a unique situation in that not many overseas plastering companies have previously been allowed to work in Japan and the Japanese Government had to grant permission for and issue work permits to enable our men to carry out the on site works. Whilst in Kobe, the men were treated very warmly by the Japanese people." http://www.georgecook.co.uk/kobe.html.

from the City of Kobe, and other government officials. The Duke of Kent cut the ribbon to officially reopen the Choueke *Ijinkan*, and all the city officials joined us in the garden for a group photograph. Helicopters snapped photos of everyone, and when the pictures hit the newspapers, crowds returned in intimidating numbers. Directly following the departure of all celebrities, government officials, and royalty from the Choueke house, I returned to conducting business as usual.

Goodbye, My Friend

This is not one of those stories where the beautiful protagonist dies tragically as the stage lights dim for theatrical effect. I am still doing fine at ninety-nine years old. Thank you for asking!

In my Aleppo days, Auntie Latife had often told me, "Eat while you can... Dance while you can... Sleep while you can... And laugh while you can..." I smiled at her and nodded my head in agreement, although I was completely unable to imagine a time when those simple things would no longer be possibilities. It took me over seventy years to finally understand her point.

I have vivid memories of my hunger for *choux a la crème*, chocolate cake, orange juice, grilled meat, pita bread, and hummus when the holes in my pockets wouldn't allow me to enjoy them. Now I can afford to buy anything but can't taste the most luxurious Kobe beef, *yakitori*, sushi, *soukiyaki*, *kibe*, or *mechshi*. I always loved to dance, but first I was limited by society and second by marriage. Now I am limited physically. Sleep came plentifully almost my entire life. Now, I need medication to spend half the time doing what came naturally before. That only leaves laughing... Well... thanks God I can still laugh, although the losses of many of my friends, in addition to my family members, have lowered its volume and frequency.

Osakabe-San visited me often until he passed. After his retirement from the police force, the Jewish community, as a token of gratitude, supported him for the rest of his life. A few times a year he would visit the museum, where we would have a coffee and some chocolate, talk about our children, and discuss the paths of our old friends. He was really as good and honorable a man as there ever was.

I think about Ezra many times a day. It took me close to thirteen years to understand why he finally let his sickness interfere with his work. Now, like him, I have trouble sleeping, can't taste my food, and am not all that enthusiastic about leaving my room. It's not that I don't have the ability... I can function very well. The only way I can explain it is to say that I have lost interest.

Someone once told me that it is better to suffer when you are young and rest when you are old than to do the opposite. I suffered in my youth but am happy with my accomplishments. I grew up poor, was married against my will, moved to a foreign land, fought with my mother-in-law, survived bombs being thrown on my head, struggled to resurrect our business, raised four children during and after the war, breathed life and meaning into our house, and buried many family members as well as friends. I thought my time for hardship had finally come to an end when suddenly I received a phone call from America.

I cried for months after my Frieda passed away. Her hardworking, intense lifestyle had caught up with her in the form of a heart problem. I couldn't understand why God had let me live and let Frieda die. I would have gladly changed places with her in an instant. The pain of a mother outliving her child is more suffering than anything else I experienced in Aleppo or Japan. Unfortunately, there is no deal I can make to change the course of fate.

They say if you can look back two generations and forward two generations, you are blessed. I have known my grandparents,

parents, children, grandchildren, and great grandchildren (although I expect more to arrive). That makes two back and three forward—I know that I am more than lucky.

I personally feel fine most days. I don't know why God still needs me on this earth, but I am hanging around for now. Occasionally, people from the government come to the house to check on me. They want to make sure that I am still alive. It took me about ten years to pay off the inheritance tax bill when Ezra passed away. I suppose they are waiting for me to depart so they can collect the other half. I will leave that project in the capable hands of my surviving children. But, even though I have no fear of dying, I am not ready to go. Given the options, I would rather stay in my bed than underground on cold Lake Futatabi. My bed is warmer and doesn't have any flesh-eating bugs slinking around.

I have stopped giving tours of the museum, although we occasionally open it for special events or charitable endeavors. I am pursuing my interests in literature and handing off all responsibilities to the children. The way I see it, I have already told my story to millions of people. By putting it down on paper, I will hopefully communicate it to anyone else still interested. The museum and these written words will continue their dialogue, while there is something else to be said and while there is someone else who is willing to listen. Forgive me, but I have lost interest in repeating my story over and over hundreds of times a week. I am interested in the stories of other people. So while I occupy the upstairs of the Choueke *Injinkan*, and while you may see me from time to time walking through the house, excuse me for my lack of patience. Most of the people that gave my stories meaning have long since departed. The telling and retelling of the stories has therefore become more painful, as I have to continually visit old friends who can no longer visit me.

I invite you to visit the museum and the synagogue (www.jcckobe.org) on your next visit to Kobe. My websites, www.wombofdiamonds.com and www.choueke.com, will provide you with any scheduled openings and more information regarding our family and residence. God willing, these two buildings will preserve not only our legacy but the legacies of every good foreigner that lived in this great country. And that is where I will leave my obligation to the public.

My children are not pleased with my withdrawal from society. They want me to go on trips, give tours of the museum, eat well, and enjoy myself. Unfortunately for them, I have learned all their tricks from our negotiations with Ezra. My children have given up trying to tempt me to travel. Now, they try to shame me into leaving the house with a number of taunts: "Moses had to climb Mount Sinai to receive the Torah; the mountain did not come to Mohammed; Mohammed had to go to the mountain; and Jesus had to ascend before giving his Sermon on the Mount. But despite all this, Mom stays home!" In their examples, I, of course, am being compared to the mountain, and all my righteous friends of various backgrounds need to undertake long, arduous journeys to come see me.

But I have decided to never again leave Japan... It is my home.

As for my old friends and family, nothing brings me more pleasure than to see them, share the news, and exchange a few new jokes. I have two bedrooms ready to accommodate them whenever they have time to visit. They were responsible for not only my successes in life but also my survival. In Aleppo, when a few Muslim enemies complicated our lives, our Muslim friends helped us. In Kobe, during the war, while a few anti-Semitic individuals endangered our lives, it took tremendous goodwill from the Japanese people to save them. While the Americans almost destroyed us with bombs, they saved us from the Nazis and provided a future for my family in the United States. I was also blessed to receive countless good deeds from the French army in Aleppo; the French Consul in Japan; the Catholics who

educated our children and provided us with the best medical care; the Chinese, Koreans, and Filipinos who were our
valued business suppliers; and many other honorable people
to whom I am forever indebted. Among the most welcome
in our home are our Japanese friends and business suppliers that have accompanied us in countless invaluable, loyal
partnerships for the past seventy-four years. It also goes
without saying that in the absence of our Jewish friends living in Israel and many other global communities, I would
have become lost in all aspects of life.

Now, lying in my room, as the sun makes its long arc
through the afternoon sky, I comfort myself and my critics
with these words: "*Chacun son métier, les vaches seront bien gar-
der.*" Literally, this means if everyone does his job, the cows
will be well taken care of. My job on the family farm was to
work with our factories, buy and sell merchandise, entertain
and correspond with our customers, care for our children,
and eat hungrily after a long day of fighting to make a life
for our family. Since those days have passed, my job now is
to give advice, watch the finances, and offer moral support.
"Everyone according to their position; everyone according to
what they can do."

I advise my children to be like Japan's revered carp, of
which a picture hangs in our museum. A carp first swims
downstream, encountering many difficulties, while fortifying
its body and will. When the time comes, the magnificent fish
battles upstream, leaping meters into the air, gallantly flashing its golden plates of armor, and struggling against insur-
mountable odds to reach calmer waters. The carp thrusts
with its tail, wriggles its body spasmodically, and swims
violently to avoid a premature ending at the hands of a wily
predator. However, once ensnared in a net and laid on a chopping block, the carp intuitively knows the end is near. It lies
still, waiting with dignity, for a sudden flash of silver to end
its time on Earth.

I am now waiting, like the carp, for the inevitable. I swam down through the difficulties, I came up a success, and I am lying in bed, hoping to depart with some dignity. To pass the time, I am always happy to see any of my old friends or family when they arrive in town, regardless of whom they pray to. To entertain them, I run through all my favorite old stories. I tell them about the ritual bath, school in the Allianz, Directrice Penso, Lieutenant Compagnon, Mr. Romanoff, my mother, my brothers, my sisters, milking the goats under my mother-in-law's supervision, my engagement for two scoops of ice cream, the undulating belly dancer at my wedding party, and my final departure from Aleppo. I tell them about starting our business in Japan, the funny and romantic stories involving the bachelors, falling in love with Ezra, the rationing during World War II, Osakabe-San, Dr. Sakamoto, the birth of my children, the fighting with my mother-in-law, Lily Braha, escaping the bombs, Bunkamura, rebuilding our lives after the war, our export business, buying property, building the synagogue with the community, marrying off my children, taking care of Ezra, starting the museum, introducing millions of Japanese to the lives of foreigners, becoming a minor celebrity, rebuilding after the Great Hanshin Earthquake, and anything else they want me to review.

There is also some pending business that I am always happy to discuss. First and foremost, the *dota* and *busra* for my grandchildren and great grandchildren. I warn the girls of what my daughter Frieda used to say: "Before twenty-one, you pick; after twenty-one, they pick." Secondly, I push my lazy grandchildren who have already tied the knot to create more Chouekes. I was a grandmother at age thirty-five, and most are just planning their first children at age thirty. In Aleppo, this type of behavior would have forced their husbands to acquire second and third wives. Obviously, I must prepare more embarrassing questions about their sex lives in order to jump-start the production line. Third, I confirm our children are making sound health and financial decisions. I make sure the family holdings are allocated to the purchasing of more properties. Land is the only investment I believe in. My only other daily interest is to check on the running of the house and museum—which is now in the capable hands of my children.

Whenever it comes time for a guest to leave, like you my friend, I offer them my heartfelt best wishes: "May you enjoy health, happiness, stay religious in whatever consumes you, have many children, become financially successful, and return to see me again soon, God willing!" And as my Auntie Latife said, "Eat while you can... Dance while you can... Sleep while you can... And laugh while you can..."

The End

Please see
www.wombofdiamonds.com
for some photos and Appendix 1, 2, and 3.

Appendix 1: The Path of a Few Resourceful
Refugees from Europe to Kobe, Japan

Appendix 2: Why Weren't We Killed? A Glimpse at a Few
of Japan's Jewish Policies, Ideas, and Preconceptions that
Possibly Kept us Alive during World War Two.

Appendix 3: A Review of Jewish Worship in Kobe

Auntie Latife and Uncle Halifa

*Lucie in the Professional
Photograph Sent to Ezra*

*Lucie on the Third Floor of
Her House in Aleppo*

Lucie, Linda, Vicky, & a Boy

Lucie Passing the Time in Aleppo

Ezra as a Young Man

Farida's Stamped Travel Document

Abraham Chammah (Lucie's Grandfather on Her Mother's Side)

Farida in Aleppo

*Ezra, Lucie, and Abraham
After Their Discussion*

*Lucie, Ezra, and Farida
on the Conte Verde*

Lucie and Frieda Near Rokko, Japan

Lucie and Friends at a Japanese Tea Ceremony

Party for Jack's Birth

Party for Jack and Tony's Circumcision

*The Choueke Museum Photographed from the Garden. The Kobe Officials,
Duke of Kent, and Friends of the Family All Arrived for the Rededication in 1996.*

CPSIA information can be obtained
at www.ICGtesting.com
Printed in the USA
BVHW031302280222
629529BV00012B/12/J